ACCLAIM FOR *SWIMMING ACROSS*

"Beautifully told. . . . Spare prose imbues the narrative with an understated power."

—*Wall Street Journal*

"A poignant memoir of the coming-of-age of Andris Grof, a Jewish refugee from Budapest who, as Andy Grove and head of Intel, became one of America's phenomenal success stories. The book is a moving reminder of the meaning of America and the grit and courage of a remarkable young man, marked for success."

—Henry Kissinger

"A poignant tale leading to human courage and hope."

—Elie Wiesel

"Fascinating and moving . . . dramatic and compelling . . . in tune with the times. . . . Since September 11, it is comforting to think that there are people walking among us who have persevered through events far worse than what Americans face now."

—*BusinessWeek*

"Many readers are likely to be inspired by his story, his courage, and his tenacity. Those who know Grove in the business world will be fascinated with this other facet of the tough-talking, pugnacious Intel leader—and maybe glean some insight into how he got this way."

—*San Jose Mercury News*

"Reads like a spy novel . . . a heck of a story."

—*American Way*

"Enthralling."

—*Biography* magazine

"Honest . . . riveting . . . fascinating."

—George Soros

more . . .

"Andy Grove is a tremendous role model, and his book sheds light on his amazing journey. I would choose him as my doubles partner any day!"

—Monica Seles

"Astute and personal. . . . The intelligence, dedication, and ingenuity that earned Grove fame and fortune are evident early on. He deftly balances humor with insight. . . . Grove's story stands smartly amid inspirational literature by self-made Americans."

—*Publishers Weekly*

"Wonderful . . . combines a unique and often harrowing personal experience with the virtues of fiction at its most engrossing—vivid scenes, sharply delineated characters, and an utterly compelling narrative."

—Richard North Patterson

"Polished, solid . . . a tight, simply told, extremely intimate memior with careful attention to structure and detail. Even the metaphor in the title is multifaceted, adding depth and resonance as the story moves forward."

—*Kirkus Reviews*

"Remarkable . . . a simple, powerful memior."

—*Book* biography

Moving and inspiring . . . a vivid picture of a tumultuous period."

—*Booklist*

"Poignant . . . excellent."

—*Library Journal*

SWIMMING ACROSS

Also by Andrew S. Grove

Only the Paranoid Survive
High Output Management
One-on-One with Andy Grove
Physics and Technology of Semiconductor Devices

SWIMMING ACROSS

{*A Memoir*}

ANDREW S. GROVE

An AOL Time Warner Company

Warner Books, Inc., 1271 Avenue of the Americas, New York, NY 10020
Visit our Web site at www.twbookmark.com.

An AOL Time Warner Company

Printed in the United States of America

Originally published in hardcover
by Warner Books, Inc.

First Trade Printing: November 2002
10 9 8 7 6 5 4 3 2 1

The Library of Congress has cataloged the hardcover edition as follows:

Grove, Andrew S.
Swimming across : a memoir / Andrew S. Grove.
p. cm.
ISBN 0-446-52859-5
1. Grove, Andrew S. 2. Electronics engineers—United States—Biography. 3. Executives—United States—Biography. 4. Holocaust survivors—Hungary—Biography. 5. Semiconductors. 6. Intel Corporation. I. Title.

TK7807.G76 A3 2001
943.905'2'092—dc21
[B] 2001017752
ISBN 0-446-67970-4 (pbk.)

Cover design by Honi Werner

Front cover photograph courtesy of Andrew S. Grove

TO MY MOTHER,

WHO GAVE ME THE GIFT OF LIFE,

MORE THAN ONCE.

Acknowledgments

As head of a public company, I have been in the limelight for a good number of years. I have always viewed this exposure as one due to my professional work and have maintained a separation between my work life and my personal life and background. The former was fair game, I thought, the latter, not.

The first chink in this position, which turned out to be the first step toward this memoir, was the result of my meeting Josh Ramo. Josh was assigned to write my profile for *TIME* magazine's 1997 Man of the Year issue. He was keenly interested in my younger years, convinced that they had a major part in shaping who I became as an adult. At first, I resisted his efforts as I had all other such attempts before that. Josh prevailed, however. His genuine interest in my story and the trust he earned through the hours we spent together caused me to open up. My willingness to do so led to what I thought was an excellent profile—with that, the first olive was taken out of the bottle. So, thanks are due to Josh for starting the process.

In the years after the *TIME* article, the thought of telling my own story, in greater detail and in a book form, has recurred time and again. My wife, Eva, who over the years has heard me talk about the events of my life before we met at age twenty-one encouraged me. She reminded me of my grandchildren, who may not get to hear these stories from me when they will be old enough to understand them. Her encouragement turned into her becoming a sounding board and an active participant in prompting my recollection of incidents and events; it continued in her becoming a critical editor of the evolving story.

Once I had a first draft of the manuscript, Norm Pearlstine took on a key role. Norm and I have known each other professionally for twenty years or so, but when he agreed to edit my book, the relationship took on a different form. He immersed himself in my story and spotted the places where I was still holding back, perhaps because some memories were still painful. Norm systematically analyzed my manuscript for these spots and drew me out further than I was prepared to go at first. His efforts led to a more complete and more genuine story.

Last but not least, I am grateful to Catherine Fredman who, after having helped me with *Only the Paranoid Survive,* a book on business strategy, readily shifted gears stylistically, adapting to the requirements of telling the personal story of a boy. She maintained her keen editorial instincts but also undertook to question me in detail about settings, scenes, and emotions. Cathy's pursuit of the fine detail caused me to dig into my memories far more than I thought I could.

I am very fortunate to have people like these four take a deep interest in my first twenty years. Without them this book wouldn't have taken shape.

Contents

Prologue

I was born in Budapest, Hungary, in 1936. By the time I was twenty, I had lived through a Hungarian Fascist dictatorship, German military occupation, the Nazis' "Final Solution," the siege of Budapest by the Soviet Red Army, a period of chaotic democracy in the years immediately after the war, a variety of repressive Communist regimes, and a popular uprising that was put down at gunpoint.

This is the story of that time and what happened to my family and me.

Before I tell my story, it may be helpful to provide some historical context. When I was born, Hungary was governed by the right-wing dictatorship of Admiral Miklos Horthy. Horthy's government was aligned with Nazi Germany, but it was more independent than Nazi Germany's other allies. This may have had something to do with the fact that Hungary was situated between the countries under Germany's influence and the Soviet Union.

During the early years of World War II, Hungary maintained a policy of armed neutrality. However, when Hitler's Germany attacked the Soviet Union in June 1941, Hungary abandoned that policy and declared war against the Allies. For all intents and purposes, this meant declaring war against the Soviet Union on the side of Nazi Germany.

By 1943, the Soviet army had the Germans and their Hungarian allies in retreat, and the front began to work its way through Hungary from its eastern borders toward the capital, Budapest. The Germans were concerned that Horthy might try to negotiate a separate peace with the advancing Russians. To preempt that possibility, they occupied Hungary in March 1944 and, in October, installed an extreme Fascist government under the pro-Nazi Arrow Cross Party.

While the Horthy regime had discriminated against Hungarian Jews, the severity of the discrimination and persecution skyrocketed with the arrival of the Germans. Gestapo official Adolf Eichmann, who oversaw the implementation of the Nazis' Final Solution throughout the rest of Europe, took personal charge of the deportation and extermination of Hungarian Jews. The extermination process started in the countryside and the cities outside of Budapest; within four months, virtually all Hungarian Jews living outside of Budapest had been deported. The great majority of them were killed in concentration camps.

Before the process could be extended to Budapest, the rapidly deteriorating military situation—the Soviet forces were advancing on Budapest, and the Western Allies had successfully landed in Normandy and Italy—forced a halt to the deportations. Consequently, the majority of Jews in Budapest survived. Nevertheless, before the war, there were over six hundred fifty thousand Jews living in Hungary; after the war, some one hundred fifty thousand remained.

In January 1945, after street-to-street and house-to-house fighting, the Soviet army pushed the Germans out of Budapest and, by April, out of the rest of Hungary as well. Instead of a German occupation army, there was now a Soviet occupation army.

In the immediate aftermath of the war, despite the presence of the Soviet occupying forces, Hungary enjoyed a multi-party democracy. However, the Communist Party gained more and more influence and finally consolidated its position in 1948. Thereafter, Hungary became an unquestioned satellite of the Soviet Union.

The Hungarian Communist Party was divided into two major branches: the native Hungarian Communist branch, which had remained in Hungary even after the Communist Party in Hungary was outlawed by the Horthy regime; and the Muscovite branch, whose members had escaped to the Soviet Union and had now returned with the Russian troops. Matyas Rakosi was the preeminent leader of the Muscovite branch. Although both branches belonged to the same political party, there was a degree of distrust between them that grew as they jockeyed for positions of authority in the Communist regime.

By 1949, this jockeying for position broke into the open with the arrest and public trial of native Hungarian Communists by the Muscovites. The persecution intensified during the last few years of the life of the leader of the Soviet Union, Joseph Stalin, with purges, arrests, imprisonment, and deportation affecting the lives of broader and broader circles of people.

Stalin died in March 1953, and a gradual relaxation of totalitarian controls took place. Over the next few years, this process accelerated until it culminated in a rebellion against the Communist government—the Hungarian revolution of October 1956.

The revolt lasted for thirteen days and was then put down by Soviet armed forces. Many young people were killed; countless others were interned. Some two hundred thousand Hungarians escaped to the West.

I was one of them.

Right: My father and my mother, around the time I was born. *Below:* My uncle Jozsi.

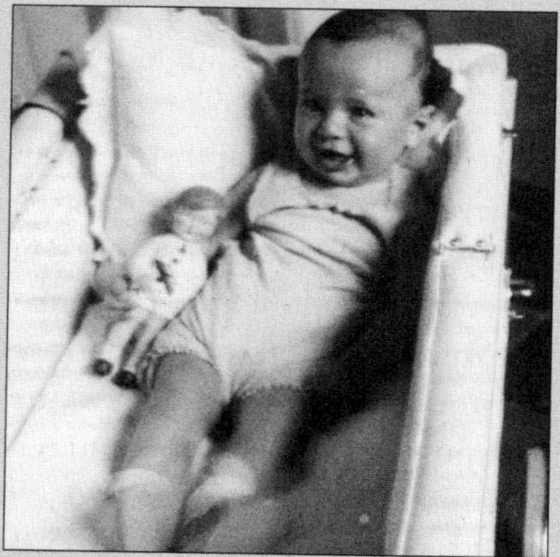

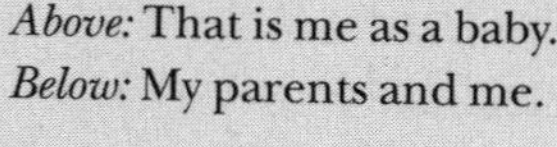

Above: That is me as a baby. *Below:* My parents and me.

Above: The house where we lived, on Kiraly Street (above the trolley bus).

Chapter One

MY THIRD BIRTHDAY

THE SEARCHLIGHTS were like white lines being drawn on the cloudy evening sky. They moved back and forth, crossing, uncrossing, and crisscrossing again. People around me had their faces turned up to the sky, their eyes anxiously following the motion of the white lines. My mother said that they were practicing looking for planes.

I paid no attention to them. I was taking my new car out for its first drive.

My car was a tiny version of a real sports car. I could sit in it and drive it around by pushing up and down on foot pedals and steering with a real steering wheel. It looked exactly like my uncle Jozsi's sports car, except that his was white and mine was red. Red was a lot more fun.

Jozsi and I had taken our sports cars to a promenade on the banks of the Danube River. I drove my car up and down, weaving between the legs of the people out for a stroll. It seemed more crowded than usual. Jozsi kept encouraging me to go faster and faster, then ran after me to keep me from bumping into people. Sometimes he succeeded. Sometimes he didn't.

But people didn't seem to mind. They barely paid any attention to me. They were mesmerized by those white lines in the sky.

My parents had come along, too. We often walked along the promenade on summer evenings. It was a popular thing to do in Budapest. Summer was over, but it was a warm evening, so I wasn't surprised that we were celebrating my birthday by the Danube. I was now three. It was September 2, 1939.

My parents had moved to Budapest the year before. My father, George Grof, whom everyone called by his nickname, Gyurka, was a partner in a medium-size dairy business that he owned jointly with several friends. They bought raw milk from the farmers in the area, processed the milk into cottage cheese, yogurt, and especially butter (they were particularly proud of the quality of their butter), and sold the dairy products to stores in Budapest. My father was a pragmatic, down-to-earth businessman, energetic and quick. He knew how life worked.

My father had dropped out of school at age eleven. My mother, Maria, had finished gymnasium, the Hungarian equivalent of a college preparatory academy. It was an unusual accomplishment for a woman at that time and even more unusual for a Jewish woman. Her heart had been set on becoming a concert pianist, but because she was a Jew she was not admitted to the music academy. Instead, she went to work in her parents' small grocery store. That's how she met my father.

The dairy business was located in Bacsalmas, a small town about one hundred miles south of Budapest, near the Yugoslav border. My father often traveled to Budapest to call on customers, the butter, milk, and cottage cheese distributors.

One day, my father called on my mother's parents' store to peddle his dairy products. He introduced himself to my mother. When they were done with their business, they stood in the doorway and talked until it was time for my mother to close up shop. Then they went for a walk through the streets of Budapest and talked and talked and talked some more.

They were different, but their differences complemented each other. My mother was cultured without being snobbish. My father was smart and energetic, with a quick sense of humor. My mother tended to be shy and reserved with strangers, but somehow she was not at all like that with my father. His energy and inquisitiveness brought out the best in her. They liked each other a lot.

The fact that my father was also Jewish helped further their relationship. It gave them a common background and a common understanding. Neither of my parents was religious. They didn't attend synagogue, and although most of their friends were Jewish, they didn't consider themselves to be part of the Jewish community. Aside from the religious affiliation that identified them on official documents, there was nothing to differentiate them from other Hungarians.

When they met, my mother was twenty-five and my father was twenty-seven, an age at which a man was expected to have found a way to make a living good enough to support a family. They married a year later and moved to Bacsalmas. It was 1932.

My mother hated Bacsalmas. She was a city girl, well educated, a would-be concert pianist, used to going to concerts and the theater. All of a sudden, she found herself in a small town out in the provinces. Not only was she living in a house with dirt floors and an outhouse, but she had to share the house with some of my father's relatives and partners. My mother was the newcomer and the outsider. She was a loner and very uncomfortable with communal living. She couldn't wait to get out of there, but she would not have a chance to do so for a while.

Shortly before I was born, my parents temporarily moved to Budapest so that my mother could give birth in a good hospital. My mother would have liked to stay, but she returned to Bacsalmas with my father and me.

She finally got her wish in 1938, when I was two years old.

My father decided to set up a branch of the dairy in Budapest to service his growing number of city customers. We moved into an apartment on Kiraly Street, a few blocks from the dairy.

Budapest is a city of two parts, separated by the Danube. The Buda side was hilly and dotted with old churches and castles and ramparts and rich homes. Pest was the commercial side, with the apartment houses spreading out from the city center. The natural setting, with its combination of the hills and the river, was beautiful and the stylish apartment houses and wide avenues lined with trees made for a pleasant environment.

Kiraly Street was a busy thoroughfare connecting the central Ring Road on the Pest side to the big City Park farther out. A streetcar line ran down the middle, making the street even busier. It wasn't particularly noisy, but something interesting was always going on.

There was a Jewish quarter in Budapest. It was located about a mile or so from where we lived. It was a strange, foreign area, where the men wore black hats and dark coats and long side curls and smelled odd. We were Jewish, too, but they were part of a different world.

Our world was a typical middle-class neighborhood. Ours was a nice street but nothing fancy. Our apartment house, too, was like many others: a ground floor with shops facing the street, topped with two stories of apartments surrounding a central courtyard. A small one-story building in the courtyard housed a photo studio. An older couple who lived in one of the ground-floor apartments in the back of the courtyard provided basic caretaker services. The man doubled as a shoemaker as well as superintendent of the building, while his wife, a kindly old lady, picked up packages for tenants, let in tradesmen, and performed other ordinary chores.

In our building, most of the apartments faced inward, their doors and windows opening onto the courtyard. A narrow balcony, maybe three or four feet wide with a wrought-iron railing, ran around the courtyard to connect the apartments on each floor. There was a communal toilet near the back of the balcony on each floor. This was for the inside apartments, which did not have their own toilets. A stairway connected the floors at each end of the balcony. In front, the stairway was wide and respectable. The back stairway was narrow and dark.

The apartments that faced the street were the better apartments. They were bigger and had their own bathrooms. Our apartment was one story up from the ground floor. Two rooms faced the street, the Big Room and the Little Room. Both were equally deep, but the Big Room had two windows while the Little Room had just one. The windows were tall and narrow and opened in the center, like doors; the sill was waist-high, so you wouldn't fall out. During the summer, the windows were always open. You could look out at the apartment buildings across the street and watch the traffic and the streetcars and the people coming and going on Kiraly Street. Even when the windows were closed during the winter, the rooms were bright and airy.

My mother's parents lived in the Little Room, and my parents and I lived in the Big Room. It served as my parents' bedroom, my bedroom, and our living room. There was a sofa bed in one corner, where my parents slept, with my crib nearby. There was also a polished wood dining table and chairs and some other furniture. The hardwood floor was covered with Persian carpets and area rugs.

A door opened from the Big Room to the hallway, a long, dark passage that led to the staircase. You could get to our bathroom from this hallway and also from the Little Room. The bathroom had a sink, a bathtub with a wood-burning stove used to heat the water for baths, and a toilet. Just before you got to the stairs, the hallway opened on one side into the kitchen and on the other side to a very small room, where our maid, a heavyset woman named Gizi, lived. Gizi cooked, cleaned the house, did the shopping, and looked after me. She eventually married a man who went only by his surname, Sinko. After they got married, Gizi and Sinko both squeezed into that little room. Sinko worked elsewhere, but when he was home, he would carve wood sticks for me and take me to the park. In her spare time, Gizi would sit down and read me the crime stories in the newspaper. I was completely fascinated.

We had frequent visitors to the apartment. Almost no one had a telephone, so instead of people calling up, they would drop in. People would come by, unannounced, and sit and talk for hours. As they were saying good-bye, they would stand in the doorway and talk for what seemed like hours more. My mother's younger brother, my uncle Jozsi, was around a lot. He was strong, muscular, and balding, and he was a lot of fun. I have no idea what he did, although judging from comments that the rest of the family sometimes made, it couldn't have been very much. But that didn't seem to matter. There was always a warm and joyful feeling about Jozsi.

That wasn't the case with my mother's second brother, Miklos. Miklos and Jozsi were twins but were very different in appearance and personality. While Jozsi was friendly and fun, Miklos was surly and seemed to carry a dark cloud around him. People didn't like him; their voices changed tone when they talked about him. Miklos didn't get along with anyone in the family, including my grandmother, his own mother. Once he was so nasty to her that my father intervened and the two of them started shouting at each other. I was afraid that they would come to blows. I had never seen my father that way before. After that, we didn't see much of Miklos.

My father was a sociable guy, and many of our visitors were his friends and business associates. Jani was one of my father's best friends and a partner in the dairy. He was from Bacsalmas, and his parents still lived there. He had his own apartment in Budapest, but he camped out in our apartment all the time.

Jani had been an officer in the Hungarian army, which impressed me. Tall and ramrod straight, he was a snappy dresser and something of a dandy, which also impressed me. He had a loud voice and a loud laugh and exuded self-confidence and energy. Jani was different in another way. He wasn't Jewish.

Another friend of both my father and Jani went by his last name only: Romacz. Romacz was as skinny as a stick, and his face was all wrinkled, like a raisin. I liked him a lot because he always talked to me as if we were equals. He, too, was from Bacsalmas and was involved in the dairy business; he managed the Budapest branch. He wasn't Jewish, either.

My father's friends knew my mother from when they all lived in Bacsalmas. If my father wasn't home, they would hang around anyway. She would serve them something to drink, smoke with them, and talk. None of the men was married, so they would recount stories of their latest romances, confide in her, and ask her advice. She was a kind of sister to them. They were like uncles to me.

Religious identity played no part in my world then. Some of our visitors were Jews, others were not. Those who were not Jewish seemed no different from us. While many Jewish people had German names, like Fleischer, Schwartz, or Klein, our name was no different from non-Jewish names. The word *grof* is Hungarian for "count." Family legend has it that an ancestor was the estate manager for a Hungarian count and somehow people started to refer to him by association as "the Count." In more recent times, some Jews changed their names to Hungarian-sounding surnames. Our family already had one.

I was born Andras Grof, but everyone called me by the more familiar form, Andris.

Left: That's me, at age 3.
Below: My parents and me, at age 4.

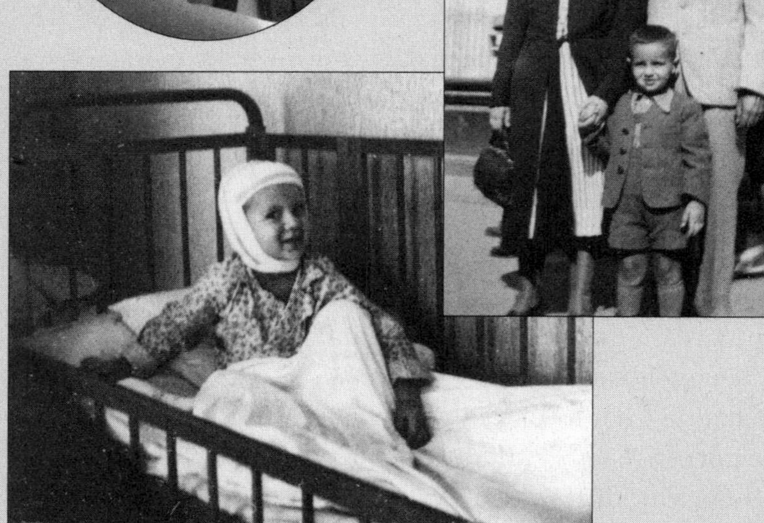

Above: I had to stay in bed for several months while I was recovering from scarlet fever. My head is bandaged because of my ear operation.
Right: My father (*top row, second from right*) is leaving for the front. He is with other members of his labor unit and some army guards.

Chapter Two

SCARLET FEVER

I DON'T REMEMBER becoming sick, and I don't remember being taken to the hospital. I don't remember anything about my illness until one day when I was four years old and found myself lying on my back, looking out of the window of a strange room. I looked upward and saw a leaden sky. My first thought was, I must be dead and in my grave, and that gray thing that I'm looking at must be the earth filled with the people who are still alive. This thought didn't exactly depress me, but I was a little sad that I might not see those people up there again. Then I looked away and became aware of my surroundings and realized that I was alive, too.

I noticed that I couldn't move either my head or my arms. There was a big bandage running around my forehead and my ears and covering the top of my head, like a turban. The turban was heavy, which made it very difficult for me to turn my head. My arms were by my sides, with tubes coming out of the inside of my elbows and running up into some contraption that was hanging on a wooden coat stand. This was the only object that was familiar to me. That coat stand was just like one we had at home. But I could not have been home because everything else looked different.

After a while, some men and women in white coats came into the room. Most of them were strangers, but one of them was my doctor, Dr. Rothbart. I was happy to see him. I loved Dr. Rothbart. You couldn't help but love him. He had a friendly, roundish face with a pockmark in the middle of his forehead. He once told me that he scratched himself there when he was a kid and that's why he had that pockmark. It always fascinated me that Dr. Rothbart was once a kid, too.

He told me I had had scarlet fever but that I was now recovering. I couldn't hear him very well. I thought it must have been the turban over my ears. He sat down on my bed, took my wrist in his hand, and counted my pulse. I watched him. His lips moved silently as he counted. I thought that was funny.

I saw a lot of Dr. Rothbart in the days and weeks after that. After some time, he helped me sit up in bed and I could actually look out the window and see something other than the sky. There was a courtyard with some bushes and trees in it. He took the tubes out of my arms; that hurt, but not as much as when they changed the bandage on my head. When it was time to change the bandage, I always begged him, "Please don't hurt me." He always promised that he wouldn't, but he always did.

One nice summer day, the nurses put me in a chair with wheels and wheeled me outside into the courtyard. I sat there in the sunshine and realized that I hadn't been outside for a long time. I was looking around, seeing people come and go on the paths between the bushes, and at one point I noticed a pair of feet in blue-and-white women's shoes under one of the bushes in the garden. I was sure they were my mother's. I called out for her: "Mama, Mama!" The shoes moved away. I called out again and the nurses came running. They told me that I should calm down, it wasn't good for me to get excited. Then they wheeled me back to my room. I couldn't calm down. I kept twisting my head, calling out for my mother: "Mama, come here! Mama, come here!"

The next day my mother visited me in my room. I reached out to her, but the weight of the turban kept me from turning to her, so she held my hand and stroked the back of it. She told me it was indeed she who had been standing behind the bush. The nurses thought that seeing my mother would get me all worked up and that would be bad for my heart, so she had been told to keep out of my sight.

After that, she came to visit every day. She brought me a copy of *The Jungle Book*, by Kipling. She sat by my bed and read me story after story, then read the stories that I liked over and over until I could almost recite them along with her. She also taught me how to tell time. First, she used a big wall clock to explain it. One day, she brought me a little wristwatch. A real wristwatch! Its brand was Marvin, and that became its name. I endlessly practiced telling the time and showing off my newfound knowledge to the doctors and nurses.

There was a blond nurse with big blue eyes whom I particularly liked. She was lively and paid a lot of attention to me. I felt warm every time she came into my room. My uncle Jozsi also liked her a lot. After he met her in my room, he came to visit very often, but he seemed to spend more time with her than with me.

One day, two of my nurses came to my room in great excitement. "Andris, you're going home today," one of them said. I was ecstatic. Then they continued, "But before you go, we have to clean you up." That part was not fun. First, they put me in a bathtub and scrubbed me from head to toe, except for my turban, with a soap that stung and a hard brush. Then they took me out of that bathtub and dried me, moved me to another bathroom, and let me take a real bath, all along admonishing me to keep the turban from getting wet. At last they dressed me in my own pajamas and took me to a room where my mother and father were waiting.

They greeted me with great excitement. I looked at their hands; they were empty. I asked them, "Aren't you supposed to have flowers for a sick kid?" My father turned around, ran out, and came back in a few minutes with a bouquet of white lilies. I took the flowers. They smelled good. Then my father picked me up and carried me to the exit with a whole retinue of nurses trailing behind.

We got into a taxi to go home. The taxi was boxy, with a glass window separating the passengers from the driver, and it had a leathery smell. I loved taxis, and the ride home was too short for my taste.

When I got home, a present was waiting for me. It was a little toy car track. You put the car on the top of the track and it would zoom down, twist around, and jump over a break in the track to the other side. My father showed me how it worked and kept playing with it until I complained, "Isn't that mine, Gyurka?" (I had called my father by his nickname ever since I learned how to speak. Nobody ever corrected me, so he became and remained Gyurka to me.)

After that, my mother put me to bed. As she explained to me, my heart had been damaged during my illness and it had to heal. I also found out that the scarlet fever had led to an infection in my ears and that my ears had had to be operated on. The bones behind my ears had been chiseled away. I shuddered at that description. To make matters worse, during surgery a blood clot started to travel toward my heart, but the surgeons noticed this and interrupted the operation. They cut a vein in my neck and got rid of the clot before it could do any harm. All in all, I was told, I had spent six weeks in the hospital. Now I would have to stay in bed for nine months. I didn't know how long nine months were going to be, but I was so happy to be at home with my family and in familiar surroundings that I didn't care.

My bed at home was a large crib in the Big Room. In short order, it was equipped with a board that ran from one side to another. If I sat up, the board served as a table. My food was placed on it, but more important, so were my toys.

Because I liked *The Jungle Book* so much, my parents gave me little animal figures—tigers, wolves, giraffes, and a wonderful lion that I called Lion *bacsi.* Children were expected to call adults *bacsi,* or "uncle," and *neni,* or "aunt," as a sign of respect. Lion *bacsi* was clearly a figure of great respect. I played with my animals for hours on end. I also had a set of very realistic, modern toy soldiers. I played with them, too, but I liked the animals better. From time to time, I had to endure the torture of my bandage being changed, but otherwise I was comfortable and feeling increasingly frisky.

During my long confinement in bed, I discovered an activity that made the time go faster. I started playing with myself. I found that it felt good and my mind always roamed when I did that. Little fantasy scenes ran in my mind, usually involving my blond nurse.

My mother caught me in the middle of one of my reveries one day and asked me rather harshly what I was doing. I was startled but told her, "I was telling myself stories."

My mother grabbed my hands, put them by my side on top of the covers, and in a tone of unusual disapproval told me to stop. I was taken aback. After that I told myself stories only at night when it was dark.

That didn't work all the time, either, because as I moved, the crib moved with me and made a telltale creaking sound. My mother would emerge from nowhere and yell, "Andris, stop that!" So I learned that I could only tell stories to myself very, very quietly.

Luckily for my mother's peace of mind, I had another playmate—a real one. My grandmother had died before I got sick, but my grandfather was very much alive. He had infinite patience, which made him the perfect playmate. We played the same games over and over, and each time he participated with as much excitement as if it were the first time we'd ever played that game. My favorite game was to play the conductor on a streetcar; he would play the passenger and hand me a ticket, which I'd carefully punch with my toy puncher. We also played barber, and once he actually let me cut his hair.

After months had passed, I was allowed out of bed for a few hours at a time, but I had to stay home in our apartment or nearby. Then, finally, the day came when Dr. Rothbart cheerfully told me that he would take the turban off one last time and I would not have to deal with it again. This turned out to be only partly true, because while the turban was gone he covered the wounds behind my ears with a sticky bandage that hurt almost as much when it was removed for cleaning. But eventually that, too, went away.

However, even though my turban and the bandage were gone, I still didn't hear as well as I used to. I could understand people only if they talked directly to me. After a while, people around me learned to speak louder, so I never felt I missed anything. I understood women's voices better than men's.

Ears and ear troubles preoccupied me for a long time. My mother brought me a hand puppet, a little bear that you slipped over your hand and moved around with your fingers. She used to entertain me by doing makeshift puppet shows for me. When I got my hands on the little bear, I cut a hole in its skull behind its ears, then I bandaged it so that he looked just like me.

In 1942, when I was five years old, my father was called up into the army. He was not really a soldier; he and other Jewish men were conscripted to serve in labor battalions clearing roads, building fortifications, and the like. He had been called up for short periods of time before, and each time he came home in a few days or, at most, a few weeks.

This time, though, was going to be different. When he came home with the news, he was trying to smile, but there was something wrong with his smile. His unit was to leave for the Russian front, and he would not come back any time soon.

My mother and I went down to Nagykoros, the town from which my father's unit was to leave. Nagykoros was about sixty miles from Budapest, and we had to take a train to get there. When we got there, my father's train was being readied for departure.

Most of the cars in which his unit would travel were open freight cars, without roofs and with sides that were only half as high as those on regular cars. One car was packed with kettles and stoves and cooking equipment; it was the kitchen unit. One of my father's cousins by marriage, who was also named Miklos, was the cook, and my father was helping him out. My father already knew many of the men in his unit. It looked like fun, almost like a bunch of friends going camping.

There was a crowd around their train. My father and the other workers were wearing their regular clothes, as were the women like my mother who came out to say good-bye. They looked like any normal crowd of people out on a summer day. But there were also soldiers, dressed in ill-fitting uniforms and carrying rifles. These soldiers guarded the workers' unit. The guards and the laborers mixed freely. The soldiers even helped me climb up on the kitchen car and let me hang from it. It did not feel as though the workers were prisoners—in fact, the soldiers looked like a bunch of sloppy workmen, but the uniforms and the rifles were a constant reminder that they were different.

Then it was time for all the men to get on the train. I held my mother's hand, while my mother talked with my father and my father's friends and we got ready for the final good-bye. After a couple of toots, the train slowly started to move out of the station. My mother's hand tightened on mine. I didn't see her expression because I couldn't take my eyes off my father. He was waving good-bye with a smile that looked a little too cheerful. As they were moving out of our sight, my father gestured to my mother, using his fingers to pull his mouth into an even wider grin to try to cheer her up. Then the train was gone.

We headed back home to Budapest. It was a couple of hours on the train. My mother was very quiet.

When we got home, we were greeted by more bad news. My grandfather, my mother's father, was in the hospital. We immediately went to visit him. He was in a room with several beds. He had an ice bag on his forehead, and he was mumbling incoherently. On our way home, my mother explained that my grandfather had had a stroke. A few days later, he was dead.

I was about six years old when this picture was taken. People told me it made me look older but, they shrugged, it didn't matter: I would grow into it.

Chapter Three

THE WAR ARRIVES

After my father left, Jani and Romacz continued to drop by to chat with my mother, but now we also had a new set of visitors: the wives of the men in my father's labor unit. Their husbands' absence brought the women together, and they visited each other frequently. Often, they came to our house.

The women would stand around in the Big Room, talking and sipping cognac and smoking cigarettes. After the initial greetings, I was ignored. I felt left out and after a while would slink off to play by myself in a corner of the Little Room. With my grandfather dead, no one lived there anymore, so it was used as a guestroom. Someone was always sleeping over, generally one of my father's friends from the dairy or rug business. One formerly frequent visitor who was now noticeable by his absence was my mother's brother Jozsi. Like my father, he, too, had been conscripted into a labor battalion and sent away to the Russian front.

The women would stay until late in the afternoon, talking and drinking, talking and drinking, and chain-smoking until the air in the Big Room was hazy from their cigarettes. Visitors had often smoked, but I didn't remember anyone ever drinking at our house before. The mood was different, too. Instead of the laughter and animated conversation I had been used to, everyone seemed preoccupied.

I noticed that my mother drank more than the other women. After they left, she often continued to smoke and drink by herself as the light dimmed in the Big Room; it seemed as though her thoughts were very far away. I knew she was thinking about my father.

The letters had stopped coming shortly after he was taken away. Then, in the spring of 1943, my mother got an official notification saying that my father had "disappeared" at the front. I didn't know what that meant. I didn't know how people could disappear. I wondered, "Isn't it better to be lost than to be found dead?" But I didn't dare ask my mother. So through those long afternoons, she smoked and drank in the Big Room and I played by myself in the Little Room.

Smoking was a constant in our house. The smell of cigarettes was pervasive throughout the apartment, but especially in the bathroom, where people always lit up to mask other smells. I disliked the smell of cigarettes, but I was fascinated by the ritual of smoking. One day, as I watched my mother chat and smoke with Jani, I sidled up to them and asked to be allowed to try it. They laughed at me, which just made me dig in my heels and insist that I really, really wanted to. The two of them discussed it for a while, then my mother said, "Okay, Andris, you can try. Let's see if you like it."

I reached victoriously for her cigarette and pulled in one puff. Immediately my stomach got queasy. I dropped the cigarette and dashed to the bathroom and threw up in the toilet. When I came out, my mother and Jani with straight faces offered me another smoke. I shook my head. I couldn't even look at them.

When there were no visitors, the Big Room was my playground. With my interest in jungles piqued by *The Jungle Book,* I imagined that each of the area rugs represented a different exotic island. An older boy in our apartment house frequently came to play with me. With the help of a map of Southeast Asia that he had studied, the two of us would go island hopping. We would start on the rug designated as Borneo. We would put Lion *bacsi* on the rug designated as Sumatra, and we would hop over the South China Sea of the polished hardwood floor from Borneo to Sumatra to kowtow to Lion *bacsi* and ask for his friendship. Then we would hop over to Java and all the other far-off islands that my friend culled from his map. We would spend the afternoon doing this until Gizi started cooking dinner and it was time for him to go home.

In the mornings, I went to a kindergarten in our neighborhood. There were maybe ten or fifteen kids in my class. We were all Jewish, as was our teacher. We often played with wooden blocks that fit together, but I rarely made them fit the way they were intended to. Instead, I preferred to build contraptions of my own.

I made up my own games, too. Once, when my mother was talking with the other war wives, I overheard a phrase that intrigued me. The phrase was, "They will put the Jews in a ghetto." I had no idea what a ghetto was, but for some reason the phrase stayed with me.

One day, I dragged some of the kindergarten tables and chairs over to the wall to make an enclosure. I declared that that was the ghetto and we would put all the Jews inside it. A few of my playmates and I started chanting, "They will put the Jews in the ghetto, they will put the Jews in the ghetto." We grabbed some of the other kids and dragged them, slipping and sliding on their behinds, inside the enclosure. Pretty soon we were all chanting in unison, "They will put the Jews in the ghetto, they will put the Jews in the ghetto." When my kindergarten teacher heard us, she sharply told us to stop saying that. But by then the entire class had picked up on the phrase, and the more she protested, the stronger the chanting got. She looked at us helplessly, then shrugged silently and let us be. We played the ghetto game over and over again for weeks.

Once in a while, my mother and Jani would take me on a picnic to one of the outlying parts of Buda. They would settle down to talk, and I would run around and play. I had a little metal drinking cup made of rings that telescoped down to a flat circle. I was very proud of it and loved to fill it with water from the fountain.

One time, I went to the fountain, opened my cup, and filled it with water. When I turned to run back to my mother and Jani, I couldn't see them. I turned and ran in a different direction. I kept running around until I realized that I was lost. I was terrified. All of a sudden, the woods around me seemed cold and menacing now that I couldn't see my mother. I ran faster and faster looking for her until I lost my breath and started to cry. Some strangers knelt down and tried to console me. Nothing worked until my mother and Jani emerged from the woods, looking for me. I ran to my mother and clung to her legs, sobbing. It was a long time before I calmed down.

Across the street from our apartment house was a pastry shop that served ice cream during the summer. When I was good, my mother took me down for a scoop. During the winter, instead of ice cream, my treat consisted of puree of chestnut with whipped cream both inside and on top.

I loved ice cream, but my love was seriously tested in the summer of 1943 when Dr. Rothbart decided that my tonsils needed to come out. My mother took me to a hospital, which didn't alarm me particularly, because she promised that I would get to eat a lot of ice cream. In the examining room, I was put in a big leather chair and covered with a heavy rubber sheet from my neck to my knees. A doctor who was wearing a round mirror with a hole in it over his eye told me to open my mouth really wide. When I did, he and a nurse propped it open even farther with a metal bracket. It strained my jaw and I tried to complain, but my words came out "Ah, ah, ah." The doctor nodded in reply, made some reassuring sounds, and reached deep into my mouth with a long metal instrument. I didn't feel any pain, but after a while blood started spurting from my mouth all over my chest and onto the floor. It was very scary.

After that, I was kept in the hospital for a few days. My mother slept next to my bed on a mattress on the floor. The promised ice cream did, in fact, materialize. I was given as much ice cream as I wanted to eat, but it didn't taste so good.

That was not my only experience with doctors. Although the wounds behind my ears had healed, I was left with holes in my eardrums, and my ears drained fluid more or less all the time. We went to see a doctor who lived outside of Budapest. We took one tram and then another tram and yet another tram to get there. The house didn't look like any of the doctors' offices I'd been to before. Those had been in hospitals or big apartment buildings. This house was surrounded by a big, fancy garden, like a castle in a picture book.

Inside, the office was full of strange boxes, with knobs and wires sticking out. The doctor didn't do much to my ears; instead, he made me listen to all kinds of sounds that he made by twisting the knobs. I was to signal when I heard them.

At first, I was curious about these contraptions and participated in the tests as if they were some kind of a game. After a while, the game became tedious, but I soldiered on, pushing the button when I heard the sounds. Every once in a while, I daydreamed and missed my moment to push the button. Then I hurried up to push it later, hoping that it still counted.

The doctor told my mother that I had lost about 50 percent of my hearing and that the draining needed to be looked after. The doctor who had operated on me had since died, so my mother found a very highly regarded expert in Budapest to replace him. He was called Dr. German.

Dr. German had a fancy office on the banks of the Danube in an especially ornate building in a neighborhood of many ornate buildings. It was much more elegant than where we lived. We visited Dr. German every week, and we always had to wait. The waiting room and the examining room were both painted a deep green color. Everything, wherever I looked, was the same deep green. I was told it was meant to soothe people's nerves while they waited to be treated. When I heard that, instead of being soothed, I got worried. I didn't want to be hurt.

I needn't have worried. Dr. German had a collection of metal instruments, but all he did during each visit was look inside my ear, wrap an instrument with cotton swabs, and dry the discharge. Then he patted me on the head and told us to come back in a week. As we left, my mother would mutter about Dr. German driving us to the poorhouse with his high fees.

Dr. German was married to a famous actress. That was the first thing everyone mentioned when they talked about Dr. German, even before they mentioned his fees. She acted only in grown-up plays, so I had never seen her. But I was impressed by the way her reputation seemed to enhance his. Once Dr. German asked me what I wanted to be when I grew up. I said I wanted to be just like him. He laughed and asked why. I said, "Because I want to marry an actress, too."

SWIMMING ACROSS

Starting in 1943, from time to time we had air raids. They always happened in the middle of the night when I was sleeping. My mother would reach into my bed and drag me to my feet and dress me while I was still half-asleep. I would hear the howling of the sirens as I came awake. If I stood in bed and looked out the window, I could see a streetlight hanging from the wires that were strung across the street. I thought the siren sound came out of the streetlight.

My mother had already thrown on her clothes and had her overcoat on. We hurried down the long, dark hallway and ran down the stairs to the air raid shelter. The shelter was in the cellar that ran under the apartments. Other people streamed out of their apartments, hurrying downstairs to the cellar, too. Before the war, each apartment had its own designated section in the cellar to store coal or wood for the stoves. The air raid shelter was a walled-off section. It was painted a drab color, with naked light bulbs suspended from the ceiling. There were rows of wooden benches with no backs.

Everyone filed into the room and took their places on the benches. People would be wrapped in their overcoats, whether it was warm or cold. They sat side by side, hunched over on the benches, sleepily staring ahead or occasionally looking up nervously at the cellar ceiling. Most raids lasted about half an hour, sometimes an hour. Nobody talked much. I huddled against my mother, drifting back to sleep for little bits of time, jerking awake on the hard bench, then drifting back to sleep again. We waited—either for the bombs to hit us or for the steady siren sound that signaled the end of the air raid.

We never did get hit, but an apartment house maybe half a dozen blocks from us did. It looked like a big knife had sliced off the front half of every floor. You could see into the apartments on all four stories, like a doll's house. In the back part of each room, the furniture was still in place and the pictures were still on the walls. The front part had fallen into a big heap of bricks, stones, and unidentifiable rubble.

Rumors abounded. Some people said the planes that caused the destruction were English. Someone told my mother that the air pressure from the bomb blew goose down from a storage area into the air raid shelter next to it and it suffocated a lot of the people hiding there.

My mother and I passed the ruined building every time we went to the City Park. The sight made me very uneasy, but by the time we got to the park, I usually had forgotten all about it.

My favorite place to play was near a statue of George Washington. The statue was a big bronze figure of a soldier on a rearing horse. I thought this statue was made of iron because the Hungarian word for "iron" is *vas,* pronounced "vash." So I assumed that the soldier's name was "Vashington" and he was named for the material his statue was made from.

There was a sandy area near the statue. One day, a little girl was playing there. We had never seen each other before, but I had sand toys and she had a doll, so we started to play together. We were busily building sand castles and putting the doll next to them when she suddenly turned to me and said, very seriously, "Jesus Christ was killed by the Jews, and because of that, all the Jews will be thrown into the Danube."

My mother was sitting on a bench nearby. I jumped up and ran to her, bawling my head off. I told her what the little girl had just said. My mother put her arm around me and said it was time for us to go home. We picked up the sand toys and left. That was the last time I played in this park.

In the fall, I turned seven and started going to elementary school. Most of my schoolmates were only six, but since I was born in September, I hadn't been allowed to start real school until now.

My elementary school was affiliated with a Jewish orphanage. Some of the children were orphans and wore a uniform. Others like myself were day students. We did not wear a uniform. Everybody at this school was Jewish. After my encounter with the little girl in the park, I found this reassuring.

My teacher was called Magda *neni*. She was a redhead. Because of my bad ears, I was placed in the first row so I could hear her better. I liked sitting there; it felt as though she was talking mainly to me, and I loved the attention. When we weren't participating, we were supposed to sit upright with our hands crossed on the small of our backs. We leaned back against the bench, our hands cushioning us against the hard wood.

I was usually the first one to have my hand in the air when she asked a question, and she called on me often. I frequently had the right answer and enjoyed the praise and further attention I got for doing so well. It also allowed me to break out of the uncomfortable sitting position.

There were girls in the class, too. I particularly liked a girl named Aniko. Another girl, Eva, liked me. But I was so intrigued with Aniko that I didn't pay much attention to Eva. We always raced to help each other into our overcoats. I was usually the first to get Aniko's overcoat. Meanwhile, Eva was usually the first to get mine. But I would wait until Aniko took the overcoat from Eva so that she could help me into it.

One time, Aniko didn't come to school for a few days. I found out that she was ill. My mother took me to her house so I could visit her. When I walked into her room, she jumped out of bed and hugged me, wrapping her legs and arms around me like a monkey. I was very excited and pleased.

In March 1944, the German army occupied Hungary. There were no announcements and there was no fighting—they just came in. My mother and I stood on the sidewalk of the Ring Road, watching as the cars and troop carriers filled with soldiers drove by. The German soldiers didn't look anything like the soldiers who had guarded my father's labor unit. Those soldiers slouched a bit, and their uniforms were wrinkled. The German soldiers were neat and wore shiny boots and had a self-confident air about them. They reminded me of my toy soldiers; they had the same kind of helmet, the same color uniform, and the same type of machine gun. I was impressed.

The sidewalk was lined with passersby, all watching the procession of soldiers, all looking very serious. My mother was also very serious. I looked up at her. Her face showed no expression at all, but she squeezed my hand tightly. There was no sound, except for the engine and tire noise from the cars and troop carriers. My mother started pulling me away. The procession hadn't ended, and I didn't want to go. I was fascinated by what I saw.

German soldiers became a regular sight all over the city. Some were in big groups marching in unison, some in small groups walking in single file with machine guns strapped across their chests. Trucks and troop carriers moved around the city, particularly on the Ring Road. They set up a headquarters a few blocks from our house. Soldiers and officers came and went in our neighborhood streets all the time. Like the soldiers in the procession, they were always neat, their boots were always shiny, and they always acted self-confident.

Once I encountered an officer on Kiraly Street near our house. I was coming home from school by myself. He was walking in the opposite direction. He moved deliberately, his steps firm. There was something overwhelming about him. I averted my eyes and flattened myself against the wall to try to make myself invisible.

That spring we had many thunderstorms. There's a feeling before a storm breaks that the weather is about to change. You know something is going to happen. The wind stops, the temperature drops, the air gets more humid. Something is going to burst out. That's the kind of feeling there was in the air that spring, even on clear days. I didn't know what was different, I just knew that something was.

That June, my first year of school came to a close. Magda *meni* handed out our report cards and we ran down the stairs to our waiting mothers. I had the highest grades in all of my class. I happily showed my grades to my mother. She was pleased, too.

My mother, in 1944. By fall, all Jews had to wear a yellow Star of David on their clothes.

Chapter Four

LIFE GETS STRANGE

THE SUMMER OF 1944 started out in a strange way. Soon after first grade ended, with very little preparation, my mother shipped me off to Bacsalmas. She explained that Budapest was not a good place to be that summer.

In addition to being the location of the main branch of my father's dairy, Bacsalmas was also the hometown of my father's friend Jani. I stayed with Jani's parents, who lived in a peasant house with earthen floors. There was no running water; you got water by pumping it out of a well with a long-handled iron pump. There was a dog, a cat, and chickens. But Jani's parents were old and quiet, and I had no other children to play with. Life was dull after Budapest, and the days moved very slowly. I was lonely and missed my mother.

I didn't have to miss my mother very long. Early one evening, less than a week after I had arrived, Romacz unexpectedly showed up. He, too, was from Bacsalmas and was friendly with Jani's parents. I was happy to see him, but I was told to go and play while he and Jani's parents had a long and serious discussion. Afterward Romacz told me to go to sleep but added,

"During the night, I'm going to take you home to your mother." I was delighted.

Sometime in the night, Romacz woke me up and helped me dress, then we got on the train to Budapest. He wrapped me in a blanket and I fell asleep and didn't wake up until the next morning, when I woke up in my own bed in the Big Room. I was very happy to be home with my mother. She was a little embarrassed about my sudden trip to—and even more sudden departure from—Bacsalmas. She explained that Romacz found out that Jewish people were going to be taken away from Bacsalmas. That's why he went down there to bring me back.

This was only one of the strange things that happened that summer.

Before that summer, listening to the radio was an ordinary thing. Now it became a complicated ceremony. The radio sat on a table in a prominent position in the Little Room. It was a large wooden box with shiny black knobs on it. The sound came through a cloth that was stretched over the front. By turning the knobs, you could listen to all kinds of foreign-language programs mixed with mysterious squeaks and whistles. I knew that these strange languages and the noises signified that the programs were coming from far away, so I always was a little awestruck when I listened to the sounds emanating from the box.

Before that summer, listening to the radio was an occasional thing. Now friends came over almost every evening to listen. People started paying a lot more attention to the radio than they had before, but at the same time my mother didn't want anyone outside our apartment to see or hear us listening to it. She would pull down the blinds and draw the curtains, then turn the radio on at a very low volume. She and her friends would huddle around it with very serious expressions. I think they were listening to Hungarian programs transmitted from England. The programs always started with four rhythmic thuds: dit-dit-dit-dah. I couldn't hear anything else, but the adults must have heard something they liked because occasionally they would cheer silently.

I was confused by all these goings-on and annoyed that I was kept away from the radio. The radio used to be my toy; I used to have access to it any time I wanted. Now the adults had taken over my radio and it was no longer available for me to play with.

Later in the summer, the radio disappeared. Jews were no longer permitted to own a radio. Now I missed the listening ceremony that used to symbolize the end of each day.

Certain elements stayed the same. Jani and Romacz still visited frequently. Gizi was still living with us, and meals continued in a regular fashion. Nighttime air raids occurred periodically. But life was getting more tense all the time.

Government posters appeared on the walls of buildings, describing the latest regulations applying to Jews. Jews were not supposed to mix with other people. Some stores started to carry signs: "We don't serve Jews." When we took the tram, we could board only at the back and we had to stay standing even if there were empty seats. We could have tried to cheat, but everyone seemed to know who was and wasn't Jewish, so it didn't seem like a good idea. We stayed close to home. I wasn't in touch with any of my school friends. No one seemed to know anything about anyone else.

Then something even stranger happened. There was a man who ran one of the shops on the ground floor of our apartment building. We knew him only to say hello to, but near the end of the summer, he became much friendlier toward us than ever before. He would frequently show up at our door with flowers for my mother. I didn't think much of it. My mother was a beautiful woman: She had very fine features, big blue eyes, soft brown hair. I thought giving flowers to beautiful women was what people did.

One day, this man rang our doorbell and I answered it. He had a box of chocolates and he said it was for me. I loved chocolates and I hadn't seen any for a long, long time. I took the box, thanked the man, and danced back to the Big Room, calling for my mother: "Mama, Mama, look what I got." My mother took one look at the chocolates in my hand and asked me where I had gotten them. When I told her, her eyes flashed, and in one swift, firm motion, she slapped me across my face. She grabbed the box of chocolates and ran out of the apartment after the man who had brought them. When she returned a few minutes later, I was crying in the corner of our room. I didn't know why she had slapped me. She bent over me and said, "Andris, you don't understand what is happening." Then she explained that the man had offered to take her and me away to his hometown as if my mother were his wife and I were his child.

"But he's already married," I said. I knew this because I had met his wife.

My mother just stared at me. Then she told me, "Do not, under any circumstances, ever take anything from him or talk to him again."

Shortly after that, at the end of the summer, our lives changed in a major way. Jews had to move out of their apartments by a certain date and into special buildings that were designated as houses for Jews. People called them "Star Houses" because a big yellow Star of David was painted above the entrance of each of these houses. The Star House that we moved to was just a block and a half away on Eotvos Street.

We moved into a very small apartment that had one room, a kitchen, and a bathroom. It had been Jani's bachelor flat for many years before he moved to a larger apartment. Jani still owned it, and he made it available to us when the building was designated a Star House. Gizi had to return to her home in the country because Jews were not allowed to have domestic help. We shared the apartment with two other women. One was an acquaintance, the other one was a stranger. The acquaintance was the wife of one of my father's former business partners. The wife was Jewish; the husband was not, so he continued to help run the dairy and live in their old apartment, while she moved into the Star House.

Some furniture was already there. We had no room to take any of our belongings with us, which was just as well, since we weren't allowed to anyway. We just took some suitcases filled with clothes. I took my school knapsack with some books and a few stuffed animals.

The new apartment was on the ground floor, looking out onto a narrow side street. It was small and a lot darker than our old apartment. We slept on sofa beds and cots, which were folded up during the day. Cooking was very clumsy because of the lack of room. Instead of a stove, there were only two hot plates, so the women took turns.

Nobody complained or commented much. We made do, because there wasn't much else we could do. Things were happening to us one after another. Just when we got used to one thing, another thing happened.

The next thing that happened was that we were all required to wear a yellow Star of David on our jackets over our heart. I remember my mother stitching the cloth stars on some of my clothes. We were forbidden to step outside the Jewish house without wearing one. It was just one more of those things to accept numbly and silently.

One day, a friend of mine, also Jewish and about my age, showed up at our doorstep wanting to play with me. He wasn't wearing his yellow star. I was frightened—frightened for him and somehow for us, too. When we started playing, I forgot about it, but after a few hours, he set off to go home. His home was in another Jewish house some blocks away. My fear returned. My friend just laughed, shrugged his shoulders, and ran off into the street. I was afraid for him, but I was also impressed by his cocky courage.

Whenever we went out, we wore our star. But we didn't go out very much. There were few places we could go to, and the hours when we could be on the street were limited. Many stores would not serve people with a yellow star; besides that, it was a very strange feeling to walk on the streets wearing it. People avoided looking at us. Even people whom we knew wouldn't meet our eyes. It was as if a barrier was growing between us and everyone else.

In addition to the German soldiers on the street, we saw members of the Arrow Cross Party. I didn't know much about the Arrow Cross Party, except for their uniform, which was black and militaristic. They wore armbands with their emblem, two crossed arrows, one vertical, one horizontal, with points on both ends. I had seen Arrow Cross members on the street before, but I never had anything to do with them. Now I didn't want to look at them; they frightened me. I was told that they were the Germans' closest supporters in Hungary and they hated Jews.

At one point, I got sick. I had a bad case of diarrhea. My mother didn't have the ingredients or the means to cook me a proper chicken soup and mashed potatoes, which was what I craved the most. Fortunately, she ran into the wife of the superintendent of our house on Kiraly Street, who readily offered to make these things for me and bring them over. As a non-Jewish person, she was free to move around.

I got my chicken soup and my mashed potatoes and enjoyed every bit of it. But the next day there were loud knocks on our door. When my mother opened the door, a strange man stood there with a grim look on his face. He showed my mother something, and words were exchanged between the two of them. My mother came over to me and said, "I have to go away for a while. Stay here and wait for me."

There was no one else in the apartment. I didn't know what was going on. All I could do was wait. I played with my toys to pass the time, but I wasn't really interested in them. I was wondering where my mother had gone.

My mother returned in a couple of hours, shaken up. She told me that the man who came for her was a policeman who arrested her along with the superintendent's wife. Feeding Jewish people was against the law, and my mother had broken the law by allowing the super's wife to provide us with food.

My mother said that she was incredibly lucky to be back. As the policeman was taking her in, he told her that she should have bade me a more proper good-bye because she probably would not see me again. They happened to walk by the storefront that housed what used to be my father's dairy, and as luck would have it, one of my father's former partners was sitting in the store and noticed my mother walking by with the policeman. He was the non-Jewish husband of the woman who shared our apartment, and he recognized my mother. The policeman was in plain clothes, but the police station wasn't too far, so the man put two and two together and figured that my mother was under arrest. This man had a friend in the police force, and he instantly telephoned him. The friend pulled some strings, and after being made to cool their heels for a while, my mother and the super's wife were both released with a stiff warning.

From then on, it was predominantly boiled beans for me.

Early one evening in October, my mother came to me with a very serious look on her face. "Andris, we have to get out of here," she said. My father's sister's husband, Sanyi, had come by a few hours earlier. He was not Jewish, so he was able to move around the city and talk to people. He had heard rumors that the Arrow Cross Party was going to overthrow the Hungarian government the next day. After Sanyi gave us the tip-off, he disappeared.

My mother told me that the Arrow Cross Party thought that the government had been too easy on the Jews. If they took over, things were going to be a lot tougher. I listened without saying a word, as she explained that we both needed to disappear from the Jewish house. Immediately.

She told me I was to go to Jozsef *bacsi,* another of my father's former business partners and a Christian. I would stay with him and his wife until she could come and get me. Meanwhile, she had made other arrangements for herself, and as soon as I was packed off, she would disappear, too. But, she assured me, she would visit me as soon as she could.

We left our apartment within an hour of Sanyi's visit. I put on some extra clothes and gathered up a few of my favorite books in my school knapsack. We dressed in overcoats without our yellow star. Then my mother took me by the hand and we walked the half block or so over to the store. It was dark outside, and I was so confused that it never occurred to me to be scared about being outside without a yellow star. My mother said a quick good-bye, then Jozsef *bacsi* took my hand and we walked to the tram. We got on at the front entrance this time, which reminded me that I was supposed to act as someone other than who I was. We rode a couple of miles to his house.

Jozsef *bacsi* and his wife lived four floors up in a big apartment house that was similar to ours on Kiraly Street but bigger. I was put in a room of my own. There were only the three of us in their spacious apartment, so in one way, it was a pleasant change from my previous surroundings. But I couldn't really enjoy it because my mother wasn't there. I was numb with loneliness.

My mother had told me while she was getting me ready that if anyone asked, I should say that I was from the country and had escaped from the Russians who were bombarding our town. But I didn't know what the name of the town would be or anything else. There had been no time to come up with a more detailed story in the few minutes she'd had to prepare it. Jozsef *bacsi* explained to me that the best thing for me was to stay out of sight so that nobody could show an interest in me.

The weather was gloomy and the curtains were often drawn. Jozsef *bacsi*'s wife was often around the apartment, but though she wasn't unfriendly, she tended to her own affairs. So I sat in the dim main room, day after day, and read my books over and over. One of them was about a little kitten who goes out to play in the snow and gets very, very ill. I read it a million times, and every single time, my heart would break over the kitten that was going to die. Even though I knew it would get better, I would have to finish the book to get out of my funk.

The days moved slowly, interrupted only by an occasional air raid. The air raids were becoming more frequent, often occurring during the day. I took my books to the air raid shelter. I read them with a great deal of attention, not because they were so interesting—after all, I'd read them a lot of times already—but because that way I could avoid catching the eye of anyone who might be looking at me.

My mother did come to visit. One of the workmen from the dairy had taken her in. They pretended that she was a refugee from the countryside. The workman's wife was the superintendent of an apartment house, and my mother worked alongside her, lugging garbage, dumping ashes, and sweeping the stairways. She wore a kerchief over her head, like our super's wife in the apartment on Kiraly Street. I had never seen her wear a kerchief before. It made her look plain, but it didn't matter to me. The only thing that mattered was that she was there.

But no sooner did she arrive than the air raid sirens went off and we had to go to the shelter, all four of us. I wasn't supposed to recognize her, and it took all the effort I could muster for me to avoid talking to her or even looking at her. Then, when the air raid was over, my mother had to go. She gave me a quick hug, and kissed me, and told me she would be back. Then she left.

When I got bored or lonesome, I looked out the window, which overlooked a square. One day, I was alone in the room and was staring out the window when I noticed a commotion at the entrance to the apartment building across the street. German army trucks were lined up, covered with dark green tarps. German soldiers were standing in two lines, forming a passage between the first truck and the entrance to the apartment house, and people were filing out of the apartment house and onto the trucks.

This was a Jewish house; I could see the yellow star over the entrance. The people filing out were all wearing yellow stars. They all had their hands up in the air, even the little kids who were being carried by their parents. They came in an unending flow, filling up one truck after another. I watched from the unlit apartment window on the fourth floor. I was too high up to see their expressions or hear any noise through the closed windows, but I could see that the German soldiers weren't shouting. It all seemed very orderly. Tears started to stream down my cheeks.

All of a sudden, the door to my room opened. I turned around and there was my mother in an overcoat with the kerchief covering her head. I ran to her and grabbed her around the waist and buried my head in her overcoat. As I recognized her scent, I buried my nose even deeper. She didn't say anything, just held me very, very tight. Then, after a little while, she said good-bye and left again. When I looked out the window, the trucks were gone. There was no sign that anything had ever happened.

The third time my mother came, she came to take me away. Nobody else was around. She sat down with me on a sofa and explained that she now had official papers for us. According to those papers, her name was Maria Malesevics—the papers kept her real first name—and I was her son, Andras Malesevics. I was to forget that my name was ever Grof, and I had to absolutely, positively learn this new name, Andras Malesevics, and the story to go with it.

We were going to pretend that we were from the town of Bacsalmas—the papers said so—and we were escaping from the Russians. If anybody asked about my father, I was to say I didn't know who my father was. Men were always coming and going, visiting my mother. I didn't know which of them might have been my father. We were going—together!—to a suburb of Budapest called Kobanya, where Jozsef *bacsi*'s parents would take us in as refugee relatives from the country.

I didn't care where we were going. I cared only about two things: I was with my mother, and I had to learn a new name. I understood that I had to memorize it to the point where it was a part of me; I couldn't make a mistake. The name was hard—Malesevics is a Slavic name that I had never encountered before, and I was afraid that I would forget it. So all along the interminable tram ride to Kobanya, through the winter evening, I looked out the window, watching my reflection in the glass appearing and disappearing with each streetlight we passed and muttering inaudibly, "Andras Malesevics, Andras Malesevics, Andras Malesevics."

We took the tram to the last stop, and after walking some distance, we arrived at our destination. This whole neighborhood consisted of small one-story apartment houses. They looked shabby compared to our old neighborhood. The building we went to had perhaps a dozen units surrounding a courtyard. Jozsef *bacsi*'s parents lived in one of these units. Their apartment had one room and a kitchen. My mother and I were to sleep in a folding bed that was stashed in a corner of the kitchen.

Jozsef *bacsi*'s parents greeted us warmly enough. His mother toasted slices of bread on a pan on the gas stove, spread some lard on top, and gave them to me. I ate them with gusto while she and my mother went about setting up the cot we would share in the kitchen.

Before I went to sleep, I had to use the toilet. There was no bathroom in this apartment. You had to go outside to the courtyard, where there was a communal toilet with stalls shared by men and women. My mother warned me, never, absolutely never, to pee in front of anybody or to wash myself in front of anybody. I had been circumcised, as Jewish boys in Hungary typically were, but Christian Hungarian boys were not. If anybody saw my penis, it would have given me away instantly. I took this to heart and became extremely private.

The next morning, my mother heated a pan of water on the stove and I washed myself. Then I got dressed and ventured out to the courtyard. Another boy my age was playing there. His name was Jozsi. We started playing together. There were a few other kids in the apartment building, some younger, some older than we were, but the two of us became inseparable buddies.

Romacz visited us a few days later. He was wearing a backpack, from which he took a couple of loaves of bread, some lard, and some other food, which he gave to us. My mother took it with profuse thanks and made it our contribution to the household food supply. Romacz kidded around with me a little.

It was a welcome change in an otherwise quiet and serious environment.

Jozsef *bacsi*'s parents were about my grandparents' age. They never called me anything but Andris, and they acted without exception, unfailingly, as if I were Andris Malesevics. I wondered if they knew who I really was, but they never indicated that they did.

Ordinary life ceased to be. The apartment was like a village, with regular residents and a transient population of people displaced from the countryside because of the fighting. There were more women than men, and the men were mostly older; all the young men were in the army. People came and went, tending to the daily chores of getting bread from the bakery and finding firewood. We didn't spend much time with each other, but there was still a sense of belonging to the apartment unit.

My mother helped with cleaning the apartment and cooking. I was never hungry, but the food was always the same: dried beans or lentils and bread, if we could get it. In addition to the gas stove used for cooking, there was a wood-burning stove used to heat the apartment. But there wasn't much wood, so the stove was lit only part of the day. We generally wore our overcoats even inside.

It was November, and the weather was cold and dark. Occasionally, it would snow. Things were gloomy. But my mother was there, and that made me feel there was something warm and normal at the center of this strange existence. Her constant presence reassured me enough so that I could have fun with Jozsi. My days consisted of playing outside with my friend, coming in from time to time to warm up a little, then going outside again. Our friendship was the only spark in this dreariness.

I wasn't going to school, and Jozsi had no school, either. There was not much else to do but play in the courtyard. Every once in a while, my friend and I would go outside the courtyard and play in the street. We were told not to go very far. That was fine with me because I did not feel comfortable being far from my mother.

I noticed big posters plastered on the walls. There was a colored one showing English or American planes flying overhead in the background; the foreground showed a little girl who had picked up a doll that exploded and blew her hands off. The little girl was looking toward the planes, a question printed next to her face: "Why?"

But that wasn't the poster that made the biggest impression on me. That one warned in big bold black letters what would happen to people who harbored Jews or Communists. The warning stated that people found doing that would be—and then came a word that I didn't recognize but that sounded very, very scary. One night, I whispered to my mother, "Mama, what does *folkoncoljak* mean?" My mother put her finger on my lips. Later, when no one was in the apartment, she told me it meant "to slaughter." Somehow, it sounded even worse to me.

I never said anything about these posters. Jozsi didn't, either. Some mornings, I would notice that somebody had used a rubber stamp to stamp red Communist stars all over these posters. Of course, I didn't know who it might have been, but the appearance of those red stars gave me a warm feeling. They suggested I was not alone. But I never looked at the posters for more than a second, because I was afraid that I would give myself away to my friend.

We weren't the only refugees living in the apartment building. There were several others, mainly women, who boarded with some of the tenants. One of these women had red hair, which almost got her into trouble.

One day I was playing with Jozsi in the courtyard. It had snowed and people had shoveled the snow into a big mound in the center of the courtyard. Jozsi and I were trying to slide down the mound in an old sled when the redheaded woman came through the entrance with a German soldier. He stood in the courtyard while she went into the apartment where she was staying. She reemerged shortly afterward with her identification papers in her hand. The German soldier examined the papers very thoroughly, then eventually folded them up and handed them back to the woman, saluted, and went away.

After he left, all the other residents came out to find out what was going on. My mother was among them. The woman told them that because of her red hair, the soldier thought she was a Jew, and whatever papers she had with her were not sufficient to convince him otherwise. I continued playing with Jozsi in the snowbank, as if what I had heard had nothing to do with me. But my heart beat rapidly for a long time.

Above: The remains of barricades set up in Budapest by the German army. (Sovfoto/Eastfoto) *Right:* A square in the center of the city after the Russian army took it over. (Sovfoto/Eastfoto)

The retreating Germans blew up all the bridges connecting Buda with Pest. (Major Edward Czerniuk)

Chapter Five

CHRISTMAS IN KOBANYA

I ENCOUNTERED MY FIRST Christmas ever in Kobanya. I didn't know much of anything about Christmas, but I knew it had to do with gifts. Jozsi's family had a makeshift Christmas tree, and I was invited to come and exchange gifts. I was impressed with the Christmas tree. It was a small branch of a pine tree that they had propped up on a table. It was overloaded with decorations, all the decorations that would have gone on a much bigger tree.

You couldn't buy any presents. Nobody was working anymore, and even if they had some money, no stores were open. Jozsi had some homemade small gifts for me. With the help of my mother, I worked up some gifts for him, too. I gave him police paraphernalia: a makeshift badge, a whistle, and a few other things. We played around the tree and then went outside and used our new gifts in our games. Christmas was fun.

A few days later, I woke up to a strange sound. It sounded like someone was dropping planks of wood on top of each other. Three or four planks would drop with loud thuds, then there would be some minutes of quiet, then the thuds would start again. When the planks were dropping, the adults around me stopped talking. It looked to me almost as if they were holding their breath. My mother told me that what we were hearing was the sound of Russian artillery. I was fascinated and went outside with Jozsi to be able to listen better to the sound of the big guns.

One morning, shortly after I came back from the toilet, there was an explosion outside in the courtyard. It didn't sound like a plank dropping at all. It sounded the way I imagined an explosion would sound—a big, long, loud, reverberating bang, followed by the random, rattling noise made by the debris of roof tiles, bricks, and pieces of wood flying around. The silence after the explosion was deep. People sat frozen in place, as if waiting for more explosions to come. After a while, when nothing else happened, we went out and noticed that fragments of a shell had torn into the door leading into the toilet. I stared at the fragments; I had gone through that door just a few minutes earlier.

The adults decided it was time for us to move to the wood cellars, where we would be safer from shells like this. As in Kiraly Street, there was a central cellar area, and each apartment also had its own storage cellar. People dragged their cots and belongings down from their apartments and set up housekeeping. We shared a cellar with the redheaded woman who the German soldiers thought might have been a Jew, and another woman.

It was just as well that we moved, because things were getting worse by the day. First the electricity went out. Then a day or two later the water stopped flowing. It would come back on from time to time, then go out again. When it did come on, everyone stockpiled water in every pan and bucket they could find. The only reason people left the apartment building was to attempt to get bread or other food. Most of these trips were unsuccessful, but every once in a while, one of the women would find an open bakery that had just finished baking bread and would rush home to tell the others to get some before it ran out.

The cellars were dark, with wood and coal piled up on the side. The coal dust covered everything, including our clothes and belongings. Each cellar had a naked light bulb hanging from a wire in the ceiling, but since there was no electricity, the cellars were lit by kerosene lamps. The smoke from the lamps added to the grime. Most people had small stoves to cook the beans that made up our diet, but the stoves didn't do much to combat the cold and damp, so we wore our overcoats all the time, even to bed. We had no choice. We adjusted with numbed resignation.

Time went by slowly in the cellar. There wasn't enough light to read. Some of the men played cards. The women looked after the necessities of eating, scrounging up supplies, and cooking. The few kids there were just hung around underfoot. We weren't allowed to go outside. The sound of the artillery was a continuous backdrop. At first, it was a shock, but within a few days, we were so used to it that we hardly paid it any attention.

One day, the father of one of the children decided to engage us in a useful activity. He gathered all the kids together in a corner of the cellar where a stove was lit, so it was fairly pleasant, and told us that it would be a good idea for us to practice our catechism. All the kids nodded. I did, too, but I was frightened out of my wits. All I knew about catechism was that it had something to do with the Catholic religion, but that was about it, and I was sure that my lack of knowledge would give me away in an instant.

The man started questioning one of the children. I avoided looking at him, so that I wouldn't catch his attention. The answers were satisfactory, so the man moved on to the next child, one closer to me. When the question moved to the third child, I would have been next. I got up and excused myself and said, "I have to go to the bathroom." The man nodded, then turned his attention to the child he was questioning.

I ran to my mother, buried my face in her neck, and whispered to her what was going on. She hugged me firmly and said, "You will not go back." Then, out loud, she told me that it was about time I gave her a hand and started bossing me around. I never made it back to the catechism.

This experience made me avoid the other kids a bit more. I did not want to get caught in another educational exercise.

A week or two after we settled into the cellar, a group of Russian soldiers showed up at our apartment house. There was no shooting or fighting; they just walked into the house and found their way down into the cellar. They came in casually, but each of them carried a machine gun. The Russian machine guns were different from the German kind. They were like a rifle, but the bullets were stored in a circular drum that was attached to the barrel of the rifle.

The Russian soldiers had stubble on their faces and looked rumpled and tired. There were maybe ten or fifteen of them. The soldier who was in charge didn't seem much different from the rest. He spoke German, which made it possible for some of the tenants to communicate with him. Several of the other Russian soldiers also spoke a little German. One old man in the apartment building came from a part of Hungary where they spoke a dialect of Russian, so he became something of a translator for the Russians who didn't speak any German.

The soldiers checked out the cellar, then they settled in the vacated apartments upstairs. They weren't too friendly, but they weren't unfriendly, either. They left us some of their bread. It was different from Hungarian bread; it was shaped like a brick, was very dark, and had a sourish taste. But we were very happy to have it.

After this initial encounter, they pretty much left us alone. They left the apartment house very early each morning and came back late in the evening. It was just as if they went to work.

The artillery fire continued and we were still living in the cellar, but I felt a little more secure now that the Russians were there. They weren't Germans, and they had pushed the Germans out.

The soldier in charge—my mother told me he was a sergeant—often chatted with my mother in German and came down a number of times to visit with us in the cellar. I had never heard my mother speak anything but Hungarian before, so I was very impressed by how fluently she seemed to be able to talk with him. At one point, my mother, the sergeant, and I were alone in our cellar and my mother, after exchanging some words with him, turned to me. She said, "Andris, do you remember *'Modim anachnu lach'*?" This phrase was the beginning of the Hebrew prayer I had learned the year before in first grade and recited every morning at school. I froze. I wasn't supposed to remember things like that. My mother said, "Just for now, it's okay. If you remember it, tell it to the sergeant." I did. A big smile spread on the sergeant's face, and he patted me on the head. That night, my mother and I snuggled up in our cot, and she whispered to me that the sergeant was a Jew and his family had been killed by the Germans in Russia. His name, she said, was Haie.

Another night, we were settled in our cot and I was asleep when someone came into the cellar. I drowsily saw by the light of the lantern that it was the old man who occasionally acted as a translator. The old man said something to my mother and the two other women. An argument ensued. I couldn't follow it, but I could tell that the women were very upset.

A Russian soldier came in and waved the old man and the two other women out of the cellar. He closed the door and fastened it from the inside and propped his machine gun against it. He sat down at the side of our bed. He was grinning. My mother was telling him things in Hungarian, then in German, but he just continued to grin. He poked his forefinger against my mother's chest, then pointed it at himself and said, "Andrei," as if his name were Andrei. My mother pointed to me and also said, "Andrei." I figured that "Andrei" must be the Russian version of "Andris."

The Russian soldier kept grinning and again poked his finger against my mother's chest. My mother got out of bed and picked me up. The soldier moved his gun and opened the door and let my mother carry me out. She handed me to one of the women in another cellar. Then she went back to our cellar. The neighbor woman took me into her bed and put her arm around me. I lay there, stunned and full of apprehension. I had no idea what was happening to my mother or what would happen to us both. There was so much pressure in my chest that I could barely breathe.

After a while, my mother came back for me. She was very tense and angry. She picked me up again, which was unusual, because I was too big for her to carry me. She carried me to bed and we went to sleep. Later on that night, some more Russians came into our cellar. My mother yelled at them something about how all three of the women had already done it today. After some hesitation, the Russians left.

The next morning, my mother had a frighteningly determined look on her face. She brusquely told me to get dressed quickly. I knew better than to argue. She grabbed me by the hand and took me out of the cellar, out of the house, and started walking very fast on the street until she ran into a Russian patrol. She walked right up to them and started gesturing, asking about something called GPU. The Russians gestured in some direction and we went on. I had no idea what was going on and had no idea what GPU was about or who GPU was.

After several stops to ask for directions, we ended up in another apartment house filled with Russian soldiers. My mother seemed to be asking them something. Then, still holding on to my hand, she was brought up to an apartment where there was an officer. The officer spoke German, so a rapid exchange took place. The officer nodded and said something. My mother seemed to be thanking him. We turned and went out. The soldiers in the courtyard stared at us without saying anything.

We returned to our apartment building. I was panting because my mother was walking so fast. When we got back, Haie was waiting for us in the courtyard. He had a very serious look on his face. He gestured for my mother to follow him. I was sent back to the cellar.

Later, my mother joined me there, clearly upset. That evening, Haie came for us in the cellar. We followed him to one of the apartments. It was full of his group of soldiers and also with several strange soldiers, including the officer with whom my mother had talked earlier in the day. My mother faced our Russian soldiers, then one after the other, she looked each one in the eye and shook her head no. I was holding my breath when she faced Andrei. Andrei himself was beet red, and it looked like he wasn't breathing. After a very brief pause, my mother shook her head no. I yanked at her hand. She yanked back and said to me, "Quiet," in a fierce tone that forbade an answer. The examination continued until my mother shook her head no to each of the Russians in our house. After some discussion, the other Russians turned around and left. We went back to the cellar.

That night in bed, my mother explained to me what had happened. Haie told her that if she had pointed out Andrei, Andrei would have been shot on the spot. But his comrades for sure would have thrown hand grenades into the cellar and killed us all. So she had decided not to recognize him.

After a while, the artillery exchanges subsided. The Russians moved on and we moved back upstairs. It was mid-January. One day, I was alone in the courtyard, building a snowman, when my mother came out of the apartment and beckoned me over to her. She looked different. She pulled me into the apartment and closed the door. She told me that Haie had come back to tell her that as of yesterday, there were no more Germans on the Pest side of the city. They had retreated to the Buda side and blown up all the bridges over the Danube after they left. This was intended to make it hard for the Russians to chase after them, but it also made it very unlikely that the Germans would come back. The wave of relief that swept through me was so strong that I felt dizzy. It was as if after holding my breath for a long time, I could start breathing again.

But I could see in my mother's face that there was something else. She went on, "I think it's time for you to become Andris Grof again." I was stunned. I had become Andris Malesevics so through and through that for a moment I was confused. But only for a moment. Then the significance of being free to use my real name engulfed me.

Just then, I heard my friend Jozsi calling me to go sledding with him. I went. I wanted to tell him my news, but I couldn't find the right words or the right moment. So we just sledded and played in the snow on the street around the house, and I didn't say anything. When we had enough and were heading back to the house, without looking at him, I burst out, "You know, I didn't tell you the truth. I am not who I said I was. I'm not Andris Malesevics. My name is Andris Grof. I had to change it because I'm Jewish and they would have taken me away if I kept my real name."

He didn't react at all. He dragged the sled toward his apartment, waved good-bye, and went inside.

I stayed in the courtyard to finish building my snowman. Half an hour or so later, Jozsi's father appeared in his doorway and called out to me, "Andris, come in here." I went. I didn't know what to expect. He had not been unfriendly to me, but other than at Christmas, he had never invited me in before.

When I came into their kitchen, the father told me to sit down on a stool by the kitchen table. He pulled out another stool for himself and brought out a sheet of paper and a pencil. "What did you say your name was?" he asked.

I could feel the heat rising in my face. Andris, I told him, Andris Grof. I sat there looking at him. He went on, "And where did you live?" My face got hotter. But I told him. "And where is your father? What did he do before the war?"

And so it went, question after question. Slowly, carefully, he wrote down each answer I gave him on the sheet of paper. Then he looked at me and without a word folded the paper and got up and went to a cupboard filled with shirts and slid the folded paper below the stack of shirts. He thanked me without a smile. I told him he was welcome—also without a smile.

I got up and left. Once outside, I began trembling with fear and from the hatred welling up inside me.

I found my mother in our apartment and burst out with what had just happened. I was panting so hard, I could barely speak. When I was finished, we stared silently at each other for a long moment. I was still breathing heavily; she didn't seem to breathe at all. Then she said, "It won't do him any good. The Nazis are gone. Gone." I nodded. I couldn't say a word. I was choking with hatred.

A couple of days after Haie told my mother that the Germans were chased out of the Pest side, my mother decided it was time to go home to Kiraly Street. The trams, of course, were not running, so going home meant walking ten miles through the snow-covered streets.

The night before, we carefully made our preparations. My mother borrowed a backpack and put all of our clothing and some food into it. Early the next morning, after saying goodbye to the neighbors and hugging Jozsef *bacsi*'s parents, we set off.

The streets were empty and covered with snow. Tanks and troop carriers had chewed up the snow, and the tire tracks had frozen into hard, icy ruts. At first, there was not much sign of the war, other than occasional Russian patrols. But as we kept walking, the street scene started to change.

We saw streetcars standing abandoned in the streets. The overhead power lines were broken, and the wires lay twisted on the ground next to the trams. Burned-out military vehicles, both German and Russian, were scattered around. As we got closer to the center of town, the houses started to show signs of fighting. Some buildings had big round holes in them, through which we could see destroyed apartments. Broken bricks and pieces of mortar were strewn over the street. Everywhere, the plaster on the outside walls showed bullet marks. And all the windows were blown out, with broken glass everywhere crunching under our feet.

There was an eerie quiet in the streets and no traffic. The few people out moved furtively, trying to make themselves inconspicuous. They were mainly women, who were bundled up, their kerchief-covered heads bent down so you could hardly see their faces.

We kept walking. At one intersection, I saw a man lying in the street facedown, his legs and arms sprawled out. It was the first time I had ever seen a dead body. I kept turning my head to look at him. My mother yanked on my hand and growled, "Look where you're going."

We kept walking. Down one street, I could see a strange shape. As we got nearer, I realized it was a dead horse sprawled by the side of the street. An old man crouched next to it, sawing away at the horse's frozen leg with a kitchen knife, cutting off slivers of meat and dropping them into a bucket that was next to him. He didn't look at us as we walked past.

The closer we got to the center of the city, the worse was the devastation left behind from the fighting. I kept looking around with a sense of wonder. I felt as if I were in a dream. The city didn't look like the Budapest I'd left behind just a few weeks before. In barely two months, it had become a different world.

The sensation of being in a dream kept me from feeling fatigue and also kept me from wondering what would await us at the end of our journey. I just kept walking, numb. After a while, I was neither particularly surprised nor unsurprised by anything we encountered.

To break our trip, we stopped at the apartment of a friend of my parents. This friend was a Jew who had been a highly decorated officer in the Hungarian army. Because of that, he did not have to move into the Jewish houses or a ghetto, and he and his family were exempt from the regulations that governed the rest of the Jews. My mother was confident that he would still be in his apartment. We were looking forward to a break in our journey.

We went up to the third floor of the building where he lived and knocked on his door, but neither he nor his family were in that apartment anymore. Some neighbors heard our knocking and came out to tell us what happened. The Arrow Cross had taken him and his wife and his children, who were younger than I, out to an empty lot nearby and shot the entire family, decorations notwithstanding. After a moment of silence, my mother turned around and left, pulling me by my hand.

We headed to the last place we had stayed, in the Jewish house on Eotvos Street. The house was largely untouched by the fighting. Somebody else was already in our apartment when we arrived. We put down our backpack and immediately went over to our real apartment on Kiraly Street. There was no glass in any of the windows, but the apartment house was still standing.

We knocked on the superintendent's door, and his wife answered it. After a startled pause, she hugged both of us. She was genuinely glad to see us. She said, "People didn't expect you to come back."

My mother looked at her for a moment, then said quietly, "We are back."

The super's wife told my mother that somebody had moved into our apartment and that most of our furniture was taken away. Then she said, "Let me have some time to take care of things." We went back to the Jewish house and spent the night with the strangers who had moved into the apartment where we had stayed.

The next day, we returned to Kiraly Street. Our apartment was vacant. The windows had been covered with thick tan packing paper. It kept the cold air out, but it also kept out the light, so the apartment looked as gloomy as if it were dusk. Some of our furniture was missing. Other pieces were in the wrong place, so our apartment didn't look like home. And it was filthy, with everything covered with dust and dirt and grit. One of the beds was outside in the corridor. The bed had a huge gash in the middle of the mattress. My mother pressed her lips together but didn't say anything.

Bit by bit, our belongings surfaced. I didn't think we got everything back, but it started to look like our old apartment.

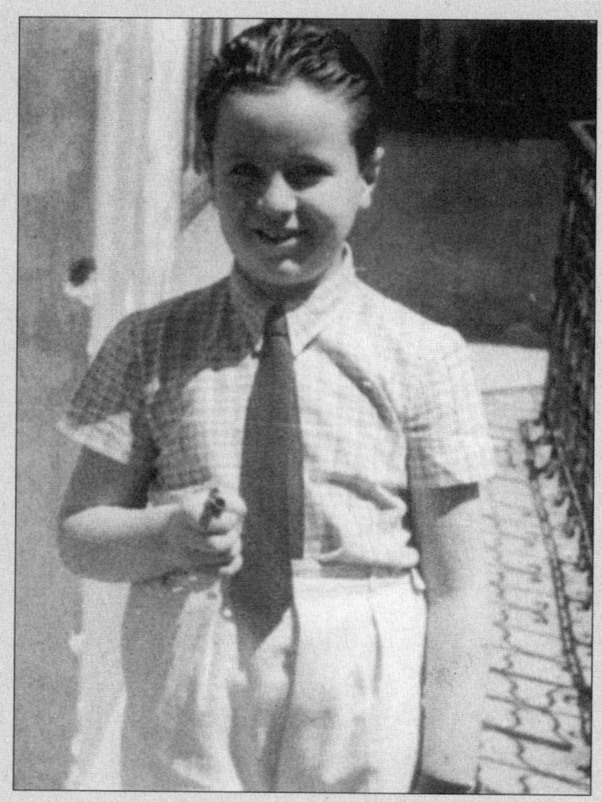

Right: Me, at age 10, standing on the walkway in front of our apartment. *Below:* I graduated from the fourth grade (I am the third one from the left in the third row). The girl I had a secret crush on is the second from the left. Margit *neni* and the school principal are in the middle.

Chapter Six

AFTER THE WAR

THE FIGHTING was over, but Budapest was still occupied, this time by the Russian army. No sooner had we settled back into our apartment than the super passed the word that the Russian authorities wanted us all to go out into the streets and shovel the snow. Even though I was only eight, I had to go, too. They couldn't find a shovel small enough for me, so I was given a sharp hoe with which to chip off bits of ice and frozen snow from the pavement.

We were called out for similar snow-shoveling exercises frequently during the rest of that winter. No one ever worked too hard. People shoveled because they were ordered to, not because they were enthusiastic about it. However, it was a good opportunity to talk and exchange news. That's how we heard that Jani had been picked up by the Russians and taken away to a prison camp.

My mother buttonholed everyone she ran into to ask if they had heard anything about my father. The answer was always, "No." But that didn't stop her. She asked about my father all the time. She would interrupt ordinary conversations to question people she had already asked the day before. I found her insistent inquiries as annoying as a fly buzzing around my head and, it seemed to me, about as productive. We never got any news.

Normal life returned in fits and starts. Soon after we returned home, Gizi and her husband, Sinko, returned and settled back in their room next to the kitchen. Reassured that there was someone to take care of me, my mother took a trip to Bascalmas to visit what used to be the main branch of the dairy. She packed her bag full of extra clothing, silverware, and china to barter for food. She returned a day or so later with fresh cottage cheese, sour cream, salami, and other things that I hadn't seen for months. I jumped up and down with joy when I saw them.

My mother told a harrowing story of her trip. Train service had started back up, but it was sporadic and the trains were crowded beyond belief. My mother traveled both directions on the top of a train along with a lot of other people, all of them hanging on to the roof and to each other to keep from falling off.

After a while, Sinko and my mother started making these trips regularly, and eventually my mother reopened the storefront that used to be the dairy distribution outlet. (Like other stores in Budapest, it had closed as a result of the fighting. Luckily, unlike many, it was not damaged.) My mother started to sell the dairy products she and Sinko brought back from the country. This way, in a very modest fashion, the dairy business started back up again.

When Sinko wasn't busy with the dairy or getting the apartment back in order, he occasionally took me to City Park. He had an old, beat-up bicycle, and he let me ride on the crossbar as he pedaled down Kiraly Street. Sinko liked to go fast. The streets were rutted and full of potholes from the fighting, and on every bump the crossbar bit into my bottom. But I didn't care. These outings were always very special.

We didn't do much when we got to City Park. I had no friends my age and Sinko didn't qualify as a playmate, so we just rode around, bumping along on the unpaved paths. I desperately wanted to learn how to ride a bike. Once in a while, Sinko let me sit on the seat while he walked the bicycle, but my feet didn't even reach the pedals.

By the time spring came around, my mother was very busy with her trips to Bacsalmas and the business. School had reopened. Even though some kids went back to class, my mother figured that I might as well skip the entire year and make it up later.

My mother and I had decided that I would have the Little Room as my own, but soon the novelty of having my own room wore off. I was pretty much left alone, and I was bored and a little lonely just hanging around. However, hanging around became much more fun when I hooked up with Gabi.

Gabi Fleiner was not related to me, but he might as well have been. His mother was one of the daughters of the owner of a neighborhood tobacco shop. The shop had been around forever. It supplied my mother with cigarettes, postcards, and stamps, and me with occasional candy. The smoke shop owner's family and my mother had a cordial relationship that went back a long way. Our families had something else in common: Like my father, Gabi's father had been taken away to a forced labor battalion and had not returned. Gabi and I had known each other before the war, but we had not been close friends. Now we became inseparable.

Gabi and I were the same age and about the same height. I was a little pudgy, while he was quite skinny. He had light brown, straight hair, and I had curly dark hair. Gabi was the more enterprising one of us, and he became the leader in our adventures.

Our first mission was to explore the neighborhood. The streets were a big playground of rubble and bombed-out buildings. We poked around the piles of rubble and gawked at the damaged buildings, returning to our apartments only to grab a bite to eat. It was like being on permanent vacation. Meanwhile, all of the adults were preoccupied with getting their lives back to normal, so they didn't pay much attention to us.

One day, Gabi took me to a little general store that had sprung up in a bombed-out storefront a few blocks from home. The glass had been blown out from all the windows and hadn't been replaced yet. The goods were displayed in the window opening, protected by a chicken-wire screen. There were potatoes, cabbage, and onions and other staples, and there was also some candy.

Gabi and I looked in through the chicken wire. Then, while the store owner was busy with a customer, Gabi nudged me with his elbow, quickly reached in through the chicken wire, and grabbed a handful of candy. I did likewise. Nobody saw us, but we pounded off down the street as if we were being chased. When we ran out of breath, we stopped and ate some of the candy; the rest we stashed away in our pockets. It wasn't very good candy, not as good as I remembered from before the war, but being stolen gave it extra flavor. Then we sauntered home.

My mother was home when we arrived. She had an uncanny ability to know when I was up to something or when I was telling less than the truth, and this case was no different. She eyeballed us sternly and with a few pointed questions quickly found out what we had done. She erupted. Then, still breathing fire, she ordered us to take back the candy we had left and apologize to the storekeeper. She gave us some money to pay for what we had eaten.

We went back to the store, much more slowly than we had come. My mother followed at a distance, close enough to ensure that we did as we were supposed to but far enough away to let the storekeeper speak her mind to us freely. It didn't take a lot of explanation for the shopkeeper to get the picture. She knew the whole story as soon as we opened our grubby hands and handed her the candy and the change. She accepted them and our apology, and we left. That was the end of my life as a criminal, but not the end of my adventures.

In the absence of school, organized activities, or much in the way of toys, we had to be inventive to entertain ourselves. Sometimes it didn't take much. The main staircase in our building spiraled all the way from the ground floor to the top. One rainy day, Gabi and I went up the main staircase to the top floor, and we peed down the stairwell, marveling at the shape of the falling streams and the way the drops hit the stone floor two stories below.

When my mother came home that night, I knew I was in big trouble. Someone must have spotted us and told her what we had done. She called me into the bathroom and yelled at me, and before I knew what she was doing, she started beating my bottom with the handle of a wooden spoon. Although I'd had an occasional slap, I had never been beaten before. It hurt. It hurt a lot. I started bawling and tried to make myself as small a target as possible by clinging to the towel rod and plastering myself against the wall. But my mother kept yelling and the wooden spoon continued to find me.

Finally she stopped. No one said anything. After her yelling and my bawling, the silence throbbed as painfully as my bottom. I went to my room and lay down on the bed, trying to find a position in which my bottom didn't hurt. I didn't succeed. I tried to read. I read the same paragraph over and over many times before I gave up. I put my head down on the pillow, feeling very sorry for myself. Finally, I went to sleep.

The next day, I had black-and-red-striped welts all over the backs of my thighs. Some of them showed beneath the hem of my shorts. When I went to visit my mother in the store, her coworkers noticed them and gave my mother a hard time. This consoled me some. Meanwhile, I learned my lesson. I never peed in the stairwell again.

As the weather became warmer, Gabi and I would go to City Park to play. One time, I found a cartridge of rifle shells. There were six bullets, all shiny and clearly live. It was a real treasure.

I took the cartridge home and studied our apartment with a purposeful eye. The windows from the bathroom and Gizi's room both opened onto an airshaft, which allowed light to come in from above. Since the building next to us had been demolished, light also came in from the side. The bottom of the airshaft was on the level of our floor. I could climb out through the bathroom window and pretend that I had a private little courtyard. But I had to be very careful that I didn't fall out of it. This area was maybe six feet square, with concrete on the bottom and bricks on three sides. It was the perfect hiding place.

I climbed out of the bathroom window, clutching my cartridge of bullets, and looked around. I noticed that some of the mortar under the bathroom window was loose. I picked at it with my finger and was able to dislodge a chunk, exposing a hole under the window. The cartridge fit perfectly. I slid it in, then replaced the mortar to hide it. After that, I snuck out of the bathroom window periodically to examine my treasure. I was always very careful. There were all kinds of rumors about kids playing with unexploded munitions and blowing their hands off. I didn't want that to happen to me.

The war was effectively over in early April of 1945. By the middle of April, the last of the Germans and the Arrow Cross retreated from Hungary. Budapest was gradually returning to the life of a functioning city and becoming recognizable again. Little by little, the paper in the shattered windows was replaced by real glass and the piles of rubble in the streets were cleared away. Some of the streetcars began running again. Stores started to open for business, in a rudimentary fashion. Food was rationed, but peasants from the countryside brought produce to the city to sell, so there was a growing variety of food available. The Russian soldiers were still there, marching around and standing guard, much as the Germans had done a year earlier. I could barely remember a time when soldiers hadn't been a backdrop to my everyday life.

One of the first signs that life was returning to normal was the reappearance of newspapers. They were sold by boys my age, who ran up and down the streets shouting out the headlines in order to promote sales. One day in August, the kids were madly waving the papers and shouting, "Auto bomb dropped on Japan! Auto bomb dropped on Japan!" I didn't know what an auto bomb was. When I asked, I was told it was a very big bomb, so big that the war might be over. And in a few days the newsboys were shouting that it was.

My mother and I didn't celebrate in any particular way. It wasn't new news. For us, the war had ended back in January, on the day Haie told us that the last of the Germans had been pushed out of Budapest.

People began to surface from wherever they had disappeared to. The Russians let Jani go fairly soon after they took him away. He dropped by, not particularly worse for the wear.

My mother questioned him as she did everyone who came from anywhere else: Had they seen or heard anything about my father? The answer was always, "No." I was getting impatient with her obsessive questioning; it was obvious to me that she would never get a satisfactory answer. I could barely remember my father, and now his memory, faded as it was, was tarnished by my mother's obsession. It was one more thing to be irritated by. It got so that every time she buttonholed and interrogated yet another person about him, I cringed.

Then my aunt Manci came home. The last time I had seen her was at Nagykoros, when my father and her husband, Miklos, left on the troop train to the Russian front. She showed up at our house one afternoon in August. She said she had just arrived on a crowded train from a camp and come to our house before attempting to go back to her own home in Kiskoros.

Manci looked awful. I hardly recognized her. She'd been a small woman to start with, but now she was reduced to skin and bones. She was tense and strangely distant. She told us that her aunt, my father's mother, and all the other members of my father's and Manci's family who lived in Kiskoros had been taken away with her. They'd ended up in a place in Poland called a concentration camp, a concentration camp called Auschwitz.

Gizi made a big pot of noodles, and I watched transfixed as Manci finished off almost all of it. Later, she told my mother her story, then my mother told me. She had been separated from the rest of her family. She had protested because she wanted to go with them, but the Germans wouldn't let her. She was a skilled seamstress before the war, so they shipped her off to a factory to sew for the Germans. The rest of the family was sent to the gas chambers. Only Manci survived.

Manci stayed with us for a while. Trains were coming in almost every day, bringing returning prisoners of war from the Russian front. My mother and Manci established a routine. The trains always seemed to arrive in the afternoon. Manci and my mother, usually with me in tow, would go to the Western Railway Station in the late afternoon, hoping that a train would come in. Hundreds of other people did the same. Most often there was a train. Decrepit, skeletal men in rags would stream out of the cars, their eyes searching for a familiar face in the waiting crowds. We, in turn, were also searching for a familiar face. We were hoping to see Manci's husband, Miklos, and my father.

They didn't come.

After a while, Manci went back home to Kiskoros, still not knowing if Miklos would show up. My mother and I continued to meet the trains almost every afternoon. But we never recognized anyone.

In early September, my mother got word that trains were coming from the prison camp in Russia where she somehow thought my father had been. So we again went out to the railway station to look for my father. The train station was a distance away, and we had to walk both ways. I was getting very impatient. I was tired from the long, fruitless walk and from standing on the hard concrete platform, getting jostled by the crowds, watching the men streaming by, and looking in vain for my father.

The next day we did it again. I didn't want to go. I didn't think I was much use anyway because I had no recollection of my father. But my mother took me by my hand and pulled me along. Again, we didn't find him.

We got home tired and thirsty and wearily sat down in the kitchen to have something to drink. All of a sudden, my mother sat bolt upright in her chair and stared at the wall so intently that you would think it had just spoken to her. I asked her, "What's the matter?"

She hushed me and continued to listen. Then she said, greatly agitated, "I thought I heard your father's whistle." My parents had a private signal between the two of them; they would whistle the first few bars of a popular song.

I was annoyed and protested that she was imagining things. She ignored me. She jumped up from the table and ran down the hallway to the Big Room. She leaned out of one of the open windows, bending out over the railing to look up and down the street. I reluctantly followed her and looked out the other window. The street in front of our house was dark and empty. I straightened up and said irritatedly, "I *told* you you were imagining things."

Just then the doorbell rang. My mother turned and ran back down the hall. I followed her. Gizi had just opened the door. An emaciated man, filthy and in a ragged soldier's uniform, was standing at the open door. Gizi was standing to the side, staring at him speechlessly. My mother stopped as if she had turned into a statue, then in a moment took off and leapt on the man, embracing him in an all-encompassing hug. I stood there, alone and forgotten. I thought, This must be my father.

They were still locked in this desperate embrace in the open door of the apartment when two spinsters who lived on our floor came by on their way out. They glanced through the open door, then stopped and stared. When they realized what was going on, they apologized for intruding and disappeared. Nobody paid them any attention anyway.

Eventually my father came over to me and patted me on the head. I was bewildered. This was supposed to be my father, but I didn't know him. I was supposed to love him, but I wasn't sure what I felt. All I knew for sure was that after I had been so emphatic about telling my mother that he wasn't coming, he wasn't coming . . . now here he was. I was embarrassed that I had been wrong.

He suddenly turned and went into the Big Room. He

walked directly over to the wardrobe, opened it, and flipped through his suits. He seemed to be looking for one in particular. When he found it, he pulled it out into the light and examined it carefully, paying close attention to the buttons. He examined a button that had a crack in it, then he broke into tears. Later he explained that as he was recovering from a deadly illness in the prison camp, he would check on his sanity by picturing his own clothes. He specifically remembered the suit with the cracked button. Finding that his recollection was correct was important proof that he hadn't lost his mind.

By now Gizi was building a fire in the bathroom stove and drew a bath for my father. Soon he was in the tub, covered in soapy water. My mother sat next to him on the side of the bathtub. I peered in from the door, not knowing what to feel or say. His arms and legs were like sticks, with knobs where the joints were. His face was covered by stubble. He looked worse than a beggar.

After a while, he turned to me and asked me with a slight smile, "Andris, whom do you like best, your mother or me?"

I swallowed hard. I knew what answer would please him, but I couldn't give it to him. I looked to one side and said, "I know my mother. I don't know you." He seemed satisfied with the answer. He motioned me over and patted my head again.

Initially, my father was a stranger around the house, but not for long. As soon as he was nursed back to reasonable energy, he returned to the dairy business. Later, he also moved into a regular job as manager of a government-owned department store. My mother, meanwhile, continued to help out in the dairy business. The routine of the household changed. Jani and Romacz continued to pay frequent visits, but now the rest of my father's friends also dropped by often. The apartment was much more lively. It was almost like before the war.

But not everything was the same.

Little by little, news trickled in about people who were still missing. There was never any official notice. It was always someone who had been in a camp with someone else and came back and told the relatives of that person's fate. That's how we got word of my mother's brothers, Miklos and Jozsi. Miklos survived, but Jozsi died.

A few months after my father got home, something happened to my mother. She seemed to have gotten sick, although she didn't really look sick. My parents had a lot of deep discussions that I couldn't follow. After a while, my mother told me that they would have to visit a doctor specializing in women's illnesses.

The trams were not running that day, so they walked to his office. Then they walked back home, my father supporting my mother by her arm. My mother was pale. My father helped her to the sofa in the Big Room. She lay down and closed her eyes.

Sometime later, I learned that my mother had gotten pregnant but that my parents felt it would be wrong to bring a child into the chaotic world we lived in, so they had decided she would have an abortion.

I didn't know what an abortion was. I vaguely understood that my mother might have had a baby. Somehow, and for no particular reason, I always assumed that the baby would have been a girl—a sister I was not to have.

Later in September, after I had turned nine, school started. I was enrolled in third grade at the school attached to the Fasori Jewish boys' orphanage where I had gone for first grade. I had skipped second grade, so every afternoon I went for tutoring in what I should have learned in second grade. My tutor was Margit *neni,* who was also my third-grade teacher. Consequently, she knew what I needed to catch up on.

The second-grade makeup stuff was boring. It was mainly improvement in reading, which I was already pretty good at, and multiplication tables, which I just had to memorize. Fortunately, my third-grade class didn't know the multiplication tables, either, and a lot of our third-grade classes consisted of chanting in unison, "One times one is one, one times two is two," and so forth. After a month of tutoring, Margit *neni* thought I was ready to pass second grade. She told the principal. He sat me down and gave me a test, which I passed. The afternoon tutoring sessions stopped. I was now a full-fledged third-grader.

The kids in my class were different from the ones I knew in first grade. There were about thirty of us. As in first grade, the class was made up partly of boys who boarded at the orphanage and partly of day students. The orphanage boys all wore uniforms and had their hair cut very short. They were always hungry and frequently mooched lunch from the day students.

There was a new set of girls in the class, too. I had a crush on one of them. Her name was Jutka. She had blondish brown long hair that she wore in braids. She was very serious and aloof. I never actually talked with her; I just threw her glances from afar. I don't think she had a clue that I had a crush on her.

School was interesting enough. The principal came into our class every once in a while to deliver lectures about the value of good study habits and good behavior and that sort of thing. One lecture that caught my attention was about different learning aptitudes. There were students who learned quickly and retained what they had learned for a long time, said the principal. There were students who didn't learn quickly but also retained what they had learned for a long time. Then there were students who learned quickly and quickly forgot what they had learned. He urged us to be, if not the first type of student, the second. Without realizing it, he pushed me into a funk, because I had an easy time picking things up, but I forgot them just as easily.

Going back and forth to school was an adventure in itself. To walk to school, I would head toward City Park on Kiraly Street. Halfway there, Kiraly Street changed its name to Fasor Street. Fasor translates to "A Row of Trees." My school was halfway to City Park on Fasor Street.

Fasor Street, as its name suggests, was lined with trees—horse chestnut trees. In the fall, the horse chestnuts grew ripe and fell off the trees onto the pavement. The first chestnuts of autumn represented a much coveted treasure, and all of us raced to pick them up and put them in our bags. We would push and shove each other to get to the precious chestnuts. I hoarded my collection jealously and lined the chestnuts up on my windowsill at home in nice, even rows. I loved to watch the sun shining on their polished red brown shells. But as more and more chestnuts ripened and fell to the ground, they lost their intrigue and currency. I went home and tossed my precious collection of chestnuts into the garbage.

Sometimes after school, a group of us would head off to City Park, just a few blocks from the school. The closer the street came to City Park, the more palatial the houses got. Some of the very fancy houses were occupied by Russian dignitaries and their families. Although all kinds of political parties were operating in Hungary, there was no question that the Communist Party had Russian backing. Russian soldiers still patrolled the streets. Everyone knew that the Russians called all the shots.

Once, a group of Russian boys came running out of one

of those houses as we passed by. They surrounded us and started taunting us in Russian. We didn't understand a word they said, and we stared at them, bewildered and scared. The Russian kids closed in on us and started pushing us around. The kids were no bigger than we were, but they were Russian. None of us dared to push back. We kept moving, and eventually we broke away from them. After that, every time we went to City Park, I was worried that something like this might happen again.

That winter, it snowed a lot. Fuel was still scarce, and the classrooms were heated only some of the time or not at all. It wasn't uncommon for us to sit at our desks, fully bundled in winter coats, hats, scarves, and gloves, with our breath visible in the cold air. At times like that, I hated the cold. But on the way home, at least we could play in the snow. Snowball fights were common.

Once, one of the snowballs went astray. It flew through the open door of a passing streetcar and hit the driver in the face. To our amazement, the streetcar screeched to a halt and a very angry driver came tearing after us. I was the one he caught. He grabbed my hat and yelled at me, then got back on his tram with my hat in his hand and drove off again. It was the only hat I had, and it wasn't easy to get another one. I trudged home, upset and shivering.

When I got home, I sheepishly reported what had happened. I stressed that I wasn't the one who had thrown the offending snowball. My father nodded matter-of-factly and said, "Let's see if we can get your hat back." He put on his coat and hat, and the two of us trudged back out into the snow to try to retrieve my hat from the streetcar driver. That particular streetcar line didn't go by our house, so we had to walk to its terminal. It was a long way, and it was getting darker and colder by the minute. When we finally got there, we asked the dispatcher if anyone had brought in my hat. Miraculously, the hat appeared. After getting a lecture from the dispatcher, I was allowed to put it on my head, and my father and I trudged home. I held his hand part of the way; it felt good to have him with me.

Another time, some of my friends were talking about a whorehouse. I didn't know what it was, so I decided to ask my mother. She was combing her hair in front of the bathroom mirror, and I was crouched on the closed toilet. When I asked my question, my mother continued to comb her hair very deliberately and didn't look at me for a while. Then, addressing her response directly to her image in the mirror, she rapped out in a no-nonsense tone that a whorehouse was where men went to put their penises in women and pay them some money, after which they closed their pants and went home. I sat on the toilet seat, dumbfounded. I felt that I had been thwarted somehow, but I didn't even know what other questions to ask.

A few days later, a couple of school friends and I were hanging out in the doorway to my apartment house on our way home from school. One of them was holding forth about how babies are made. He said, knowingly, that babies were made when a man put his thing into a woman and shot one of his balls into her. I considered this thoughtfully. On the one hand, this matched my mother's description of what people did in a whorehouse. On the other hand, something didn't add up. I knew for a fact that some people had more than two kids, but all of us boys had only two balls. I asked my friend about this inconsistency. He clearly hadn't thought of it and was stunned. These matters remained confusing for some time to come.

In the spring of 1946, my father decided that it would be good for me to learn English. He quoted a Hungarian saying: "You are worth as many men as the languages you speak." He told me that one of his big regrets was that as a child he had never learned another language. He believed that this made it difficult for him to learn languages as an adult. During the war, he had tried to pick up German and Russian but had not succeeded. He particularly wanted me to learn English because he figured that since both the English and Americans spoke it, it might in time become the most widely spoken language in the world.

My mother found a middle-aged spinster who spoke English fluently and taught it as well. She lived by herself in a once grand but now old and decrepit apartment house on the Ring Road. My mother negotiated for a series of lessons; she paid with links from a gold necklace that she broke up for this purpose.

English was boring, and I didn't like the teacher or her decaying apartment. I thought she was weird and her apartment depressing. I was always eager to escape back to the street. But my parents had their hearts set on my participating in this stupid activity, so there was no alternative but to go along with it. Even though I didn't like it, English lessons became a regular part of my life and continued so for many years to come.

As if the English lessons weren't bad enough, a bit later, a big black piano appeared in our living room. My parents' sofa bed was moved under the window to accommodate the piano. My mother explained that it was time for me to learn to play. At first, I was intrigued. I picked out a few simple melodies and played them endlessly. But then an old lady piano teacher appeared, carrying an enormous purse big enough to put a loaf of bread in. She sat down at the piano and started to coach me in the mysteries of scales. She made me play the stupid scales over and over; then, after she left, my mother made me practice them again and again. After a lot of scales, I got as far as

Mozart's "Turkish March," but I never became very good. I detested practicing. I had put up with English without too much resistance, but piano was really too much.

My mother wasn't much inspiration. Every once in a while when friends came over, they would sing songs and she would accompany them. I marveled at her effortless skill. But she never played for her own pleasure, nor did she work with me.

When I wasn't in school or taking English or piano lessons, I read quite a bit. My favorite books were by Karl May, a German who had written a popular series of novels that took place in the Sierra Nevada mountains of the American West. The key characters in all of his books were the noble Indian chief Winnetou and an equally good-hearted cowboy, Old Shatterhand. Old Shatterhand and Winnetou always, always let the bad guys go even when they should have known they would come back to haunt them in the next chapter. I didn't care. For me, the books were full of suspense. Some of my friends told me that Karl May had never visited America, in fact had never left Germany and had written these books while in prison. I didn't care about that, either. Karl May's America was a world where wrongs were always righted and justice always prevailed. I liked that.

While my ordinary routine of school and after-school lessons was being established, Budapest, too, was returning to a routine existence. Some of the damaged buildings were being repaired. Others were demolished and turned into empty lots. The first bridge across the Danube was restored. It was a makeshift affair of wooden beams, but it reestablished the link between Buda and Pest. There was a parade to celebrate the event.

In the summer of 1946, I went to Kiskoros to stay with my aunt Manci. Kiskoros was my father's hometown. My father had been part of a big family. His father had died around the time that I was hospitalized with scarlet fever. Family legend had it that he lingered between death and life while I was lingering between life and death. He hung on to life just until I turned the corner, then he died. But there had been others: my father's elderly mother, two brothers, a half sister, and various cousins, including Manci. (Manci was really a cousin but because of the age difference I always thought of her as my aunt.) All of them were taken away to Auschwitz. Manci was the only one who came back. She had a sister, Lenke, who, with her husband, Lajos, had immigrated to America in the 1930s; and my father had an older sister, Iren, who, with her non-Jewish husband, Sanyi, lived in Budapest and survived. They were all that remained of his family.

By the summer of 1946, Manci was settled back in her own house in Kiskoros. Her husband, Miklos, was rumored to be alive but still in a Russian prison camp. My father was lucky to have gotten out so quickly.

Manci supported herself as a seamstress. She had acquired a puppy. I had never had any pets in Budapest, so the puppy was a major attraction in my agreeing to stay with Manci for the summer.

Kiskoros was south of Budapest, in the same direction as Bacsalmas, but not as far. At nine, I was very proud of being old enough to take the train by myself. My parents put me on the train in Budapest, and Manci was to meet me at the Kiskoros station. By the time the train arrived, it was dark. I couldn't find Manci. The train pulled away, leaving me alone on the platform with my bags. I panicked and yelled at the top of my lungs, "Manci, you stupid ass, where are you?" Manci heard this and burst out laughing. She had, in fact, been there waiting; she just hadn't seen me in the dark. She retold this story many times, deeply embarrassing me each time.

Life in Kiskoros was very different from life at home. Like Bacsalmas, Kiskoros was a small provincial town, tiny and backward by Budapest standards. The houses were all small, one-story structures, many of them with thatched roofs and outer walls plastered with clay. In the more prosperous houses, the plaster was whitewashed, while elsewhere the walls were left their original muddy color. The houses were crowded together on the narrow, unpaved streets, where the dust turned to slick clay when it rained. There were no streetcars or buses. Instead, there were horse-drawn carriages and loaded-down bicycles that people pushed through the rutted streets. There was a small town square with a drugstore and a movie theater. Once a week, the square was the site of a market to which peasants brought their horse-drawn wooden carts piled high with cabbages, onions, potatoes, and other food.

Manci's house had a yard and a little one-room shed, which was empty and became a kind of playhouse for me and a few neighborhood kids whom I befriended. We turned the yard into a playground and sculpted the black earth into moats and castles. In the process, we would get utterly muddy, much to Manci's chagrin. She was obsessed with cleanliness.

Another boy and I decided to build a balcony on top of the shed. To do that, we had to take some of the tiles off the roof. We were very efficient about it—we loosened the reddish clay tiles and dropped them to the ground, watching in fascination as each tile crashed and shattered, scattering sharp-edged pieces of glazed ceramic over the black earth. Manci did not appreciate our efforts and yelled at us.

My quick pass through second and third grades had left me wobbly in my multiplication tables—at least in my father's eyes. As a child, my father had been something of a math wizard, and he measured my skills by his own standards. He arranged with a friend of his who lived in Kiskoros to tutor me in math during the summer. I liked the man a lot. He was friendly and a lot of fun. He would sit me down a couple of times a week and practice math problems with me. In the warm summer weather, he often rolled up his shirtsleeves. He had strong forearms, one of which showed a tattooed number. He, too, had been in Auschwitz.

I had plenty of opportunities to practice my math. Inflation was raging in Hungary, and the value of the pengo, the unit of currency, shriveled daily. On market days, I was amazed to notice that the price of vegetables changed in the course of the few hours that the market was open. Inflation introduced new bills with incredible denominations—thousands, tens of thousands, and hundreds of thousands of pengo. Prices were so astronomical that people carried piles of bills in baskets to pay for goods.

The little cinema in town showed films once a week. Most of the features were prewar American cowboy movies. Manci usually took me to see whatever movie was playing. The price of the tickets, along with everything else, escalated as the summer progressed. By the end of the summer, people were paying for the movie tickets with produce. Like most people in Kiskoros, Manci kept a few chickens. We set aside some of their eggs for admission to the movies. While the price of the ticket in pengos changed from one week to the next, once we switched to paying in eggs, the price stabilized. It was my job to carry the eggs in a little basket and hand them to the man in the ticket booth. It cost us one egg apiece to sit on rickety seats with ripped upholstery and see a scratched version of Tom Mix.

Manci also taught me photography. She had an elaborate camera, made in Germany before the war. You aimed it by opening the top and looking down at a screen that showed the scene in front of you. Putting in the film was a tricky matter, and something Manci would never let me do.

Manci also had a boxy old Kodak camera. Taking pictures with this one wasn't difficult at all; you pointed it and pushed a button, and it clicked. Manci gave me this camera and the two of us took pictures often, she with her camera, I with mine. We took pictures of the fortresses I built in her yard, of the puppy, and of each other. Then we developed them and I sent them home to my parents.

Kiskoros was the birthplace of Sandor Petofi, perhaps the most prominent poet in Hungarian history. He was prominent not only because of his poetry, but also because he was killed as a young man in the abortive Hungarian revolution of 1848. The house where he was born was on a little side street; it was a tiny house with dirt floors, very small windows, and a thatched roof. It was just like every other house in town, only older. It was the most distinguished site in Kiskoros.

We visited Petofi's house several times. I had read his poetry in school and liked it. I found it awe-inspiring to step inside the room where Hungary's greatest poet was born. One time when Manci and I visited Petofi's house, we were stunned to see in front of it a figure familiar from hundreds of photos in the newspapers and posters plastered on buildings. Matyas Rakosi, the head of the Hungarian Communist Party, was visiting with his wife. Rakosi was well-known. He had been imprisoned for Communist activities by the Hungarian government before the war and was later exchanged for some high-ranking Hungarian prisoners of the Russians. He lived out the war in Moscow and came back to Hungary with the Russian troops. Since he was the head of the political party backed by the troops that now occupied Hungary, he was unofficially the most important politician in the country.

I almost stumbled over my own feet when I saw him. I stared

at him with my mouth open, watching him through the viewfinder on my box camera, until Rakosi noticed me. He said in a friendly way, "Would you like to take a picture of me?" I said yes, and he and his wife posed for me. But much as it was a simple matter to take a picture with this camera, I was so nervous that my hands shook and I ended up taking a picture of the sky above their heads. Manci was watching from the side and found the incident very amusing; she couldn't wait to write to my parents about it.

Late in the summer, I returned to Budapest. There were still some weeks before fourth grade began. Manci had let me keep the Kodak camera. With it and my newly acquired expertise, Gabi and another friend, Ungar, and I went into the photography business. Ungar knew how to develop black-and-white film and make contact prints. The prints were not very good. Not only were they gray all over, but we didn't know how to flatten them, so they dried curled up. Still, we formed a firm named Unfleigro, a contraction of our three last names: Ungar, Fleiner, and Grof. We went around to all of our friends and relatives and offered to take pictures of them. We had a few takers, but even we were embarrassed about the product.

Ungar was a very handy boy. He had a movie projector and a few strips of 35mm black-and-white movie film that someone had managed to salvage from a cutting room floor. The three of us would darken a room and project these movies onto a wall. The strips were short, so the segments were only a few seconds long, but we rewound the strips and watched them over and over again in fascination.

Fourth grade was very similar to third grade, even a little easier because the school routines were well established and I didn't have to make up any lost years. I was with the same group of kids, and I had plenty of friends to talk to. I talked to them so often in class that I was frequently reprimanded for being a chatterbox. Once again, I got good grades without having to work hard. The only subject in which I was marked down was "Behavior." The teacher's commentary that accompanied me throughout school was, "Andris is too lively."

At first, my parents didn't react. They might even have been a little amused by these comments. But as the comments kept coming, the amusement gave way to serious disapproval. I dreaded the occasions when my mother would go to school and talk with my teachers. Once I ran into her in the school hallway after such a meeting. I was surprised to see her and greeted her with a big smile. She glared back at me in such a way that I seriously considered not going home after school. But I didn't know where else to go, so I dragged myself home.

The inevitable lecture followed: I wasn't taking life seriously and would pay for my casual attitude later and so on. I'd heard this lecture many times before. I would quiet down for a while, then inevitably drift back to being "too lively" in class again. But if I was immune to the lecture's message, I was not immune to the unpleasant atmosphere that its delivery generated.

I didn't generally have a lot of run-ins with my parents, but when I did misbehave, my parents were a united pair: My mother lectured and my father yelled. My mother never beat me again after the stairwell incident. My father never beat me at all. He used a different method of keeping me in line. He had a favorite pair of leather slippers that he kept by his bed. The slippers were there even when the bed was folded into a sofa during the daytime. Whenever I didn't mind him, he would wave one of his slippers at me in a threatening manner. If I still didn't respond, he actually threw his slipper at me, although he never hit me with it. I never knew if he purposefully avoided me or if his aim was bad.

They also expressed their approval in their own different ways. When my mother liked something I did, she would hug me and look at me with a warm expression in her eyes. My father would come behind me and gently whack the back of my head three times, saying, "Good, son," while patting my head.

As I got pudgier, kids at school started to call me Pufi ("Fatso").

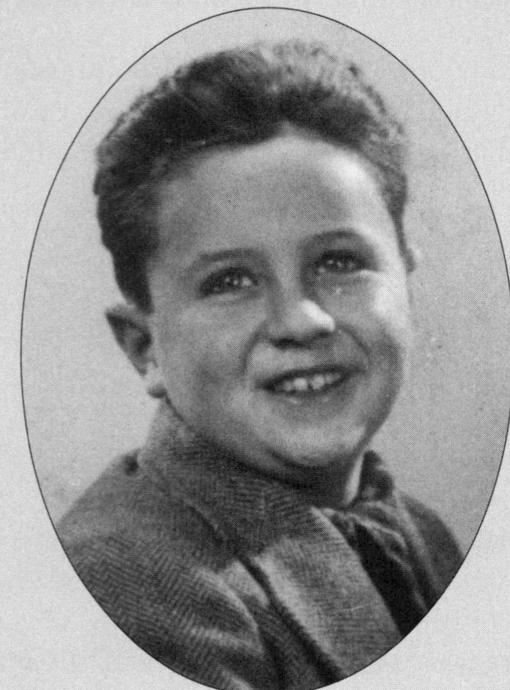

Summer vacation at Kiskoros. *From left,* Kehl *bacsi,* my aunt Iren; my mother is the second after Iren.

Chapter Seven

GYMNASIUM

FOURTH GRADE was the end of grammar school. Now it was time to decide how and where I would continue my education. Those children who wanted to go on to university typically attended gymnasium, a traditional institution that taught an eight-year curriculum of liberal arts and sciences. About half the kids at the Fasori school went on to gymnasium; the other half went to technical schools that trained them for more specific job-related employment.

People said that gymnasiums affiliated with a religious order were the better ones. My parents decided to send me to the Evangelikus gymnasium, an institution run by the second largest Protestant branch in Hungary. (Hungary was an overwhelmingly Catholic country, so even a large Protestant branch represented a small minority.) Evangelikus had a very good academic reputation and had the added benefit of being located just a couple of blocks from the Fasori elementary school, within easy walking distance of our home.

This would be my first experience going to school with non-Jewish kids, but Evangelikus had a reputation for keeping religion to the religious instruction courses and not forcing its beliefs down students' throats. When the Protestant kids attended their religion classes, I would attend Jewish religious instruction along with the other Jewish boys. Other than that, no distinctions were made among the student body.

I started at Evangelikus in September 1947, shortly after my eleventh birthday. There were a few significant differences between grammar school and gymnasium. For one thing, the student body was all boys. Consequently, I lost all contact with girls my age. I didn't really miss them and soon forgot all about them. The teachers also were all men. There was a seriousness to the classes that distinguished gymnasium from grammar school. Evangelikus was all business.

All students going to gymnasium wore a special cap. Every gymnasium had its own particular design. The Evangelikus cap was dark blue, peaked at the front and back like a soldier's cap, with a special school badge on it. I was very proud to attend the school and proud of my cap. I wore it all the time.

One day, I was chasing around on my way home from school with a couple of friends. We were cutting up on the sidewalk near our house when an older boy came by. He was wearing the Evangelikus cap and must have been an upperclassman. He stopped me and, in a very serious tone, told me that as a student at Evangelikus I represented the school wherever I went and that I gave people the wrong impression of the school by behaving like a wild man on the street. I was quite humiliated by this comment and quieted down, at least for the rest of the afternoon.

Once again, my ears gave me a front-row seat in my classes. My ears still drained and I didn't hear very well, but if I sat in the front row and the teacher stood right in front of me and spoke loudly enough for the whole class to hear, he was loud enough for me to hear him as well. My schoolmates, my parents, and my parents' friends already knew to speak louder than normal to me. And according to a theory put forward by Jani, I may even have benefited from my bad hearing. Jani hypothesized that I compensated for my deafness, just as a blind man compensates for the loss of sight, by developing other senses. I had to be quicker at processing nonverbal signs and more attentive to signals, and most important, because I often understood only parts of sentences, I had to exercise my mind constantly. I took it to mean that Jani thought my bad hearing made me smarter. I liked this theory.

I was a good student. I liked my teachers, I liked my classes, and I liked most of the subjects. We studied Hungarian literature, geography, history, math, and one foreign language. I chose to study English. I particularly liked my English teacher, Mr. Endrodi. He was an elegant man, always well dressed and neat, with a pleasant, round face. He spoke with great confidence but always had a gentle manner. He impressed me tremendously.

Even though I had been taking English lessons privately for a couple of years now, I was lackadaisical about studying. But enough had rubbed off so that I made a good start in Mr. Endrodi's class. Because I liked him, I wanted to impress him. That inspired me to do even better, and my performance in English picked up.

Mr. Endrodi became my ideal. With great disappointment, I realized that I couldn't emulate him in looks, diction, or dress. But I noticed that he signed his name with a special curlicue on the E, so I adapted that curlicue to the G when I signed my name.

Mr. Endrodi was my favorite teacher, but the others were good, too. They weren't particularly formal, but they expected discipline in class and they usually got it—although not always.

Good student though I was, much to my mother's chagrin I remained, as they put it in parent-teacher conferences, "lively."

In my mind, I didn't deserve such criticism. I just exchanged an occasional comment with my deskmate—two boys shared a bench and a double desk—or with the boys behind me. My mother thought differently. She thought that I should have left my rambunctious behavior behind in elementary school. Parent-teacher conferences continued to be the same tense events that they had been in elementary school. My grades continued to be the same, too: straight 1s (on a scale of 1 to 5, with 5 being a failing grade) in all the academic classes and 2s in behavior, with the ever-present comment about my lively nature.

The only class I disliked was religion. I never took to it. It struck me as a bunch of fairy tales, and I resented having to listen to and believe in them. I started pushing back. One time, the teacher was telling us how Joshua stopped the sun during the siege of Jericho. I raised my hand. "Yes, Grof?" (Our teachers always called us by our last names, and for the most part, we called each other by our last names.) As was proper etiquette, I slid out from behind my desk and stood in the aisle to respond.

"How could Joshua stop the sun if the sun isn't moving?" I asked. "After all, we know that it is the earth that orbits the sun and the sun is stationary."

The teacher glared at me. If the sun had been moving, his look might have stopped it. He opened his mouth and closed it, then barked at me, "This is religion, Grof! You either believe it or you don't! You never—*ever*—argue with it."

The other students snickered, which made the teacher even madder. I sat down, inwardly pleased with myself. I thought I'd scored a point. Grof 1, religion 0.

When I got home, I told my father what I had done. He patted me on the back of my head, his usual sign of approval. "Well done, kid," he said.

Before I could get a grade in religion, which might have cooled my self-satisfaction, new rules came down. Religious instruction was no longer compulsory. I was out of that class as soon as I was allowed.

As I said, most kids called each other by their last names. Unfortunately, I was in a minority. In the years after the war, I had gained weight. First I got pudgy, then I got even pudgier. Kids at school started calling me a variety of nicknames, ranging from Pufi (which means "Fatso") to Rofi (the sound a pig makes). I didn't like being called these names, but the more I protested, the louder the other kids shouted them at me across the schoolyard. So I resigned myself to being Pufi or Rofi. They became my names even in my own thoughts.

A bigger problem was that I was not particularly athletic in the first place, and the heavier I got, the less athletic I became. Whenever teams were chosen, I was always the last kid to be picked. The game we played most often in exercise periods and after school was soccer. I wasn't particularly skillful, and I was slow. I came up with a convenient excuse for my poor performance: It had been seven years since my bout with scarlet fever, but I didn't know whether my heart had fully recovered. I declared that it would be bad for my heart if I strained it. I was exempted from strenuous exercise and consequently was perennially relegated to the role of goalie in our soccer matches. Goalies didn't have to run around much.

I was a mediocre goalie. I neither helped nor harmed our team in any big way. But my career as a goalie was soon cut short. One time when we were playing soccer in the schoolyard,

I tripped over the metal rod that served as our goalpost. I landed on my left arm. It didn't hurt, but when I got up, I was stunned to see that my forearm was bent—it looked like a V. I stared at it, and the other kids all came around to look. Soon the teacher, who had been overseeing another team, came over to ask what was wrong. "My arm is bent," I said.

He walked me off the playground and took me to the school office, where he called my mother at the dairy. It so happened that there was a hospital next door, so he walked me over there. The nurse gave me some water and entertained me while I waited for my mother. I got more and more worried about my arm. It didn't hurt and I could wiggle my fingers, but the bent shape concerned me. When my mother arrived, she had a private talk with a doctor, then she told me the diagnosis: My arm was broken. I thought they would straighten it out like a piece of bent wire. Instead, I was told I would have to be put to sleep so the doctor could set the bone straight.

The prospect of being put to sleep scared me. My mother explained that setting my arm would hurt, but I wouldn't feel it if I was asleep. I didn't have a choice. As she was explaining this, the nurses took me into another room, helped me onto a table, and covered my entire face with a tentlike mask. They told me to start counting from one to ten. A sweetish smell was coming through the mask. Before I could get to ten, my tongue stopped moving and I was unconscious.

I came to with a combination of sensations. As I opened my eyes, I could see daylight through the mask over my face and I could feel something warm moving up on my arm. I had a flash of terrible sadness. I thought, They must have decided to amputate my arm, and that's my mother kissing it good-bye. Then somebody removed the mask and I could see that a white cloth, soaked in warm water and wet with plaster, was being wrapped around my arm. My arm was straight once again. The doctor told me that once the cast was completely hard, it would make an excellent weapon to elbow other kids with. Then my mother and I walked home.

I immediately put the doctor's advice into practice and whacked my classmates with the cast whenever I could. But the best part about breaking my arm was that I couldn't play the piano. I hated piano lessons, but I couldn't get out of them until I had the good fortune of tripping over the goalpost. Six weeks later, when the cast was cut off, I used the excuse of the break in my practice to stop piano lessons for good. To my surprise, my parents didn't protest a lot. It turned out that they had wanted to get some new furniture in the Big Room anyway. A short while later, they sold the piano and it was gone from the room and from my life.

The new furniture made the Big Room more attractive. Even before, it was the best-looking room in our apartment. While my father was gone during the war, his partners in the dairy business had expanded into an undertaking selling Persian rugs and, later, paintings by Hungarian artists. It was never more than a sideline to the dairy business. There was no display area; the canvases and rolled-up rugs were housed in a storefront adjacent to the dairy. The business never amounted to much, and some time after my father returned, he and his partners liquidated it. As part of the liquidation, some new Persian rugs appeared in our apartment, covering much of the floor in the Big Room. They were like the Oriental area rugs that I had played on during my island-hopping games with Lion *bacsi* years ago, only much bigger. In addition, half a dozen paintings appeared on our walls.

The paintings captured my imagination. One was of an old man sitting in a doorway of an alley in a small town that reminded me of Kiskoros. There was a small country scene that reminded me of the countryside that I'd seen from the train going to and from Kiskoros. There were a couple of bigger works, too. One was of a young woman sitting on a wheelbarrow, as if waiting to participate in a picnic. Judging from the way she was dressed, with a colorful hat with a wide brim, she must have lived long ago.

The picture that attracted me the most was a painting of a ballerina lacing up her toe shoes. The ballerina was very pretty. She looked a little bit like my mother. She lit up the room and attracted my eyes every time I entered. The painting was hung on the wall so that I faced it when I played the piano; having it there didn't help my concentration during the few months that I took lessons. Fortunately, the ballerina survived after the piano went.

Unfortunately, the dairy business didn't.

While I was struggling with piano lessons, religion class, and a broken arm, there was a growing din of political events going on around us. Even though the Hungarian Communist Party had the support of the Russians, it was just one of many parties that made up the political scene after the war. It didn't gain a majority in either of the first two postwar elections, in 1945 and 1947. In August 1948, however, the Communists won and took charge of the government. Soon, private companies were taken over by the state. First, large companies were nationalized, then they moved on to smaller companies. In short order, our dairy was nationalized.

The immediate impact on my life was the disappearance of the ready supply of fresh cottage cheese, butter, and yogurt that we were accustomed to. Even before the dairy was nationalized, my father had started a new job working for a state-owned department store, and he was able to continue to work there after the nationalization. I don't know exactly what he did, but he was some kind of a bigwig. I could tell because whenever I visited him at his office, it seemed that people were overly nice to me. They paid too much attention to me and complimented me when there didn't seem to be any reason for it. This made me uncomfortable. I did not like it.

Once I went to a winter party thrown by the department store for its employees. There were so many people that I was able to get lost in the crowd. Mostly, I sat with the drummer of the band and watched the celebrations. I had the feeling that my father was being treated with special attention. He seemed to be having a good time, dancing very energetically with my mother and also with other women. He danced to both Western dance music and Hungarian songs. But I had the impression that people were watching him all the time.

Sometime after this party, my father was promoted. He became the director of a state company in charge of livestock breeding and exports. Now he had even more signs of importance. He had an elegant secretary and a car with a driver. My mother never liked his secretary; consequently, I had an uneasy feeling about her. When I visited my father, the secretary was awfully sweet and attentive to me, but I had a feeling that her smiles and interest, as well as everything else about her, were for show. The driver, on the other hand, was a lot of fun. He let me ride up front and answered my questions about the workings of the car seriously and patiently.

Even as the nature of my father's work changed, things were changing at home, too. Gizi had to leave us. Increasingly, employing somebody was considered the same as exploiting them. It was something the Communist government frowned on. So my father felt we could no longer have a maid. Gizi and Sinko went back to her hometown. I missed them both very much.

My mother first continued working at the dairy; then, when the dairy was nationalized, she got a job as a bookkeeper at a state-owned company that managed the distribution of coal and heating oil. With Gizi gone, she now had to take over in the kitchen, too. My mother's cooking was a very simple affair. She mostly made simple dishes, such as potatoes with paprika and sausage. My father loved *lecso,* a concoction of tomatoes, red peppers, green peppers, and sausage, so my mother made a lot of that. And she made goulash, a soup made of the same ingredients but with a lot more liquid. The advantage of these dishes was that she could make a big batch and warm up little portions of it for quite some time.

I got into the routine of coming home from school, warming up some leftovers, and cleaning up after myself. This was my main meal of the day.

Big family dinners had always been rare, and with Gizi gone, they became even less frequent. When they happened, they usually happened in a restaurant on a Sunday. Some Sundays my parents visited with friends, either at our house or at a restaurant, or they got together with my father's older sister, Iren, and her husband, Sanyi. Sometimes they went on an outing in the hills surrounding Budapest, always taking care to stick near the streetcar lines because my father hated walking. Sometimes I would go with them; other times I would stay home and hang around with Gabi.

I didn't see a whole lot of my parents. My mother and father returned home from work at different times, and it was our custom that everyone ate whenever they arrived home. By the time my parents came home, I'd usually be cooped up in my room, reading or doing my homework. They would always ask me how school was, and I would give them a report, either detailed or not, depending on my mood.

I rarely needed help with my homework, but whenever I

wrote an interesting composition, I showed it to my parents. They were often helpful, and I'd frequently rewrite my compositions as a result of their comments.

Having nationalized all businesses, the government turned its attention to the school system. The Communists didn't approve of parochial schools and closed them down. So two years into what was supposed to be an eight-year sequence at gymnasium, I had to change schools. Come the fall of 1949, I would not return to Evangelikus but would have to go to a neighborhood school. Even though I had no feelings about the new school one way or another, I was sorry to be uprooted. I liked it at Evangelikus. I liked the school, the students, and the teachers. But there was nothing to be done. The Communist government called all the shots.

I had mixed feelings about the Communists. On the one hand, I felt that they saved my mother's life and my own. I was very grateful for this, and my gratitude made me want to believe in them and what they stood for. On the other hand, since they had taken power, they increasingly interfered with our daily life. They took away my parents' business, they uprooted me from my school, they forced Gizi and Sinko to leave—all in the name of some political philosophy that I didn't really understand.

There were other strange goings-on with the government in the spring of 1949. Everybody was talking about the arrest of one of the top Communist ministers, a man named Laszlo Rajk. The newspapers and the radio had previously described him as a heroic freedom fighter, so it was a shock when that May he was arrested. He was charged with being a traitor and a spy for the English and the Americans. The trial was scheduled for later in the summer.

However, all these events—Gizi's disappearance, my impending change of schools, the confused political atmosphere—were dwarfed in importance because a big wish of mine was finally fulfilled. I got an air gun. I had wanted one for a long time. I ogled the ones displayed in the shop windows of sporting goods stores and imagined myself holding one in my hand. My father had said that he would let me buy one if I saved my allowance.

That spring, after a year of diligent saving, skipping numerous movies and many ice-cream cones, I had only half the money I needed. My father took pity on me and agreed to match my savings. At last, the air gun would be mine. We went to the store together. The gun I chose had a polished wood stock and a gleaming steel barrel. You broke the barrel open, inserted the pellets in a recess inside, then closed the barrel. Opening and closing the barrel pumped up the air pressure until the gun was ready to shoot. I walked out of the store, carefully clutching my new treasure. It was the most valuable thing I'd ever owned.

I took my gun everywhere. I took it to City Park to practice shooting, a bit concerned that someone might take it away from me. I also practiced at home from the airshaft window, shooting across the empty lot and watching the bullets throw up little puffs of dust as they hit the plaster on the wall of the opposite building. My father taught me never to point the gun at anyone, even when it was empty. So I would mount the tram with the gun casually slung on my shoulder, but I always made sure that the barrel pointed to the ground.

My real opportunity to learn how to use it came that summer when, once again, I went to Kiskoros. This time I did not stay with Manci. Finally, more than three long years after my father arrived home, Manci's husband, Miklos, had come back from Russian prison camp. Manci was busy nursing him back to health.

I stayed with the Kehl family, who worked a small farm that used to belong to my father's family. The Kehls were ethnic Germans. Most ethnic Germans, called Schwabs, were deported after the war, on the premise that they must have collaborated with the Germans. A lot of families who had lived in Hungary for generations were forced to move to Germany. Somehow, the Kehls managed to avoid deportation.

The farm was too small to be nationalized. It consisted of a small vineyard, a few fruit trees, and a plot of vegetables for the family. The one-story house had several rooms with dirt floors and no indoor plumbing. The yard in front was also dirt, with chickens pecking for bugs among the farm implements that were scattered around.

A deep well stood in the center of the yard, surrounded by a brick wall to keep people and animals from falling in. To get water, you let down a pail attached to a long rope, which was wound around the shaft, waited for the sound of a splash, then cranked the pail back up. The water was cold and tasted fresh.

There were chickens and dogs and cats for me to play with, but best of all, Gabi was there. He had come with me. (Unlike my other schoolmates, I called Gabi by his first name. Also unlike my other schoolmates, he called me Andris, never Pufi or Rofi.)

We had the run of the place. We dug holes and turned them into "caves." We went hunting for frogs, something I did with a vengeance, since I hated frogs and wanted to kill every one of them. And we hung around with the Kehls' son, Adam, who was eighteen years old and a man of the world. Adam was very capable with tools, bicycles, and girls, all of which Gabi and I found fascinating.

Once, we tagged along with Adam and came upon a group of girls who worked on a neighborhood plot. Adam went off to chat with them, then told us to wait while he disappeared with one of the girls into a grove of trees. A while later, he reappeared, looking very smug. He slapped Gabi and me on the back and said, "Let's go to work," as if nothing had happened. I often wondered about what Adam and that girl did in the trees, but I never had the nerve to ask.

Most of the time, Gabi and I were left to entertain ourselves. A key item was the air gun. Unfortunately, I couldn't use it as much as I would have liked because the pellets were expensive and I'd already used up all of my allowance. The pellets came in boxes of five hundred, but I was concerned that we would run out, so Gabi and I made every shot count. I was a better shot than Gabi. I shot at cans and pieces of wood, then eventually at sparrows perched on the branches of trees. After a while, I got to be good enough so that I could sometimes hit a sparrow and knock it down. I felt very powerful when it fell dead to the ground.

Once I shot a pigeon. It fell down, but it wasn't dead. When I went to look at it, it looked back at me. It couldn't move. I felt awful. I picked it up and took it back to the house, made it a nest, gave it water and seeds, and nursed it back to health. Eventually, it flew away. After that, I didn't shoot at pigeons, but somehow I thought it was okay to shoot at sparrows.

Once a week, on Wednesday, Kehl *bacsi* and Adam bicycled into Kiskoros to go to the market. Market day was a big deal at the farm. They carefully packed big wicker baskets with grapes and fruit and strapped them onto the backs of their bicycles. Gabi and I went with them. The farm was about ten kilometers outside of town, about an hour's ride on Kehl *bacsi*'s beat-up bike. You took a rutted dirt road to the main road. The main road wasn't paved, either, but it was much smoother. Kehl *bacsi* pedaled and had me perch sideways on the crossbar. Gabi rode with Adam. These trips reminded me of riding with Sinko in City Park, except that here the roads were worse so the ruts bit harder.

The market was in the main square of Kiskoros. It was the weekly market for the region and was always crowded with people from surrounding towns. Farmers and merchants spread out everything from fruits and vegetables to hardware, clothing, housewares, fertilizer, and even farm animals. The fruits and vegetables were weighed in handheld scales, then people put them directly in their shopping baskets. After the isolation of the farm, the hustle and bustle of lots of people talking and bargaining was exciting, but it was also hot and dusty and noisy. I was usually ready to go home after a few hours, but I had to wait until Kehl *bacsi* was done with his business. The ride back always seemed twice as long.

The road from Kiskoros to the farm went past what had been my grandparents' house. I always had a tight feeling in my chest when we went by, because by now I knew my relatives had been taken from that house to be killed.

In the middle of the summer, there was great excitement in the town. They were going to pave the sidewalk from the train station at the edge of town to the square in the middle. People talked about nothing but this impending project. It took a few weeks and lots of starts and stops, but when it was done, there was in fact a paved sidewalk, separated from the dirt road by a rain ditch. People from Kiskoros felt that they had made a major step forward in progress.

I myself made two major steps forward that summer. I learned to swim, and I learned to ride a bike.

There was an irrigation ditch about a mile or so from the farm. It was maybe ten or twelve feet wide and one hundred feet long and filled with brackish water. It had a slippery mucky bottom and shallow sloping sides, but it was deep enough in the middle so that I couldn't stand. The summer was hot, so Gabi and I went there often. The walk made us definitely hotter, but we could look forward to cooling off in the water, and the cool feeling lasted almost until we got home again.

Gabi knew how to swim and showed off by swimming the length of the irrigation ditch. I really wanted to learn, not only because this was a skill I wanted to acquire, but also because I was embarrassed to be splashing around on the shallow sides of the ditch while Gabi was paddling away across the middle.

My ears were going to be a problem. I was not allowed to let water in them. That was the main reason I hadn't learned how to swim. I even had to be very careful when I took baths. However, I'd found that if I cut waxy earplugs to just the right size and warmed them up by endless kneading, I could mold them to seal my ear canal. Even then, I didn't dare put my head underwater, but at least I could go in.

In anticipation, I had brought earplugs from Budapest, as well as a swimming belt made out of blocks of cork strapped together. When I strapped the belt around my waist, it kept me from sinking and gave me confidence. After I realized that I wouldn't end up at the bottom of the ditch, I worked up the courage to stand on one side of the ditch. I counted one, two . . . three! Then I pushed myself off, holding my head high out of the water to keep the water out of my ears. A push like that got me halfway to the other side. I paddled furiously, imitating Gabi's breaststroke and keeping my head out of the water to keep my ears dry. To my amazement, my body only inched forward. I was gasping for air before I got close enough to the other side that I could reach the bottom with my feet and stand up again.

Still, I had made it across. I was elated. I looked for recognition and an acknowledgment of my feat, but there was no one to give it. Gabi was off someplace else. I stood in the shallow part of the irrigation ditch, catching my breath; then, when I was breathing normally again, I set out again for the other side.

I practiced day after day, week after week, and bit by bit I managed to cross the ditch with a lot less effort and a lot less panic. Near the end of our stay, I gathered enough confidence to try it without the cork belt. To my surprise, I found it was even easier. I started swimming the length of the ditch. I was slow, much slower than Gabi, but given enough time, I could cover the same distance. I was very proud of myself. I was not good at physical activities, and it gave me great pleasure to master one. I felt especially distinguished because many of my friends and schoolmates didn't know how to swim.

The other activity that I mastered that summer was learning to ride a bike. Every once in a while, with great patience, Kehl *bacsi* or Adam put me in the saddle of their big bikes and pushed me on the rutted road so I could get a feel for how to steer. I couldn't really get a feel for pedaling because my feet didn't reach the pedals. They would let go of the bike for a few seconds at a time, and with heart pounding, I managed to keep the bike upright—most of the time. When I started to teeter, they were there to right the bike before I crashed.

Next, we went to the top of a small grassy slope. I climbed onto the bike, one of them gave me a push, and I glided down to the bottom, where the other one caught me before I crashed. Then I pushed the bike back up the slope and did it again and again until I got comfortable in the saddle.

Later, Kehl *bacsi* borrowed a woman's bike and gave it to me. Not only was this bike smaller than his, but it didn't have the center bar, so I could lower myself to pedal. The gliding exercises on the big bike had taught me how to balance, and soon I was pedaling myself along the rutted roads. Gabi joined me on Adam's bike. He was too short to sit on the seat and reach the pedals, but he was able to ride it standing up. I crashed a few times, but it never dampened my enthusiasm.

Unfortunately, there was no question of my riding a bike in Budapest. For one thing, I didn't have one. For another, my parents wouldn't hear of me pedaling down the street alongside cars and trucks and streetcars. They were concerned that with my bad ears, I would be run over by an unheard vehicle before I got a block away from home.

Swimming was a different story. This I could continue in Budapest. There was a public pool in City Park. The pool was much bigger than the irrigation ditch, about twenty-five yards wide and fifty yards long. It was a perfect place for me to practice what I had learned.

There were a couple of weeks before school started again. I would go to the pool every morning when it first opened and before it filled up with people whose splashing and playing around distracted me. At first, it was a struggle to make it across the width of the pool, but as the days went on, it got easier and easier. Within a couple of weeks, I was able to swim back and forth many, many times.

The pool was the center of my day for the rest of the summer. Later in the morning, other kids I knew would show up and we would spend the rest of the day there. I couldn't participate in most water play because I feared getting water in my ears, earplugs notwithstanding, but it was still fun. Still, the most important part of the day for me was the first hour when I practiced my swimming.

I kept hoping that the swimming would help me lose some of my pudginess, but that didn't happen. I would start a new year at a new school, but I would still be Pufi.

When I came home after swimming, I often hung around the warm, dusty apartment and listened to the Rajk trial. The trial was broadcast on the radio every day, much of the day, and everyone who could was glued to their radio set. I listened to Rajk's examination with morbid fascination. I couldn't understand how a man who fought against the Germans and was a member of the underground could turn against his cause and his country. But there it was: He had confessed it himself.

He was sentenced to death just as the new school year began.

My mother looking over my shoulder.
I was pretty diligent about doing what I had to do.

Chapter Eight

DOB STREET SCHOOL

I STARTED THE SCHOOL YEAR not just with a new school, but also with a new address. We did not move. The Communist government had decided to rename all the significant streets in Budapest with names of famous Russians. The part of the Ring Street nearest our house was renamed Lenin Ring Street. The main avenue leading to City Park was called Stalin Avenue. Our street, Kiraly Street, was renamed after the Soviet poet Mayakovsky.

Dob Street, where my new school was located, was not important enough to get a new name. It was a narrow, nondescript street in a nondescript neighborhood about two blocks back from the hustle and bustle of Kiraly Street. There was a small post office, some humdrum shops, and a neighborhood school as shabby and run-down as its surroundings.

Dob Street School was a comedown after the polish and order of the Evangelikus gymnasium. On the surface, the school was run the same as Evangelikus. The curriculum covered the same subjects, and the classes were the same size. A number of kids like me had been funneled in from other schools, but most of the students had attended Dob Street School all along. Neither they nor the teachers had the same seriousness of purpose that was so fundamental to Evangelikus. There was no question of being proud of a school cap from Dob Street. In any case, we didn't have one.

There were girls at Dob Street, but they were in separate classrooms in a separate wing of the building. We saw them only in the halls as we came and went to classes and during recess periods.

To my surprise, I ran into Eva, the girl who'd had a crush on me in first grade. If it weren't for her name, I wouldn't have recognized her. She looked very grown-up and even wore stockings to school, which was very intriguing. But beyond a pert, smiling hello, she paid no attention to me. I wondered if her lack of interest was a punishment for how I had behaved to her in first grade. Eventually, I concluded that it was more likely that my pudginess put her off.

Initially, the grading system at Dob Street School was the same as it had been at Evangelikus. Then, one day, it changed, another manifestation of the increasing Soviet influence on our lives. Whereas before the top grade was 1 and the failing grade was 5, from one day to the next the grading scheme was turned around. Now, 5 became the top grade and 1 the failing grade. This was how schools operated in the Soviet Union, we were told, so it would be how schools operated in Hungary.

But the biggest change from Evangelikus was the teachers. A number of the Dob Street teachers were obviously new to the profession. What got them there wasn't their teaching skills, but their ability to represent the Communist government point of view. We figured that they were loyal cadres who had been plucked from positions as minor Party functionaries, given some quick training in a subject, and immediately assigned to one class or another.

A prime example was our geography teacher. His name was Gonci. The word sounds a bit like the Hungarian slang word for "sperm," so after the first class, we all called him that behind his back. I don't know what Mr. Gonci did before he showed up at our school, but he seemed to have acquired his knowledge of geography by skimming the chapters he was about to teach just before he taught them to us.

Our lessons dealt predominantly with the geography of the Soviet Union and its allies, the other Communist-bloc countries. Mr. Gonci developed favorites among the countries we studied. These included, of course, the Soviet Union and, for some reason, Romania. The rest of the world got only cursory attention. I don't remember studying anything about England or the United States.

Mr. Gonci was very predictable—so predictable that the class made a standing joke of it. Whoever was called upon to recite stood at the blackboard and started listing the facts and figures about the country we were studying even before Mr. Gonci asked him to do so. The rest of the class had a fun time watching to see if Mr. Gonci realized what was going on. He never did. He merely nodded his head as the recitation continued.

The class expressed its contempt of Mr. Gonci by acting up more and more. My tendency to chat in class no longer got me in trouble. I hadn't changed; the environment was less disciplined, so I didn't stand out as much as before. We acted in ways that would have been unthinkable at Evangelikus just a few months ago. But some of these ways were fun.

Someone had accidentally kicked a soccer ball into the classroom window and broken the glass. The windows were repaired by setting new panes in the window frame with triangular nails, then wedging a soft putty at the edge of the glass. When the putty solidified in a day or so, it formed an airtight seal between the glass and the frame. As at Evangelikus, our class stayed in the same room all day and the teachers came to us. The break between the change in teachers gave us the opportunity to get to the putty.

Some students wasted no time in scraping out the putty while it was still soft. They wadded it into balls, and immediately the balls were flying back and forth across the room. Then someone made a great discovery: If you threw a ball of putty against the ceiling, it stuck for a while, then suddenly fell down and splattered all over the floor, much to the surprise of the person sitting below it. Meanwhile, the putty thrower, studiously bent over his books, got away unidentified. It was too good a discovery to go to waste.

Just before Mr. Gonci's class, some of the boys threw putty balls where they would stick on the ceiling right above Mr. Gonci's desk. When Mr. Gonci came in, we were all sitting sedately in our places, holding our breath expectantly. Mr. Gonci took his position at the desk. He actually seemed a little taken aback by the silence of the class. But the quiet was broken when the first putty ball fell from the ceiling and exploded on the paperwork in front of him. He erupted in anger, shouting, "Who did that? Who did that?" He glared at the class, his eyes terrorizing us. Then another ball splattered on his desk, and another. We couldn't contain ourselves anymore and broke out in laughter. Even Mr. Gonci's furious shouting couldn't stop us.

We didn't learn much geography.

History class was strange also, although for a different reason. In the early part of the year, we had studied the history of Hungary and its place in the Austro-Hungarian empire. Toward the end of the year, we started studying modern history, with most of the focus on World War II.

The story of the end of World War II was told differently from what I remembered. According to our history book and our teacher, the Japanese surrendered to the invading Russian army. There was a one-sentence mention of the atom bomb, which was described as a desperate attempt by the Americans to gain credit for the Japanese defeat. Yet I remembered the newsboys running up and down the street in August 1945, shouting about what I heard as the "auto bomb." Judging from the reaction of the people around me at the time, everyone thought the American atom bomb ended the war.

I was dying to raise my hand and point this out to my teacher, but I thought better of it. This wasn't religion class at Evangelikus. Contradicting a position that was even vaguely associated with the Communist Party didn't seem like a wise thing to do. I kept my hand down.

I had one very good teacher. Mr. Feldman taught physics with great energy and enthusiasm, despite having a bad leg that made him walk with a limp. Unlike many of my other teachers, he knew his subject thoroughly and really enjoyed teaching. I liked physics well enough, but then something happened that made me like it much more.

One day, Mr. Feldman called on me to explain how a siphon worked. He put a tall pot of water on his desk and an empty pot on a chair seat next to it. Then he looped a rubber tube from the pot on the desk down to the pot on the seat. He sucked on the end of the tube going into the empty pot to get the water flowing, then stepped away. To the class's amazement, the water kept flowing up the tube, over the side of the tall pot, and down into the empty pot on the chair. It seemed impossible to have water climb over a wall against the force of gravity. Mr. Feldman called on me to explain what made the water climb uphill.

I stared at the experiment, then in a flash the explanation became clear. I enthusiastically explained that the water *had to* climb up because it had no choice. Once the flow was started, if the water didn't continue to climb up the tube and over the rim of the pot, a bubble of vacuum would be created. The vacuum would then suck the water up, so water had to continue to flow upward. It was the need to fill the would-be vacuum that made the water climb over the edge of the pot.

This all made perfect sense to me, and I was quite pleased with myself. Then I looked at Mr. Feldman. His face was radiant with approval as he said, "What I like about you, Grof, is that when you figure something out, you really understand it thoroughly." I felt as if I had discovered a new law of physics. From then on, physics was my favorite class.

It certainly beat foreign-language lessons. English as a foreign language was replaced by Russian. The language teachers didn't know much more Russian than we did, and they barely kept one chapter ahead of the class.

There was a feeling of growing resentment toward things Soviet. It wasn't anything I ever heard said, but I could sense it in my classmates' surly reactions. Nothing was ever said about politics at home, either. Our discussions centered around the chores of daily living, people coming and going, my victories and setbacks at school. But the silence on this subject replaced what had been an optimistic air about a new era in politics.

In any event, we didn't get much done in Russian class, either.

At my parents' urging, I continued to study English after school. I had a succession of tutors. Some came to our house to teach me. One of them, Egon *bacsi,* seemed a little strange. My mother was afraid that he might be a homosexual and made sure that the lessons took place when she was around. Egon *bacsi* never touched me, but my mother remained vigilant.

After Egon *bacsi* moved on, I asked if I could take lessons from my English teacher from Evangelikus, Mr. Endrodi. We had heard that Mr. Endrodi had found another teaching job after Evangelikus was closed and supplemented his income by giving private English lessons. To my delight, my mother arranged weekly lessons with him.

The lessons took place at Mr. Endrodi's apartment, where he lived with his wife, a pleasant but very quiet woman. It was a big, dark apartment, bigger than ours, in an imposing building on the Ring Street. The rooms were filled with huge pieces of furniture, all dark, polished wood. The chairs and sofas were equally imposing and covered with velvet, brocade, and overstuffed pillows. The whole apartment reminded me of a stage set for a play that had long since closed.

It was good to see Mr. Endrodi again, and I made a lot of progress during the time I had him as my tutor. He emphasized reading in English in preference to conversational English. I read stories by Oscar Wilde—moving my finger from word to word and line to line, to be sure—and even stories based on Shakespeare's plays. My favorite was *Macbeth.* I was fascinated by how Lady Macbeth overcame her husband's will and drove him far beyond where he wanted to go. The idea of a villain behind a villain fascinated me and stayed with me even after my lessons.

I didn't tell anyone at school that I took English lessons. My parents never warned me, but somehow I knew that it wasn't a good thing to broadcast.

Studying English added to my homework load. While it generally wasn't very much, I was pretty diligent about doing what I had to. I would sit at my little desk by the window in the Little Room, with the window open when the weather wasn't too cold, and do my homework to the accompaniment of the sounds of the traffic on Kiraly Street. I was usually at my desk when my parents came home from work. Each of them would stop by my desk. My mother would stroke my shoulder, and my father would pat the back of my head by way of greeting me. My father expressed particular interest in my progress in math, that having been his favorite subject. He never offered to help, however, but then again, I never needed any.

When I was thirteen, my father fell ill. I came home one evening from hanging out with my friends and found him in bed. He had a terrible pain in his belly. My mother had sent for the doctor, but she was worried, so I got worried, too.

Eventually the doctor arrived. He was an older gentleman with silver hair who carried a brown leather doctor's bag with all kinds of serious instruments in it. I was sent to my room while he examined my father. I could hear my father's groans through the closed door. His pain was getting worse. The doctor ordered him to be taken to the hospital immediately, and the next morning he was operated on.

My father stayed in the hospital for a week. I visited him a couple of times. He told me he had had gallstones as big as the tip of his forefinger; the doctor had showed them to him after the surgery. He was quite weak. He couldn't sit up without holding on to a strip of bandage that was tied to the bed frame. It scared me to see my father have to pull himself up into a sitting position. I worried whether he would ever be strong again.

But he did not lack visitors. Many friends came and sat by his bedside and chatted with him. They were quite cheerful and he seemed cheerful, too, so my fear gradually dissipated.

When my father returned home, he stayed in bed for some time. His friends continued to visit him at home. He lounged on the sofa bed, the center of an ongoing series of witty, intellectual conversations. As I watched people gather around him, I realized that this had always been my father's favorite activity, even before his illness: holding court with his friends, being the center of attention, sprawled out on his sofa engaged in vigorous conversation.

The visitors were almost always men. Jani and Romacz came. But there were many new people, people my father worked with or got to know through his various jobs. These new friends brought their friends. It got to the point where I couldn't keep track of who had come with whom.

The conversations weren't so much discussions as heated arguments where people shouted, interrupted each other, and waved their hands about a lot. At first, the loudness of the arguments scared me, but then I realized that while they were excited, nobody ever got really mad at anyone else.

Sometimes I would sit in the Big Room trying to follow the line of argument. My hearing was not an impediment because everyone was yelling at the top of his lungs, but the subjects were too complicated for me to follow. The arguments were about detailed points of law under the Communist regime or about the economics of breeding pigs and cows, the job my father was now involved in. Once, my father was engaged in a legal argument with a lawyer friend. I was very impressed by my father's ability to argue his case. I was even more impressed as I could see the other man retreat into a corner.

Sometimes the visitors included Uncle Sanyi, the husband of my father's sister, Iren. Sanyi was a bit older than my father, and my father had a lot of respect for him. He was a gentle, serious man with graying hair. He was a newspaper editor, and when the subject turned to politics, he became quietly passionate.

My aunt Iren was very different from her husband. Despite being more than ten years older than he, she was a bouncing ball of energy. She was also the most educated member of my father's family and was very well read. She always questioned me about what I was reading. Iren and Sanyi lived about a mile away, out by City Park. This meant that they passed our apartment on their way into the city. Iren dropped by our house almost daily, usually on her way somewhere else, and would be in and out in minutes, always speaking very quickly and fluttering like a hummingbird.

Both Iren and her daughter, Marika, who was ten years older than I and was a medical student, were usually borrowing something from my mother. Iren was trained as a pharmacist and her expertise included making hand lotions, so she would return the favor by creating concoctions for my mother. They smelled very nice. She also often made a particular type of chocolate dessert squares and would bring us a plate of them from time to time, which made me very happy.

My aunt Manci and her husband, Miklos, had moved to Budapest and were also frequent visitors. Miklos had some kind of an office job, and Manci continued to sew and repair dresses.

Once my father recovered from his operation, my parents resumed their usual social life. During the summer, we took the tram to the outskirts of Budapest and sometimes took the funicular up the mountains of Buda; then we would sit at an open-air restaurant and the adults would argue. When the weather wasn't so good, the outings took place at the neighborhood restaurant, always the same restaurant, where my father always ordered the exact same dish, his favorite stew, and the arguments continued.

At the end of a meal, it usually was my task to figure out how much of a tip to leave. My father, who was very quick with math, would watch me do this chore. Sometimes I was fast enough to win his approval; sometimes he was impatient. He would glance over to see if I had done it right, which I usually had, and nod his approval. It was a little game for us, and we both enjoyed it.

My father was an outgoing man. I was impressed and also a little envious at how easily he struck up conversations even with complete strangers. He was able to find a common bond with everyone he encountered—the waiter at the restaurant, the conductor on the streetcar, or somebody sitting at the table next to him. He seemed genuinely interested in these other people. Every once in a while, in his enthusiasm, he got me involved in these conversations. Most of the time, I would listen for a while, but I would soon get impatient to go home.

As I got older, I stopped going on these outings and hung out with my own friends instead.

One positive result of the nationalizing of all the school districts was that Gabi and I ended up in the same class at Dob Street School. We continued to spend time together outside of class, too.

After school and on weekends, we went on long walks through Budapest. Most of the damage from the war had been cleaned up, and Budapest by now was a bustling, living city again. There were people out on the streets at all hours of day and night, some coming and going purposefully, some just strolling around. The larger streets were lined with sidewalk cafés, where people sat and talked over ice cream in the summer and cups of espresso throughout the rest of the year. I loved ice cream and the way it was served in silvery metal dishes beaded with condensation, but it was a treat I could rarely afford from my small allowance. Cafés were mostly for people with money, and I didn't have much money.

The cafés were part of the backdrop as Gabi and I walked and talked. One of our favorite destinations was Margaret Island, an island in the Danube that was a large recreational area with restaurants, sports facilities, boathouses, swimming pools, and such. In the summer, the benches around the island were filled with couples making out, adding another bit of interest to the scenery of our walk.

Gabi was interested in music, particularly opera. A lot of people were. There were two opera houses in Budapest operating almost year-round, and opera was regularly broadcast on the radio. My piano lessons had left bad memories of classical music, and after I stopped taking lessons, I was perfectly happy to have nothing more to do with it. I had even less interest in opera. I thought it was silly for people to sing through an entire story. It took a lot of prodding for Gabi to get me to agree to accompany him to an open-air concert on Margaret Island. Even then, he had to drag me along.

The concert program included a combination of musical numbers, dance numbers, and selections from operas. We sat close up so I could hear the singers. One was a man with a big voice who sang the "Toreador Song" from *Carmen*. The man's energy and booming voice and the audience's enthusiastic reaction swept me up in a frenzy of excitement. Much to Gabi's amusement, I was on my feet with everyone else, yelling for an encore.

Afterward, I sheepishly admitted to Gabi that I would like to see the whole opera. That was easy enough to do. As long as I was willing to sit in cheap seats high up and to the side, I could afford the tickets. We soon found a production of *Carmen* and went to see it. With that one experience, I was hooked on opera.

My voice was beginning to change. My singing voice, which I tried only when I was sure I was alone in the apartment, seemed to be a deep one. I declared myself a bass-baritone. Consequently, my interest was drawn to operas where the bass-baritone had a big part. *Carmen* with Escamillo the toreador was one. *Faust* with Mephistopheles was another.

I became increasingly fascinated by Hungarian bass and

bass-baritone opera singers, particularly Mihaly Szekely, who, rumor had it, once sang at the Metropolitan Opera in New York City! My all-time favorite singer was Gyorgy Losonczy, who, while he did not have Szekely's voice, was an excellent dramatic actor. I decided that he made a good all-round role model for me even though he had married a large, shrill soprano whom I didn't like.

My parents had recently replaced the old wind-up phonograph with an electric record player. It was connected to the loudspeaker of the radio and didn't sound as good as the wind-up phonograph, but it could play record after record without my having to jump up to crank up the motor.

My father's tastes ran toward Gypsy music and popular songs, not opera, so whatever records we had were of that type. My aunt Iren found out about my growing interest and told me I could have her old opera records. One Saturday afternoon, Gabi and I picked up a bunch of her dusty phonograph records and took them home to listen to them.

We were eager to examine our hoard. Working through the pile, we slapped each record on the phonograph, sampled it, then took it off and replaced it with another. Most of them were not very interesting, and we were gloomily coming to the conclusion that our expedition would not yield any treasures. Without even bothering to look at the label, I put on the next record.

An incredible voice singing a dynamic, powerful song filled the room. Gabi and I froze and listened as if hypnotized. When the song was over, I took off the record to see who it was and what he sang. The singer was the Russian bass Feodor Chaliapin, and the opera was Mussorgsky's *Boris Godunov.*

I learned everything I could about Chaliapin. He was a workingman, not musically trained. According to the stories, he never really read music and improvised beyond what the composer had in mind. He was, I thought, just like me. In my fantasies, I pictured myself as an opera singer when I grew up.

My other fantasy was to become a writer.

I went through fits of reading. There were periods of time when I read a lot and periods of time when I didn't read much at all. These reading spurts were always triggered by the discovery of a writer whose books made a big impression on me. Karl May was one of those. Jules Verne was another. Around the time I started going to the Dob Street School, I discovered C. S. Forester's books about the nineteenth-century British navy captain Horatio Hornblower.

Something about the character really intrigued me. Although I wouldn't tell anyone this, I fancied myself as a latter-day Captain Hornblower, a man of few but deeply thought-out words, carrying the weight of the world on my shoulders, pacing an imaginary deck with my hands behind my back, living a rich inner life that my classmates never suspected. Had they known what I was really like, I imagined, they would be a lot more respectful. Nobody would call a Hornblower Pufi or dare to push him around.

I borrowed the Hornblower books from my neighborhood library. Whenever I got close to finishing one, I started worrying that the next one wouldn't be available. After I finished the entire series, I went back and read them all over again. Partly because of these books, I started to think of becoming a writer. I had ambitions of expressing what I thought of as my rich and multifaceted self in writing.

The thought really appealed to me. To be able to display what I was really like by transposing myself into an imaginary person, set in an imaginary scene, undertaking imaginary adventures, excited me. However, this was a fantasy I shared with no one. It was a part of that rich inner life that I was determined to keep to myself.

Yet I liked writing and wanted people to pay attention to my compositions, so I came up with a compromise answer when people asked me what I wanted to do when I grew up. They were asking more and more frequently these days, because it was customary for kids my age to start thinking seriously about their future careers. As some of my friends had already declared their intention of becoming mechanical engineers or physicians, I felt pressure to name a profession, too. I told my parents, some teachers, and a few of my friends that I wanted to become a journalist.

I actually had the opportunity to be a journalist—at least, in a modest way. My school sponsored a gathering where students participated in a discussion of current events. Afterward, a woman introduced herself to me. She said that she was the editor of a weekly newspaper for young people and that she liked the way I expressed myself—that I seemed to have an easy time with words. Would I be interested in writing about my daily experiences for her publication? Perhaps I would like to visit the editorial offices to see what they were like.

I could barely contain my excitement.

The editorial offices consisted of two rooms of an apartment cluttered with stacks of papers and back issues of the newspaper. The editorial staff consisted of two middle-aged men, each of whom had a typewriter on which he was busily clacking away. I didn't know what a newspaper's offices should look like. This looked good enough to me.

Shortly after, I submitted my first composition. It was five or six paragraphs about what I did during my summer vacation. It was accepted! The paper was not one either I or my friends read. In truth, it wasn't very interesting. But that changed for me once I could look forward to seeing my own words in print. I became an avid reader and brandished the newspaper wherever I went. My parents were very proud of me and showed my article to my aunt Iren, who took it home to show to her husband, Sanyi, the real-life journalist. I eagerly awaited Sanyi's praise, but to my disappointment I never heard from him one way or another.

From time to time, I submitted new compositions, all brief and all dealing with my daily observations. Every one of them got printed, usually with very little modification. I was given a little identification card, with my picture pasted in it, that identified me as Correspondent #7. I proudly carried it wherever I went, waiting for an opportunity to flash the official proof that I was a working journalist. The opportunity never came. But that didn't diminish my pride.

Most of the time, I came up with the ideas for my stories. But one time, my editor—the woman who recruited me had been succeeded by one of the middle-aged men—gave me an assignment. He asked me to report on our school's participation in Budapest's first May Day parade.

All the students were required to gather at the school on the first of May and join a huge citywide parade of people—factory workers, office workers, and other students, as well as ordinary people. Attendance was mandatory. Workers were grouped according to their place of employment, students by their schools, and people who didn't work by their apartment house block.

The parade was supposed to be a happy celebration of things Communist and Soviet. In fact, it was a slow, shuffling flow of unenthusiastic people through the streets leading to Heroes' Square, a big square near City Park. There, we shuffled by a reviewing stand where the leadership of the Hungarian Communist Party stood shoulder to shoulder and waved as the masses of people oozed past. It was hot and dusty, and we were thirsty. As practically the entire city had to march, the parade took forever. And since everyone was marching, there were no spectators.

Loudspeakers were hung from lampposts along the parade route throughout the city. They blared energetic cheers: "Long live the Communist Party!" "Long live Matyas Rakosi!" "Long live Stalin!" I got the impression that the cheering and enthusiastic applause emanated from Heroes' Square and came from all the marchers who had arrived there before us. However, when we arrived at the square, the only people standing and waving were the Party members on the reviewing stand. None of the previous marchers had stuck around to watch. No other marchers were cheering. None of us were cheering.

Yet the loudspeakers continued to blare the same shouts and cheers, over and over. I realized the cheering was a recording. Gabi and I looked at each other surreptitiously. Later, we speculated that army units must have been called up and ordered to cheer, and it was their taped voices we heard over the loudspeakers.

I did not submit an article on the May Day parade. Some other kids did, and the magazine ran a collection of enthusiastic reports about how much fun it was and how the energetic march showed the support of the young people of Budapest for the leadership of the Communist Party.

The following month, in June of 1950, scary news broke. We heard that the South Korean army, puppets of the Americans, had invaded North Korea without notice. The war in Korea became the centerpiece of everything we read in the newspapers and heard on the radio. It became the subject of formal discussions at workplaces and at school, where all of us were exhorted to demonstrate our opposition to this act of imperialist aggression. Posters of the Korean peninsula were displayed all over Budapest, with stickers showing the movements at the front. Wherever I walked in the city, I saw posters about the war as well as posters demanding "Hands Off Korea!"

The fortunes of the war turned quite quickly. The lines separating the North Korean army from the South Koreans started moving southward. The North Koreans repelled the South Korean aggressors, then took over the initiative and rapidly squeezed the South Koreans and their American protectors farther and farther south toward the tip of the Korean peninsula.

I was puzzled. A few years earlier I had seen the Red Army defeat the Germans and push them out of Budapest. I had no doubt that the North Koreans were trained by the Red Army and were equally proficient and dedicated. Yet I knew that the siege of Budapest took quite some time and that even after the Germans were defeated in Budapest, it took three more months before the last German troops were chased out of Hungary. Hungary was a much smaller country than Korea. How could the North Koreans, who were caught in a surprise attack by the South Koreans, rally this rapidly and defeat an army that had the advantage of deliberately preparing for an attack for some time beforehand?

For some reason, I was reminded of my religion class at Evangelikus. While I wanted to believe what I was told, I couldn't put aside my doubts. However, I felt uncomfortable about openly discussing my doubts with anyone. I finally brought up the subject to my father. He seemed reluctant to acknowledge that things might not be the way they were supposed to be. He cut me short, snapping, "Don't be silly, Andris," and turned away.

The only other person I voiced my doubts to was Gabi, on one of our long walks around the city. He said, "Maybe it was the North Koreans who attacked, rather than the other way around." I looked straight ahead at the pavement and kept walking. Neither of us said anything. A bit later, our walk took us by the headquarters of the security police on Stalin Road. This building had an ominous reputation. People said that this was the place you were taken to if you were arrested by the security police. A couple of uniformed policemen were guarding the gate. Without a word, we stopped our conversation and crossed to the other side. It didn't seem wise to walk our doubtful thoughts right by this building.

As time went on, the front line reversed itself again. American troops landed on the Korean peninsula and the course of the war turned in favor of the South. The posters all over the city acquired a new and ominous element. Big ugly bugs appeared next to the maps of the front, portraying the use of bacterial warfare by the Americans and South Koreans against the North. Cries of "Brutal Murder!" accompanied the pictures of the bugs. Eventually these replaced the maps altogether.

As part of his job, my father inspected breeding facilities for cows and pigs in the countryside around Budapest. During the week, he had a driver take him on these visits. Sometimes, however, he went on a Sunday, and then he drove himself and would take my mother and me along for the ride. These were rare treats.

The visits to the breeding facilities were boring, hot, and very smelly, but the rides themselves were exciting and fun. I would sit up in the front, watching the road and watching my father drive. I felt like an adult.

One time, we stopped in a little village near Kiskoros at the house of an old man who used to be my father's math teacher when my father was a child. He hadn't seen my father for many, many years, but he recognized him instantly and greeted him with great warmth. We stayed for an hour or so. At the end of the visit, the old man asked me whether I was good at math. I told him that I liked math but wasn't particularly good at it. He told me that my father was a math whiz. "I hope you're going to be just as good as he was." I didn't think I could ever be as good as my father. I shrugged sheepishly.

On another trip, I was again sitting up in front. My mother was sitting in the back, reading the newspaper.

Then: "Oh, my God, listen to this!" my mother exclaimed. She proceeded to read an article that reported on a speech by a Party functionary in which he accused my father, among others, of bending the official rules in favor of "bourgeois elements."

My father had been put in charge of the government's animal breeding program, but he didn't know anything about the subject, so he hung on to people who were experts in their field, even if they were holdovers from the previous regime and not Party cadres. Now it seemed that my father had recommended someone for a particular post and the government didn't approve.

Criticism in the newspaper was something to be taken very seriously. It usually signified trouble ahead. My father gripped the wheel and stared straight ahead on the road. He kept on driving but was clearly in a state of shock, worried or possibly very angry. I couldn't tell which. This outing turned out to be not much fun at all.

In early 1951, my uncle Sanyi and his son-in-law were arrested in the middle of the night. My aunt showed up at our house the next morning, frightened and utterly helpless. Nobody would say where they were taken or why. There were no charges and no one to inquire to. They were just gone.

None of it made sense. There was nothing we could do, except wait to see what would happen next.

A few days later, my father was fired from his job. He was

also told that in any future job he would not be allowed to earn more than one-fourth of his previous salary.

People stopped dropping by our apartment to visit my father. Jani and Romacz still stuck around, but most of the others disappeared.

Life at school didn't change, but after a while it dawned on me that the last several articles I had submitted to the newspaper had not been published. When I asked my editor why, he waved me away impatiently and said, "You just don't write as well as you used to." I asked him what his complaints were. He mumbled something incomprehensible and told me not to waste his time. I was stunned and embittered.

Walking home from the editorial offices, I was struck by an incredible thought: They don't like my writing because my uncle is in jail. It didn't seem that this connection could be possible. But when I got home, I went to my mother and asked if she thought this might be true. She listened to me quietly, then nodded. Her eyes were moist.

A career in journalism suddenly lost its appeal.

Above: Mr. Volenski, who taught physics, was my favorite teacher. He was also a character.

Above: My friend Peter was a serious student. He was the chairman of the literary circle.

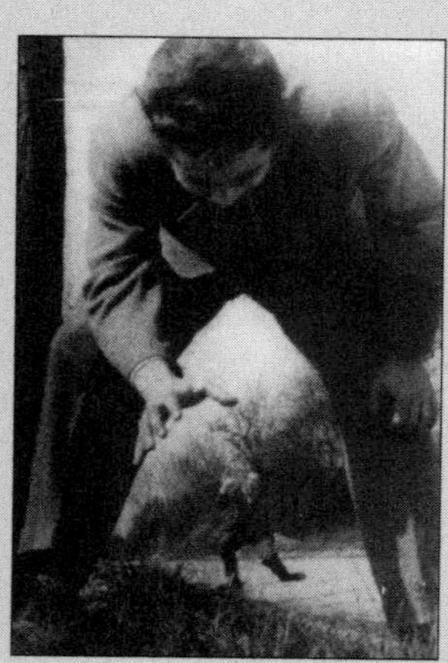

Above: My best friend Gabi. I missed him when we started going to different schools.
Left: One of my new buddies was Bubi. Here he is a willing subject of my trick photography attempt.

Chapter Nine

MADACH GYMNASIUM

NOT EVERYONE from the Dob Street School went on to gymnasium. Gymnasium was secondary schooling for students around age fourteen who intended to go to university. For other students, there were technical secondary schools called *technikum.* Those students still had the option of going to university after graduating from *technikum,* but they had professional training to fall back on if they chose not to. Some kids went to *technikum* to study electronics or the machine industry. Gabi had always been interested in working with wood, so he chose to go to a *technikum* that trained people for work in the wood industry.

I was in a quandary as to what I wanted to be. My dreams of becoming a writer and journalist were demolished. However, without being entirely sure what I wanted to study, I knew I intended to go on to university, so I chose to go to a gymnasium.

Madach gymnasium, the neighborhood secondary school I was assigned to, had once been a school well-known for its academic excellence. Like Evangelikus, it, too, had once offered an eight-year curriculum. But as a result of the nationalization of the schools, it had been restructured so that it now covered only the final four years of what used to be a traditional gymnasium.

Madach gymnasium was a twenty-minute walk from my home. It was an ornate building with wide staircases and lots of tall windows. The building had obviously once been very impressive, but now it was in decay, with the paint peeling down to the mortar.

Upon registering, we were broken into three classes of about thirty students each, called 1A, 1B, and 1C: 1A and 1B were boys' classes; 1C was the girls' class. As it turned out, the two parallel boys' classes, A and B, had distinctly different personalities: 1B was a more serious, academically inclined class, while 1A was rowdy, a class of troublemakers. Purely by chance, I landed in 1A.

Soon after the school year began, 1A was taken on a field trip to the Budapest zoo. The zoo was in City Park, quite a distance from the school. Nevertheless, we walked. We lined up in formation, four across, with the teacher in the lead. We started out in an orderly fashion. Soon, however, the ranks broke down, and we clustered into groups, shuffling along, poking each other, and taking up most of the sidewalk.

When we got to the zoo, our teacher left us alone while he went to the ticket booth to arrange for our admission. We were milling around the entrance, restless and barely controlled. Suddenly, a few boys broke ranks and ran toward the zoo fence. In an instant, they were over the top and inside the zoo, running out of sight.

For a brief moment, the rest of us were paralyzed by indecision; then, like a herd of wild horses, we, too, broke and ran. We scattered along the fence until we were out of sight of the main gate, then clambered over the iron railing. I was apprehensive about getting caught on the metal spikes of the fence, but I managed to avoid them by boosting myself up on one of the stone pillars that held the fence in place. Some frantic scrambling, a big jump, and I was in.

Once inside, I was caught up in the same exhilaration that had infected the rest of the class. With a group of three or four other boys, I ran from exhibit to exhibit, panting and flushed with excitement. People turned to stare at us as we went hurtling past. Here and there we saw other small groups of our classmates, all wildly chasing around the cages, some running to the left, some to the right, until we were dispersed throughout the zoo. None of us paid any attention to the animals.

This being a weekday in early autumn, there weren't too many people at the zoo, and we easily stood out from the rest of the visitors. It didn't take long for uniformed zoo personnel to start rounding us up. In short order, we were corralled, marched out the main entrance gate, and led back to our glowering teacher. After the last delinquent was caught, we reassembled in formation and marched back to school. The teacher paid a lot more attention to us this time. When we got back to school, we were told to line up in the courtyard. We waited in silence, a bit deflated after all the excitement. Soon the principal showed up, a short but burly and intimidating man. Glaring at us with fiery eyes, he berated us and told us that he would not stand for us turning into hooligans. Behavior like this, he warned, would have terrifying consequences.

By noon recess, the news of our escapade had raced through the school like wildfire. Kids from the other classes, including even respected upperclassmen, gathered around us in the schoolyard, demanding all the details of our escapade. Our reputation was established.

Even though I had fun in the zoo escapade, I wasn't very happy about being in this class. I missed Gabi and found it hard to make new friends. Most of the class was not interested in the subjects we were to study; I was. But the more they cut up and got rowdy, the more difficult it was to stay interested in the teachers and what they taught.

The wild kids took over the class. They taunted the few of us who did any work and didn't think anything of copying our homework. They asked for or simply took it from us, even as they mocked us for having done it.

Soon a small group of us, characterized by more interest in studying and less interest in rabble-rousing, started to hang out together.

My new buddies included a short boy nicknamed Bubi (a condescending nickname for someone of short stature). Bubi was good in math and physics, and he loved to tinker with gadgets. He may not have been tall, but he was a bundle of muscle and quite good at sports, which helped deflect some of the taunting.

Another friend, Imre, was a complete contrast to Bubi—tall, skinny, and very awkward. He was interested in literature and cultural goings-on. I could count on being able to discuss anything I read with him. Chances were he had read the same book a couple of times already.

A third member of our gang was the math wizard of the class. He was always way ahead of what we were studying and genuinely fascinated by advanced and abstract mathematics. He looked repulsive—unkempt, oily hair, snot in his nose, dirty fingernails. He had acne, too. Our class had started the year by learning about Greek mythology, and in short order he was nicknamed Minosz, after the ugly minotaur. The nickname stuck.

I also became friendly with a boy from the 1B class called Tamas. He was as good at physics as Minosz was with math. Tamas was also an accomplished violinist and a fair piano player.

I felt distinctly inferior in comparison with my friends. I didn't play the violin—or any instrument, for that matter—and I wasn't a math or physics genius. While I was a good student, I wasn't particularly outstanding in any one area. And I was still bad at all sports except swimming. But they accepted me as their equal. I think that the main asset I brought was that I was more comfortable with the rest of the class than they were. I served as their bridge to the wild bunch.

We had something else in common: All five of us were Jewish. We weren't the only Jews in the class. There were a few more whom we had not become friendly with. But as we gravitated to each other's company, and hung around with each other at recess and after school, a subtle wall formed around us. No explicit acts of anti-Semitism were ever expressed toward us. But the separation was real.

We never discussed the fact that we were Jewish. We just knew that we were, just as the other members of the class knew it, too. Hungarians almost always knew who was or wasn't Jewish, kids or adults. It became a sixth sense for all of us, never a subject of explicit discussion, but one of constant tacit awareness.

The classes at Madach operated pretty much the same way as at Dob Street. Students were settled into a particular classroom and never left it except for recess breaks, physical education, and physics and chemistry labs. Every hour a different teacher would come to our room to teach.

The teachers at Madach were better than the ones at Dob Street. One of the more interesting ones was Mr. Telegdi, the Hungarian literature teacher. He was a tall, balding, stooped older man. While the other teachers all wore ordinary street clothes, Mr. Telegdi always wore an old-fashioned, threadbare black smock over his clothes. He carried himself with an old-fashioned dignity that seemed as out of place as his smock.

Most of the teachers had nicknames. Mr. Telegdi had two. Sometimes we called him Tade, after the luckless character in the opera *Pagliacci,* which was popular enough in those days in Budapest that a lot of people knew the story, if not the actual music. When he listened to a boy answering a question, he would tilt his head inquiringly to the side, tuck his right hand behind his back to grasp his left elbow, and shift his weight into an awkward stance that matched the bemused and somewhat distant look on his face. That gave rise to his other nickname, the Sparrow.

Tade loved literature. When he got going about Hungarian novels or poetry, his face would start to glow and passion would creep into his voice. Most of the kids in the class, however, thought his enthusiasm was funny. They cut up mercilessly in Tade's class, whispering, making faces, and dropping pencils throughout the hour.

The cutting-up took a different turn one day when one of the boys came to class with a pocketful of little pebbles. Tade had his back turned to the class, writing something on the blackboard. The boy started throwing the pebbles one by one to bounce off the blackboard, taking care not to hit Tade, but being sure to disrupt the lecture. Each time a pebble clacked onto the floor, Tade would turn around, shift into his sparrow-like stance, look around the class with a mournful expression on his face, then wordlessly turn around and resume writing until the next pebble hit again.

It was irresistible for the class cutups. The next day, more boys came armed with pebbles; the day after, more still.

On the fourth day, after more pebble throwing, Mr. Telegdi left the room. The principal returned in his place. He delivered another intimidating lecture, then announced that we were confined to class during recesses until Mr. Telegdi gave our conduct a passing grade. The pebble throwing stopped at once.

At the end of the class, I was commissioned by my classmates to ask him whether we had behaved well enough to have our punishment rescinded. He sternly admonished me, "Not throwing pebbles is not the same as good behavior. I expect much better."

Class after class, he did not waver from his stand. He did not release us until we had a totally quiet classroom—no pebbles, no shuffling, no talking.

It was always strange to see our teachers outside of school. One time, to my amazement, I spied Mr. Telegdi in the opera house. I was in my usual place in the cheapest seats right under the roof, and I recognized him sitting with a group of people in the opera director's box right over the stage. He was wearing a suit, not his usual smock coat, and seemed to fit right in. I couldn't wait to talk to him the next day.

Yes, he said, he had been at the opera. The director was a friend of his. I asked him how he liked the performance. It was a Hungarian classic that featured my favorite bass-baritone, Gyorgy Losonczy. Mr. Telegdi gave a very sophisticated assessment of the performance, but he crushed me by not being as impressed by Losonczy as I was. He said, "The man is a good actor, but he sings as if he had a dumpling stuck in his throat." Thereafter, I thought of his comment whenever I heard Losonczy and had to concede that Mr. Telegdi was right.

A month or so later, he invited Imre and me to visit him at his apartment to talk about literature. He lived in a couple of shabby rooms facing the inner courtyard of a run-down apartment house. There were books scattered all over, piled on the floor and tables. Everything was covered with dust. Mr. Telegdi sat on an old sofa, we pulled up two kitchen chairs, and we all talked about literature. The conversation was very interesting, but I found the overall atmosphere incredibly sad and depressing. To my surprise, I realized that I felt sorry for Mr. Telegdi. It bothered me even more that I, a student in the disrespectful 1A class, should dare to feel sorry for him. After Imre and I left, I tried to wash the picture of Telegdi's sad apartment out of my head, and my confused feelings with it.

Mrs. Vasarhelyi, our history teacher, was quite a contrast to Mr. Telegdi. She was young, good-looking, and animated. Even though she was supposedly married to a Party functionary, she was a good teacher. Before history class, all my rowdy classmates got busy combing their hair and checking out their reflection in the window. We had no trouble keeping quiet for Mrs. Vasarhelyi.

As always, I sat in the first row because of my ears. Sometimes, when the student whom I normally shared the bench with missed class, Mrs. Vasarhelyi would perch on his desk, with her feet on the seat next to me. She was close enough that I could smell her perfume. She wore open-necked blouses, and from my seat, I could see her neck and the underside of her chin. I felt I was staring at her, but I didn't know what else to do with my eyes, so I stared at her neck. I was terribly embarrassed, but I was always happy when my seatmate was out sick.

Every once in a while, during recess, we would see Mrs. Vasarhelyi and Mr. Telegdi chatting together. They kept their voices low and leaned toward each other intimately. Each sighting ignited a speculative buzz in our class. It was hard to think of them as being romantically interested in each other, yet the possibility was intriguing.

My favorite teacher of all was Mr. Volenski, the physics teacher. He was a small man, older than most teachers in the school, with thinning reddish brown hair that he combed straight back over his head. He was a very good teacher, and physics was one of my favorite classes. But above all, he was a character.

He always regaled us with stories about his dog, Muki (an affectionate slang word meaning "Little Guy"). The stories often involved physics, as in, "I threw this object to my dog, Muki. Would it be easier for him to catch it this way or that way?" Sometimes, our performance in class was compared unfavorably to the performance of Muki.

Everybody in the class got a kick out of Mr. Volenski's stories. Perhaps that was why he never had a hard time keeping discipline.

Mr. Volenski had a fantastic memory for things that happened twenty years ago, but he forgot who you were even if he had seen you just a few hours earlier. I liked him a lot. I think he liked me, even if I wasn't always sure he could identify me. Then one day, I knew that he could.

At a parent-teacher conference that fall, Mr. Volenski told the assembled parents, "Life is like a big lake. All the boys get in the water at one end and start swimming. Not all of them will swim across. But one of them, I'm sure, will. That one is Grof." Both of my parents were there, and when they returned home, they told me about it with great pride.

They also told so many other people about it that over time, my swimming across the lake of life became a family cliché. Even though the story grew a little tiresome and I was embarrassed by my parents' insistence on repeating it, I continued to get some encouragement from each telling. I hoped Mr. Volenski was right.

Mr. Telegdi also spoke highly of me at the conference, but his description troubled me. In front of all the parents, he said, "Someday we will be sitting in Grof's waiting room, waiting for him to see us." I imagined him huddled in this waiting room, ignored by the secretary and other people, and felt sorry for him. I already felt sorry for him anyway because I knew he must be wrong. The notion that someday I would have a room to keep people waiting in seemed inconceivable.

My uncle Sanyi and my cousin's husband were still in jail, and my father was still officially disgraced. After my father lost his government job, a friend of his was brave enough to hire him to run a small accounting group at the state dairy organization. He was paid exactly as ordered—one-fourth of his previous salary.

The loss of my father's earnings had a significant impact on our lifestyle. To be sure, we had never spent all that my father and mother made before. Still, the cut in income was large and the little luxuries of life were gone. Eating out on Sundays was gone. Going to the theater was gone. Any notion of my getting anything better than the cheapest seats at the opera was gone. Delicacies like chestnut puree were gone. We had meat only once a week now.

A few months after my father started working at the state dairy, this friend told him about another job, also an accounting job, at a construction company that paid a little more money. After suitable applications and much checking and rechecking with the authorities, my father changed jobs. The construction company was located in the outskirts of Budapest, so my father had a long tram ride to get to work. He made the long commute without complaining.

I never heard my father complain about the loss of his job, either. In fact, I never heard him complain at all, but he became very quiet. He was a man who used to thrive on political discussions. Now he refused to discuss politics. And in any case, there was no one to discuss it with. Most of his friends still stayed away.

Some of my classmates had discovered girls. At recess and during breaks between classes, they constantly boasted about going out with this girl or taking that girl to the movies. The ones who claimed to be successful tended to be good at sports and looked more stylish than the rest of us. While everyone else wore ordinary clothes to special school events, they wore jackets with carefully padded shoulders and tapered pants. They didn't care much about getting good grades; according to them, grades were not an asset in attracting girls.

Nobody in my group of friends ever talked much about girls. I didn't want to admit that I didn't have anything to talk about, and I guess my friends didn't have much to talk about, either. However, I wanted to be the first of our group to succeed with girls, and I wanted to have something I could boast about with the other boys.

There wasn't a whole lot of opportunity to get to know girls in school because we were in separate classes. I had to figure out another way.

Some of my classmates in the "in crowd" knew how to dance. I envied them. I did not want to compromise my place among my brainy friends, but I did want to meet girls and impress them the way some of my classmates did.

The whole prospect of dancing seemed like a mystery. I couldn't imagine how people knew what to do with their feet, and the idea of walking up to a girl and asking her to dance paralyzed me with fear. But the very fact that I was puzzled and scared by dancing pushed me to learn.

There was a dance school on Kiraly Street a few blocks away

from our house. The school was one flight up from the street, and at night when I walked by I could hear the music through the open window and see the couples gliding by. I worked up my courage and checked out what it would take to register; basically, all it took was money and not very much of that, because, like many enterprises, the dance school was partially sponsored by the state.

I didn't have an allowance. The family's spending money was stashed under my father's underwear in my parents' wardrobe, and whenever I needed some, I was allowed to take it from the folded bills as long as I told my parents that I did so. I was very mindful that I was dipping into the family's living money.

But dancing lessons weren't very expensive, and with my father's new job, we had a little money for extras. My parents agreed that we could afford it, so in the spring of my first year at the Madach gymnasium, I signed up for an introductory class.

It was not nearly as difficult or as scary as thinking about it had been. The class was made up of kids my age, a bunch of boys and a few girls. The teacher was a middle-aged man, lean and craggy but with an air of assurance and sophistication. He wore a suit and tie, which added to his polish. Few men in Budapest wore suits, and when they did, their suits didn't fit well. The dance teacher's suit was obviously old, but it was so well cut and the cloth was so fine that it didn't look at all old-fashioned. His dapper elegance reminded me of my former English teacher, Mr. Endrodi. I was impressed and a little envious.

We formed in straight lines opposite a mirrored wall, and the teacher walked us through some very simple steps. We all counted "One, two, three, four" and put our left foot one way, then our right foot another way. It didn't feel like dancing. I avoided looking in the mirror and focused instead on putting my feet in the right place. Then the teacher put on a record, and as we counted to the music, everything started to make sense. We practiced over and over to the same records, playing tunes for the fox-trot, waltz, and tango. I began to feel quite confident—at least, when I was dancing by myself.

Then the day came when we were paired up, boys and girls. The instructor demonstrated with a woman who hung around the dance school and served as his assistant. She was frumpy looking, but when they danced together, they glided around the floor very gracefully. We were expected to perform the same transformation.

There were more boys than girls, so we had to take turns. Finally, the magic moment came when I put my arm around a girl's waist and held her hand. It wasn't all that magical. Both of us had sweaty hands, and I was busy counting "One, two, three, four." I couldn't wait for the dance to stop. I had the impression that my partner was as relieved as I.

Eventually, the steps came more naturally. I could do them without counting in my head. I even learned to tap on a boy's shoulder as he was dancing with a girl and cut in. But the dance school itself never delivered any kind of romantic adventure. We were so serious about learning our steps that our partners were just objects to practice with.

I liked the fox-trot, waltz, and tango well enough, but they weren't going to impress anyone. The rage in Hungary was American bebop music, which you danced to with fluid steps, swinging your partner out so that her skirt swirled up and doing intricate contortions with your feet as if your knees were made of jelly. Because of its Western origin, this kind of dancing was frowned upon by the Communist authorities. People could dance this way only in the privacy of their own homes to records that had been smuggled in from West Germany or Austria.

We all wanted to learn this kind of dancing, but, of course, it wasn't taught at the school. One day during a break, one of the students tried to perform a few bebop steps in class. The instructor frowned in disapproval. The student continued to contort himself. The instructor watched a little longer, then stopped him curtly and said, "If you've got to do those steps, at least do them right." To our surprise, he replaced the fox-trot record with a faster, contemporary song, then launched into a private dance, his legs elastic and his hips as supple as putty. We stared at him, awestruck. After a few minutes, he seemed to come to his senses. He stopped and said, "Unless you can do it like this, don't even bother." Nobody did.

After six weeks, the dance course was over. There was a graduation ceremony that the whole dance school attended, where we danced as couples under the watchful eyes of the instructor and his assistant partner. Now that I knew how to dance—or, at least, thought that I knew how—I dared to show up at school parties and special events that I had avoided before. But for the most part, I stood against the wall. I realized that there was a lot more to impressing girls than knowing where to place my feet.

Meanwhile, in addition to studying Russian in school, I had also signed up for a free class in remedial Russian. The Russian instruction at school was still so elementary that I was afraid I wouldn't learn anything. Since I had to learn Russian, I thought I might as well learn it for real.

The class met in the evening. Ironically, it was held in the building that used to house the Evangelikus gymnasium, which had been nationalized and was now used for other purposes. The class was made up of all kinds of people—mostly adults, but some other kids my age. One girl in particular caught my attention; she was short and blond and had a spunky personality. The students were expected to refer to each other by the

Russian version of their first names. This girl's name in Russian was Galina.

Galina walked home the same way I did—it turned out she lived past my house—and we fell into the habit of occasionally walking back from class together. I always looked forward to the walk. In fact, I realized that I looked forward to the walk more than I looked forward to the class. The teacher wasn't all that good, or maybe I just wasn't motivated to learn. The main reason I kept going to class was Galina. But I never managed to work up my courage to try to arrange a date.

My only other opportunity for socializing with girls was during recess at school. It wasn't easy. The girls tended to cluster together in groups that were difficult to break into. The boys hung out in groups, too, and it was difficult to break away. You might drift by a group of girls and say something, or you might catch a girl's eye on the stairs on the way to class or to recess. But there was no place in the school courtyard where you could talk without everyone noticing.

I was fifteen, and other boys my age were going out with girls. So at the end of my first year at Madach, I worked up my courage to ask one of the girls if she would meet me after school to go for a walk. To my delight and surprise, she readily agreed. We made a date for three o'clock in the afternoon the next day. The meeting was going to be under a street clock at the corner of Kiraly Street and Ring Street, near where we both lived.

I got there fifteen minutes early. I paced up and down along the busy street corner, waiting for the clock to move forward and practicing what I would say when she showed up—how I would say hello in a suave and self-possessed manner, as if I did this every day. Three o'clock came. No girl. I told myself that she would probably be a few minutes late: Girls probably tended to be a little late anyway.

Five minutes passed, then ten, then fifteen. Sour, heavy feelings started to grow in the pit of my stomach. My thoughts went from excitement and anticipation to a bitter argument with myself. As I walked up and down, I looked at my reflection in the shop windows. How could I really expect her to want to go out with me when I was so pudgy and awkward? At half-past three, I looked around one more time, then headed home. I was very down on myself and very angry at the girl—at all girls.

Back in school the next day, I forced myself not even to glance in the direction of the girl. I just hung around with my friends from 1A. There was only one piece of good news: Out of caution, I had never told anybody of my would-be encounter, so I didn't have to tell anybody about it not having happened.

I never talked to my parents about girls. They knew I had gone to dance class, but they didn't ask any questions about it, and I didn't volunteer anything. I was grateful for their restraint.

Manci's husband, Miklos, on the other hand, was very interested in my experiences with girls. I had the impression that he thought of himself as having been a great success in this arena as a young man and that he was dying to share his stories. He would put his arm around my shoulders and, with a professional look and a quizzical glint in his eye, ask, "Andris, how are you doing with girls?" He did this just about every time he saw me.

I dreaded seeing him and cringed at his questions. I didn't have much to report, and I hated to admit it. I tried to put him off with an attempt at closemouthed Horatio Hornblower–like solemnity. But it didn't discourage him from greeting me with the same winking and conspiratorial backslapping the next time he saw me. All of this left me with even more of a desire to have something to tell Miklos and more frustrated that I continued to have nothing.

SWIMMING ACROSS

That summer after my first year at the Madach gymnasium, I spent a lot of my time at the Palatinus public pool on Margaret Island. It was farther away than the pool in City Park, but I preferred to go there for two reasons: First, the pool was enormous, and if I got there early, I could swim really long laps uninterrupted; and second, it had a livelier social scene.

People came with groups of friends, and these groups settled down on the large expanse of neatly groomed grass surrounding the pool. By the middle of the day, the lawn was covered with colorful clusters of people picnicking, playing volleyball, sunbathing, and socializing. Sometimes I arranged to meet friends after I got my laps in. Other times I went by myself, but even then, I was sure to run into some people I knew and could settle in with them.

I liked to swim, but the main attraction was gawking at girls parading around in their bikini bathing suits. Looking at them from a distance was all I could and would do. The notion that I might actually talk to a strange girl never even entered my mind.

Once I ran into Galina from my Russian class. She seemed happy to see me. I was certainly happy to see her. We swam together for a while, but then when she was ready to leave the pool, I realized that I had got too excited and couldn't follow her. I energetically threw myself into swimming a couple of lengths of the pool as fast as I could in order to distract myself. It worked, but by the time I was able to get out without embarrassing myself, Galina and her friends were long gone.

It was 1952, the year of the Summer Olympics in Helsinki. The Hungarian team did quite well at these games, and the Hungarian fencers in particular acquitted themselves marvelously. I listened to the play-by-play commentary of the matches on the radio and was mesmerized. The sport seemed very Hornblower-like, glamorous and wild, yet something for a thinking man. Without ever having seen a fencing match, I decided to learn to fence.

It so happened that there was a fencing club in our neighborhood. Membership and the equipment were free because the club was supported by the state. Many sports clubs were state supported, especially those that trained athletes who one day might participate in the Olympics. Athletic excellence was a matter of pride and reflected on the superiority of the state.

I was soon enrolled as a member of the beginner's class. It started much like dance class. A bunch of boys and a few girls wearing gym clothes stood in a line in front of a mirror. A coach yelled, "Lunge!" and we lunged forward awkwardly onto our right foot. Then the coach explained what we should do with our hands and our knees and demonstrated what a proper lunge looked like. Then we did it again and again. The next morning, I could barely move.

After a while, though, as with dancing, we mastered the basic foot movements and progressed to working with a foil, the easiest of the weapons. I was disappointed. The Hungarian Olympic heroes were all saber champions, and that's what I wanted to be, too. But the progression of instruction required that I master the foil first and only then move on to the saber.

I was not much of an athlete. I hated gym at school and was poor at it. But fencing captivated me. Partly it was because of the draw of the Olympic champions. But partly it was because for once I was no worse than any of the others in class, and arguably better than most.

I attended classes diligently, practiced incessantly against my partner, and worked on my footwork at home. I even practiced my parries with my right arm as I was walking down the street until a neighbor lady commented to my parents in a concerned tone that something was wrong with Andris. She had been following me on the street and noticed me making weird motions with my wrist. She thought I was suffering from seizures.

To my disappointment, fencing didn't build muscles in any notable fashion or reduce my weight. The only visible impact it had on my body was that my right forefinger became thicker than the left one and it was bent back from supporting the weight of the foil.

In time, I was allowed to represent my club in official fencing events. These were the lowest class of competitions, but I was excited about getting ready and visiting other clubs and fencing with referees watching our bout. I soon discovered that I wasn't going to go to the Olympics any time soon. I was eliminated either in the preliminaries or, at best, in the semifinals. But I still fenced whenever I could.

That summer, at age fifteen, I got my first job. Imre's father worked for a state publishing company and got Imre, Bubi, and myself a job loading and unloading books on a truck. We managed to stick together and worked as a team most of the time.

We loaded a truck with boxes of books at the printing plant, then hoisted ourselves on top of the books for the ride to the warehouse, where we unloaded the boxes and threw them down a chute to be unpacked and stacked inside. Then we went back to the printing plant for more. It was a physically challenging job, but we made it into a sport, forming a chain and racing with each other to see how fast we could throw the boxes of books from the plant onto the truck, then from the truck down the chute of the warehouse. In between, it was fun riding on the truck bed through the streets of Budapest.

The truck driver was a permanent worker, a young man who watched our activity with older-brotherly amusement.

While we energetically threw the boxes of books around, he lounged against the side of the truck and smoked cigarettes, chatting with passersby and flirting with girls. He seemed to have a much easier job than we did. I grew quite envious of him as the summer progressed. He made me wonder, albeit fleetingly, if going to school was all that worthwhile.

Throughout my years at gymnasium, I got more and more involved with chemistry. It all started during my last year at the Dob Street School. I had come across a book of simple chemistry experiments for kids. The experiments themselves were fun, but I had additional motivation for getting interested in science: After the fiasco of my potential journalism career, I was eager to cultivate an interest in a new profession that was less prone to subjectivity.

The chemistry experiments were innocent at first, involving ingredients I could find at home. I dissolved sugar in water, suspended a string in the solution, then let the water evaporate and watched the sugar crystals precipitate around the string. I heated some sugar over a little alcohol burner and watched it melt, change color, and give off a caramel-like odor. Sugar was a delicacy, particularly in cube form, but I always managed to appropriate a bit for my scientific purposes.

After the first simple experiments, my book led me to more complicated ones. But for these I needed more specialized materials.

The book was published before the war, a more prosperous time when chemical supplies were easy to find. After describing an ingredient, the author would blithely end the section with, "This compound should be available from most good drugstores." I got increasingly annoyed with this phrase because in the world I lived in, even ordinary soap was available only intermittently.

Even the places that specialized in chemical compounds generally didn't have them in stock. In an economy that operated by central planning, shortages of just about everything were commonplace.

I had already experienced the frustrations of central planning when I tried to buy photographic paper. My aunt Manci had taught me some photography, and I also tinkered with developing my own film and enlarging photos at home. During the summer, my pictures had strong blacks and whites, and I needed low-contrast paper to print them properly. On the other hand, in the winter, when everything was in shades of gray, my pictures required high-contrast paper. Needless to say, low-contrast paper was always short in the summer and high-contrast paper was unavailable in the winter. I ended up buying my supply of paper during the prior season and then hoping I had stocked enough for my needs.

Buying chemicals for my experiments was also a hit-or-miss affair. There were no stores that sold chemistry supplies, so I went from drugstores to paint stores to chemical warehouses at the outskirts of Budapest, where I would plead with the clerks to give me small amounts of whatever I needed. People generally tried to help me out, but since no single store had everything, I had to go to a lot of stores before I could build up what I needed for the next group of experiments.

At first, I was satisfied just to mix two liquids together and watch them turn blue or purple or result in the precipitation of a white powder. I only vaguely understood what was actually happening, so the experiments had an air of magic. But as my school chemistry class began to cover the same ground, I began to understand the chemical reactions behind my experiments.

Conversely, doing the experiments at home gave depth to the formulas that I learned in class.

Then I discovered pyrotechnics.

If pouring two liquids together and seeing them change color was interesting, mixing two powders on a metal plate and hitting them with a hammer to trigger a big boom and a puff of smoke was thrilling.

I had several favorite experiments, which I demonstrated over and over to my friends after school. In one, I turned a wad of cotton into an explosive. After I performed my magic on it, it still looked like cotton, but if I set a match to it, it flamed up in a flash and was gone without even a trace of ashes. In my favorite experiment, I wadded a bit of this processed cotton in the bottom of a metal tube and dropped a marble on top of it. When I lit the cotton with a fuse, the marble shot out of the tube like a miniature cannonball.

Another experiment involved mixing a tiny amount of phosphorus with another chemical to make a powder that exploded on impact. With great care, I would sprinkle a small amount of this powder into the hollow pellets I used with my air gun, then seal it in with warmed wax. When I fired one of these loaded pellets at a wall, it exploded with a little flash and a crackling sound. This was great fun.

One time, I fired the pellets out of the window that overlooked the airshaft, where I was hidden from sight, at a building on the other side of Kiraly Street. I hit a wall not too far from where a romantic-minded couple was looking out of their window, and I watched with great amusement as they jumped apart and peered around frantically, trying to figure out what might have caused the explosion.

The highlight of my chemistry career was making real nitroglycerin. (I knew that nitroglycerin was used to make dynamite, so this was a little scary.) The process involved a complicated series of steps, each of which had to be done just so, and at the end there would be a small drop of heavy, yellow liquid that could really blow things up.

I first tried this experiment at home, when my parents were not around. It didn't work. I flushed the remnants down the toilet and tried again. It didn't work the second time, either. The third time around, I was getting discouraged. I figured this would be the last time I tried it. I followed every step precisely as the book said and ended up with a drop of viscous yellow liquid, just as the book said I would.

I put it on a metal plate and hit it gingerly with a hammer. I was very nervous. Nothing happened. Then I hit it again, a little stronger. Still nothing. I hit it again, this time like I meant it. There was a deafening bang. The force of the explosion kicked the hammer back in my hand. When my ears stopped ringing, I realized that my heart was beating madly and I was perspiring all over. I felt like I had climbed a mountain.

When my parents came home that evening, my mother immediately started interrogating me about what I had been up to that afternoon. Evidently, the superintendent's wife had heard the explosion from the other end of the apartment building. Even our neighbors, who had gotten used to my occasional hisses and bangs, announced that this was too much.

I got another chance to make nitroglycerin at, of all places, school.

Back in my first year at Madach gymnasium, I had told the chemistry teacher about my experiments at home. After that, he often asked me to help set up and break down the experiments in class. When I was in my third year, he asked me to demonstrate the making of nitroglycerin to a class of second-year girls. I was delighted and polished up my knowledge of the process.

With thirty girls watching my every move, I went through

the complicated process and produced the single precious drop of heavy, yellow liquid. I asked for a volunteer. When one came up, I handed her the hammer. She closed her eyes and timidly banged at the liquid. Nothing happened. She sheepishly handed the hammer back to me and, like a proud, accomplished scientist, I manfully whacked the drop of nitroglycerin. *Bang!* The class broke into shrieks and excited applause. I was on the top of the world!

Flushed with victory, I started up a conversation with the volunteer. Her name was Erzsi, and she was a cute, buxom girl. She continued to be friendly enough as we talked, so I worked up my courage and asked her if she would meet me after school one day to go for a walk.

I was still shy and sensitive from being stood up a year ago, but Erzsi showed up and we set off for our walk. We headed toward City Park. It was an early winter evening, and it quickly got dark and cold. Halfway to City Park, I reached for her hand. She didn't pull it away. The feeling of walking with a girl and holding hands filled me with almost as much excitement as exploding a drop of nitroglycerin.

When we got to City Park, we headed for a fake castle that housed a museum. The door was locked. We both bent forward to try to make out the sign on the door, only to discover that visiting hours were over. We looked at each other, shrugged, and laughed. Our heads were just inches apart. Still high from the electrifying feel of Erzsi's hand in mine, I bent over and kissed her on the mouth. She kissed me back.

I was stunned. I didn't know what to say. She didn't, either. We turned around and walked home, holding hands in silence.

I walked her to the entryway of her house and said goodbye, then I turned and ran home as fast as I could. As I ran, my excitement gradually dissipated. Then the thought hit me:

What kind of germs did I pick up? So when I got home, I furiously rinsed out my mouth.

Although I finally had something to report to my friends and my uncle Miklos, I never said anything. I went walking with Erzsi a few more times, but our encounters were never as exciting again. A few months later, there was a school dance. Erzsi showed more interest in a good-looking classmate of mine than in me. Soon, they started going out together. I was only a little sad.

While I was feeling that I might actually have a future with girls and chemistry, something bad was happening to my friend Imre.

Imre had started out at Madach gymnasium as a pretty good student. He was particularly interested in literature and history. But as the years went on, he slid more and more into mediocrity. He started missing classes, each time claiming some vague medical problem. But his "medical problem" never got cured and his grades slumped more and more. This got to be an acute problem in the third year, when grades took on more and more meaning as a key determinant of the looming process of university admission.

All of our circle were worried at seeing Imre slip, and I was particularly frustrated that I couldn't figure out what was going on with him. Our friendship faltered. I tried several times to rebuild our relationship. We went for long walks, but Imre didn't tell me much. Once, he let slip that when he cut class, he walked all over Budapest, exploring all the back streets and discovering old buildings all over town. Otherwise, he remained mysterious.

In my mind, I started to spin theories and possibilities that would be consistent with the few morsels of information he divulged. My imagination got going, and suddenly, during one of our walks, I felt I had Imre's story figured out. I was so sure about what was going on that I decided to write a story about it.

It was nine or ten in the evening when we finished our walk and I returned home. I put some paper into my father's typewriter, closed the door to my room, and started writing. My mind was racing. As I pecked away at the typewriter, the story started to take shape. I finally went to sleep at two in the morning and couldn't wait for the next afternoon so that I could finish spinning Imre's story. When I read it over, I was as excited as when my nitroglycerin exploded. It seemed I had an honest-to-goodness short story in my hand. I titled it "Despair."

I read it again and again, but the more I read it, the less I could tell whether it was good or not. I eagerly awaited my parents' return from work. When they got home, I shyly told them, "I wrote something I'd like you to read."

They sat down next to each other on the sofa. My mother started reading the story, and as she finished with each page, she handed it to my father. I sat in a chair, watching them. I couldn't tell anything from their faces. My heart was racing and I needed to fidget, but I didn't want to interrupt their concentration, so I made myself sit still.

When my father finished the last page, they looked at each other for a long moment. Then my mother said, "Andris, this is serious work." My father emphatically agreed.

I had passed the test with my parents. I was ready to raise the bar.

There was a student literary circle at school. Mr. Telegdi was in charge. He and the students got together every couple of weeks to discuss something they had all read. Once in a while, they read a composition or some poetry by a member of the literary circle. No one from the A class ever attended the literary circle. It was populated and run mainly by kids from the B class.

I wanted to submit my story. But I wanted to do it in such a way that they wouldn't know it was my story. I wasn't sure why I didn't want to be openly associated with the story. Perhaps it was because I'd never gone to the literary circle; perhaps it was because I carried the stigma of being a member of the rowdy A class; or perhaps it was because I was still sore about the rejection by the youth newspaper. In any case, I really wanted an objective reaction. So I worked out an elaborate ruse.

First, I showed the story to Imre. He denied that it had anything to do with him in real life but thought it was a wonderful story. I was happy to have him as an enthusiastic fan. I folded the story in an envelope, addressed the envelope with the typewriter, and asked Imre to give it to the school custodian and ask him to give it to Mr. Telegdi.

Then I waited for something to happen.

A few days later, something did. At the beginning of one of our Hungarian literature classes, Mr. Telegdi assumed his usual awkward stance, then, after clearing his throat, announced that something quite unusual would be taking place at the literary circle next week. A student had anonymously submitted a very interesting story, he said, and we should all come to hear it read.

Such an invitation was highly unusual. In fact, I couldn't think of any other time that Mr. Telegdi had invited the A class to the literary circle. I would have liked to savor the moment, but I was too preoccupied with trying to pretend utter disinterest.

At the appointed time on the appointed day, I showed up at the literary circle along with several A classmates and Imre—a first for all of us. The room was overflowing with kids to the point that a number were standing at the sides and at the back. I found a seat in the middle of the crowd.

The chairman of the circle was a serious student from the B class, named Peter. He called the meeting to order. By way of introduction, he made a convoluted speech about how this story was very unusual and, he went on, it was contemporary and interesting. In fact, he said, he was so intrigued by the fact that it was written by one of the students that he couldn't resist doing some detective work about the identity of the author. He would, he announced, share his findings after the story was read.

I didn't like the sound of this. I did not want to be identified, particularly not in front of a crowd of students. But I was trapped.

Then Peter sat down. One of the girls in the literary circle took his place in front of the class and read my story. She read very fluidly, giving it all the right inflections. The students listened intently, right up to the final paragraph, which described how my imaginary Imre character fought against the realization that he would not make it into the university:

"His head ached but he continued on. His mind turned into pulp; he could no longer think. When the clock in the other room struck one, he turned out the light and dragged himself to his bed in the dark. He undressed slowly, like a robot, put on his pajamas, and stretched out on the bed. In an instant, he was overcome by the deepest despair. He pushed his face into the pillow and sobbed until he fell asleep."

There was silence when she finished. Then Peter took center stage again and ponderously walked us through his analysis. He explained how the psychological insights of the story were so deep as to make it impossible for the author to have such an understanding about another person. Therefore, he concluded, the author must be writing about himself. And since, he went on, the story was vaguely reminiscent of Imre's school career, and the story's hero's last name started with a V and Imre's surname started with a T, both letters occurring late in the alphabet, that just about clinched the argument that the author must be Imre.

Imre, beet red, leapt to his feet and, waving his hands, protested loudly that he had nothing to do with the story, he hadn't written it, and it was not about him. Peter listened with condescending tolerance, which infuriated Imre even more. It took Mr. Telegdi's intervention to change the discussion from the identity of the author to the substance of the story.

The general nature of the comments was that the story was very realistic, that it contained bits and pieces of all of our lives. Mr. Telegdi summed up the discussion by saying, "Whoever the author is, I'm sure that this is not the last we have heard from him."

The buzz continued as people dissected the story with great gusto. After a while, I decided that I had heard enough. I stood up, and when all heads had turned to me, I said, "I just have one comment to make. I need to support Imre's protest. I know for a fact he did not write the story because I did."

Pandemonium broke out. The meeting dissolved into excited kids slapping me on the back, congratulating me, and shaking their heads in disbelief while they rehashed the events of the afternoon. Mr. Telegdi shook my hand and repeated that he thought the story was great. Then Imre and a few other friends and I left and went for a long walk. We walked throughout the city for hours.

This was the most exciting event of my life.

When I got home, I tossed and turned in bed, not wanting to fall asleep and have the feeling stop. Even though by now I was very interested in continuing on with chemistry, it was satisfying to realize that my earlier notions about becoming a writer had some basis in reality.

The next day, I walked over to my aunt Iren's apartment and gave her a copy of my story. After my uncle Sanyi, Iren was the most literary member of the family. I wished that I could show my story to Sanyi, but in the two years since his arrest, we still hadn't heard anything about him. We didn't even know if he was alive or dead.

Iren read the story while I was there and thought it was wonderful. She volunteered to pass it to a friend, a prominent writer.

In the days that followed, I often imagined how I might be discovered as a seventeen-year-old literary prodigy and get my stories published in a real magazine. Weeks went by. I didn't hear anything. Eventually, I got a one-paragraph typewritten note from the famous writer, thanking me for letting him see the manuscript. He wrote that he found the absence of the official school youth organization in my hero's life surprising. Clearly, in real life, the youth organization would have stepped in and helped my hero before he was overcome with despair. He suggested that the story be modified to reflect how that might take place. Other than that, he thought I would learn a great deal by reading the works of the people's great writers.

I was glad I liked chemistry.

One of the side benefits of my short story was that it established me as a person of some literary merit, as opposed to the rest of the A class rowdies. I now occasionally attended meetings of the literary circle. Some people with whom I had had very few prior dealings now paid attention to me. Peter was one of them.

Peter was quite different from me or my other friends. He

was very well read, and he tried to act like an adult. But we had enough common interests in literature, our school, and our classmates to bridge the differences. Eventually we found that we liked each other and became friends.

Another person I met was a girl called Eva. Eva had also submitted a short story to the literary circle that she said she had written. But after the story was read aloud, somebody found it had been copied word for word from a published anthology. Overnight, Eva became an object of derision.

I had a different reaction. After writing about Imre, I was intrigued by trying to figure out why people did what they did, and I was very intrigued by Eva.

I started talking to her during class breaks. Having become an outcast, she welcomed my attention. After a while, I offered to walk her home, and we started going on walks with each other. I found her to be quite intelligent and aware, but with a weird streak of trying to be somebody she was not. I thought this was a challenge. I thought that, like a modern-day Prince Charming, I would save her from herself.

On one of our outings one afternoon, we took a tram to the outskirts of Budapest. We walked around, then settled down on a bench, and after a while, I kissed her. Something was wrong. Eva kept her mouth wide open. Perhaps she was mimicking what kisses in the movies looked like. In any case, I couldn't get my mouth to fit hers. I reached up with my hand and gently tried to push her jaw closed. She angrily pushed me away and told me I should leave her alone. She knew what she was doing, she said.

We argued about the proper way to kiss. Whatever romance had prompted the kiss was lost. I didn't ask her out again.

Right: Me, at 18. By this time, I was no longer pudgy. *Below:* My mother was a good swimmer. One day, during a vacation at Lake Balaton, we held on to a rubber air mattress and swam far out into the lake. We drifted, talking about everything and nothing.

Right: Gymnasium was officially over. This is my graduation photo.

Chapter Ten

FOURTH YEAR

I DON'T REMEMBER exactly when the deportations started. Rumors of people being moved without notice to dreary locations in the countryside had been going around all through my years at Madach gymnasium. I didn't actually know anybody who was deported, but the rumors came from so many directions that they were hard to ignore. They seemed more frequent during my second and third years at Madach.

What the stories all had in common was how the deportation took place: There was a knock on the apartment door in the middle of the night. Someone in uniform handed the deportation order to the residents and told them to get their belongings ready before dawn. At the appointed hour, a canvas-covered truck pulled up in front of the house, loaded up the family and their belongings, and drove away.

Rumor had it that the deportations were overseen by the security police, a special branch of the police force that dealt with political offenses, and that the people selected for deportation were guilty of "bourgeois tendencies," whatever that meant. Often, though, it was implied that the real reason they were targeted was that a high-ranking Party official coveted their apartment.

The rumors of the deportations had the effect of permeating our lives with an intangible but constant nagging fear. Budapest took on a different personality. The streets, the stores, the people, our apartment, all looked a lot better to me than they had before. The possibility of being forcibly moved to the countryside and losing all this made them precious.

One night, our doorbell rang. I had been tinkering with my chemicals, which were stored in the long hallway that led from the Big Room to the entryway. I got up to answer the bell, and through the frosted glass of the front door, I glimpsed the drab brown of a military uniform.

My heart started thumping so hard I could barely breathe. I stopped in my tracks, swallowed hard, and then slowly went to the door and hesitantly opened it. A wave of relief swept over me, almost making me dizzy. The person in uniform was a distant relative, who was an army doctor. He happened to be in the neighborhood and had taken the opportunity to drop in for a visit.

One reaction to the growing political oppression was the number of jokes that sprang up about it. They acted as a safety valve for feelings that couldn't be expressed otherwise. Jokes about current events in Budapest were an art form. They were created and transmitted almost instantaneously.

Once, a rumor flashed through Budapest that a crowded city bus had crashed over the side of one of the bridges across the Danube. Everybody on board—some seventy people—supposedly died. News about local accidents was never published officially. If you believed the newspapers, accidents, floods, storms, and other natural disasters took place only in the West, never in Hungary, the Soviet Union, or other Eastern-bloc countries. So, not surprisingly, at first we didn't see anything in the news about this bus accident. Finally, there was a brief official acknowledgment that the bus had gone over the bridge, but the item stated that since the bus was heading back to the terminal at the end of its route, the driver and the conductor were the only casualties.

In a flash, a joke started making the rounds: Saint Peter is presiding over the Pearly Gates. A man in uniform comes up to him and says, "Peter, I'm the driver of the bus that went over the bridge in Budapest." Peter says, "Come on in, my son, make yourself at home." A little while later, another man in uniform comes along. "And who are you, my son?" Peter asks. "I'm the conductor of the bus that went over the bridge in Budapest," the man replies. "Welcome, my son," Peter says. "Come on in and make yourself at home." A little while later, a group of seventy men, women, and children come up to the Pearly Gates. "And who are all you people?" Peter asks with surprise. They reply, "We are the passengers on the bus that went over the bridge in Budapest." Peter pulls himself up to his full height and angrily says, "Do you take me for a fool? I read the Budapest newspapers, and there was no mention of you! Get lost!"

Telling jokes like this to the wrong person could be dangerous. This was captured in another joke: Two men are ogling a spanking new Western car. One of them says, "Isn't this car a wonderful testimony to the technological capabilities of our friendly Soviet Union?" The other man looks at him scornfully. "Don't you know anything about cars?" he asks. The first man replies, "I know about cars. I don't know about you."

I picked up these jokes from my classmates. Politics was no subject for jokes at home. But after years of it not even being a subject of discussion, politics now began to creep into our daily conversations.

My mother and I saw eye-to-eye about the seamy side of life under Communism right from the beginning. We were disgruntled with the shortages of everything from sweaters to soap; the lack of some of the more basic foodstuffs in the stores at a time when the nationalized agriculture of the country was supposed to be producing record harvests; the incessant lines you had to stand in to buy from a limited selection of inferior items; the pervasive sloganeering. (The most annoying slogan was "Work is a matter of honor and duty." It was posted everywhere—on factory walls, in stores, and even on street signs—right above the heads of people who were listlessly trying to get away with the minimum amount of work.)

My father at first tried to put a good face on things. He once overheard my mother and me comparing complaints and with great annoyance declared us "the village gossips." After that, we made sure to be more careful where and when we aired our gripes.

But his position, whatever it might have been, had been seriously shaken by the disappearance of my uncle Sanyi, with whom he had been close, and, of course, by what had happened to himself. He still didn't talk about the current political climate. But he stopped defending the indefensible and no longer remonstrated with my mother and me when we complained about it.

He also began to reveal glimpses of his war experiences. He had never talked much about his ordeal during the war, but now he let slip a few bits and pieces.

He told about the incredible cruelty with which the Hungarian soldiers treated the Jewish labor battalions. In a way, that wasn't surprising, as by now the news of what had happened in the concentration camps was known. Even so, some of the stories were so horrific that I found them difficult to digest. But the clear fact was that only 10 percent of the men in my father's worker battalion had survived, and many of the 90 percent that died had been deliberate victims of their Hungarian guards.

The story that was the most incredible to me was how in the middle of one bitterly cold winter night, my father's battalion was made to strip naked and climb trees, and the guards sprayed them with water and watched and laughed as one after another fell out of the trees frozen to death.

I had been under the impression that their suffering stopped when my father's battalion was captured by the Russians. It turned out that this was hardly the case. Their life was no better in Russian captivity.

Right after they were captured, they were locked into cattle cars and transported for days with no food, no water, and no heat, in the dead of the Russian winter. When they finally arrived at their destination, only a handful of people was alive in each cattle car. The survivors were then marched to a snowed-over campsite that had been used by the Russian troops as a summer training ground. They had to dig the snow out of holes in the ground with their bare hands to make shelters.

My father suffered illness after illness, surviving against all odds while people around him were dying like flies. This explained why he was skin and bones, a run-down decrepit shell of a man, when he returned home.

One particular story was so awful that it turned into a gruesome family joke. It was winter, and my father and the other prisoners were cooped up inside the shelter they had dug in the snow. They were too cold and weak to go outside to relieve themselves, so they used the same metal dish that they ate from, scrubbing the dish with a handful of snow in between uses. After my father told us this story, my mother and I would tease him about it whenever he didn't clean his plate after a meal.

My father brought home some pictures that he had managed to keep with him throughout all his years in the war and captivity. They were wallet-size studio photographs of my mother and me, taken before he left just so he could have a picture of us with him while he was away. My father treasured these pictures; they never left his body. They gave him strength when he needed it most. In his darkest moments, when it looked like he would not make it, he used the backs of the pictures to scribble his good-bye messages to us.

I read these notes over and over. One of them that my father wrote near the end of the war particularly touched me. It was dated April 1945. "My dear ones: Now that it looks like the end would be here and the prospect of seeing you again, I have had another setback—a new disease, some skin ulcers. It's spreading from one day to the next. There is no medicine. They don't know how to treat it. It's slow death. It looks like my struggles of the last three years were for nothing. And all I would like is to see you again, to know that you are alive. But I am destroyed. Just my love for you keeps me alive. Gyurka."

He made it home five months later.

In March 1953, Stalin died. Stalin's figure had been indelibly associated with the images of the Soviet Union in my mind. The picture of a uniformed, mustachioed man with a kindly expression had been everywhere—in offices, schools, at celebrations, hung on the sides of buildings—for, it seemed, most of my life. Even though by this time I had become deeply skeptical about the goodness of things Soviet, Stalin's death and the disappearance of that ever-present kindly face had a mixed impact on me.

I was glad and I was sad at the same time. It was very confusing.

Stalin's death was the occasion for a citywide march to Heroes' Square. Much like during the May Day parades, loudspeakers were strung up in the trees along Stalin Road. But now, instead of broadcasting cheers, the loudspeakers played the same classical funeral march over and over and over. During May Day marches, we fooled around while we shuffled along. We didn't know how to conduct ourselves now. I didn't feel comfortable discussing my confused feelings with anyone, not even with my close friends. Neither did anyone else. We couldn't talk about other things, and we wouldn't talk about Stalin, so we marched largely in silence.

At one point, somebody broke out into an uncontrollable fit of giggles. Pretty soon, a large number of us were trying to suppress giggles. Our teachers glared. Beyond a doubt, this was a dangerous thing to do, but we couldn't stop, perhaps exactly because it was so dangerous.

We eventually regained our equilibrium and solemnly continued our procession. The funeral march blared overhead. I wondered if things were going to change—and whether the change would be for better or for worse.

We got no hint from the newspapers. Previously unknown Russian politicians were propelled into periods of prominence, then faded out of sight. For a while, not much happened.

The first real hint of tangible change came in the spring of 1954. There had been some rumors about the release of political prisoners. Then, one day, without any prior notice, my uncle Sanyi was released.

My uncle had aged a lot while he was in jail. He'd always been thin, but now he looked even more ascetic and drawn. His hair had turned all white. He told my parents that they'd wanted him to confess to a bunch of things that he hadn't done, like fomenting counterrevolutionary activities. But he wouldn't.

He had been sentenced to death and for a long time was on death row, waiting to be executed. Stoically, he'd waited for whatever would happen to him. The only reaction he'd had to his precarious status was a compulsion to finish whatever book he was reading before he was executed. He would stay up all night reading in his cell.

My cousin's husband was released some time later. He had fared far worse. He had cracked under the pressure of interrogation and was a broken man when he was released. For one thing, he had no teeth; he never said what happened. For another, he now thought that he saw secret police everywhere. He remained high-strung and nervous and had to be hospitalized in a mental institution for a while.

But at least they were out and free to settle down and get on with their lives.

The summer before my last year at Madach, Gabi and I spent a week at a fishing cabin at Lake Velence, a lake about fifty miles from Budapest. The fishing cabin belonged to the state company where my mother worked. Employees could sign up to use it for a week at a time. When my mother found out about its availability, she signed Gabi and me up for a stay. It would be just the two of us, on our own without any adult supervision. At seventeen, we were eager for our first taste of independence.

It sounded very idyllic—a cabin at the edge of a lake. Gabi and I took the train down and trudged with our bags the few miles from the train station to the cabin. When we got there, we found that the cabin was just one room with some rough bunk beds in it—and nothing else. There was no stove, no table, no chairs, and no running water. Outside there was a pump and an outhouse that smelled as if it hadn't been cleaned in years. That was it.

But a path led to the lake nearby, where there was a rickety boat dock with a big old rowboat tied up to it. The shoreline was a forest of reeds. No other houses or people were in sight. It was all ours.

We quickly settled into a routine. Every morning, we walked along a footpath into town to pick up provisions. We purchased fresh milk from a little dairy, bought fresh bread from a bakery, and picked up sausages and apples. Milk, bread, sausage, and apples made up our diet for the week.

We spent the rest of each day from morning to dusk out on the lake in the rowboat, returning to the cabin only to eat and sleep. Other than the occasional fisherman, we didn't see anyone. We rowed, mostly the two of us at the oars because it was a big clunky boat and it took a lot of effort to move it along. When we got to the middle of the lake, one of us would jump in the water and swim alongside the boat while the other one rowed. Or we would just lie on our backs in the rowboat in the middle of the lake and talk and look up at the sky.

One time when we were lying on our backs, aimlessly floating around, two military planes flew by just above the water level. They were followed a second later by a horrendous roar. We scrambled onto our knees and looked after the planes. We had never seen jets before. After a moment, Gabi said, "The next war won't be fun."

We saw the planes only that one time. The rest of the week was quiet, the weather was good, and the surface of the lake was usually like a mirror, disturbed only by our movements.

The lake was about ten miles long and a couple of miles wide. One day, I set out to swim across it. It took me the better part of an afternoon. Gabi rowed the boat near me, so I felt comfortable swimming in the middle of the big lake, and I just swam and swam almost in a trance. What seemed like hours later, I reached the reeds at the other side of the lake. I clambered into the boat, feeling a little weak and shaky but proud of myself. I had come a long way since struggling across the irrigation ditch at the vineyard.

Our stay was marred only by the outhouse. Not only did it stink, but it was also the scene of a scare. One windy afternoon, Gabi and I returned from our boat trip and went to the outhouse together. As I went in, with Gabi waiting his turn, a gust of wind slammed the door on my leg, scraping my skin very painfully. The next thing I knew, I was crumpled on the floor, with a scared Gabi shaking my shoulders. I had fainted from the pain. Once I came to, I was perfectly all right except for the scrape, but some of my life disappeared into the black abyss of the faint. Gabi reassured me that I was only out for a few seconds, but to me that blackness had no beginning and no end.

Fainting aside, the week was wonderful and left me with the desire to continue doing something with boats and water.

The school year started a couple of weeks later. As I faced my fourth year, I became more and more focused on what I was going to do after graduation. About half of my class intended to go on to university. So did I.

Getting admitted to university meant the difference between embarking on a professional career and being relegated to an unskilled job. It meant the difference between doing only a month's compulsory military service in the army reserves each year and being drafted into the infantry for two years. I didn't know much about life in the army, but after hearing my father's stories, I wanted to have as little to do with it as possible. Getting admitted to university would make a huge difference in all parts of my life.

This was a crucial year. At the end of it, I would take the final exams to graduate from gymnasium and the entrance exams to enter university. These exams were a big deal, and performing well on both was a necessary condition for being admitted to university. But they weren't the only factor.

University admission was heavily based on the student's family background. The highest preference was given to students who came from worker families or whose parents were members of the Communist Party. Second preference was given to those who came from peasant stock. Third preference was for those whose parents were professional people. And last preference was for those whose parents didn't fit any of those categories and were therefore labeled "other."

There was also a category for "class aliens," the sons and daughters of parents who previously had businesses that employed other workers. Employing others, in the language of Marxism, was called "exploiting them." Students whose parents were exploiters would have a very tough time getting into any university.

My parents didn't fit into the worker, the peasant, or the professional category, so the question was whether I would be classified as "other" or whether my father's former dairy ownership would put me in the "class alien" category.

I couldn't take university for granted.

There was nothing I could do about my ancestry, so I concentrated on reviewing four years' worth of math, physics, chemistry, history, and literature with an eye toward the exams. Nobody had their mind on the fourth-year courses—neither the teachers nor the students. The end was in sight, so the attention of those students who were university-bound focused on preparing for the exams. Everyone focused on getting ready for life outside of Madach.

The week at Lake Velence had left me with the desire to continue doing something with boats and water. Once I had settled into the rhythm of studying for my final exams, I asked around and found out that there was a kayaking club located on Margaret Island. In late fall, Gabi and I enrolled in their beginner's course. (I had lost interest in fencing when I realized that I would never break out of the lower echelons of the competitive ranks.)

This was a lot less enjoyable than the rowboat in Lake Velence.

We didn't even get to sit in a kayak. Instead, we perched on stationary seats in a trough of water in a cold, damp concrete building and practiced paddling. Six or eight seats were lined up in each trough, one right behind the other, so at first we constantly got our double-bladed paddles tangled up with that of the person in front or back while a coach yelled at us. We quickly learned to paddle in unison.

When we weren't paddling in the stationary seats, we practiced lifting and carrying the kayaks from racks in the warehouse to the shore and back. The kayaks were fragile shells of wood that could be easily damaged if they were banged on the doorway of the storage house, dropped on the docks, or bumped against other kayaks. There was one right way to handle them and many wrong ways, and we had to keep practicing under the watchful eye and loud comments of the coach until we did it just the right way. We learned to lift single kayaks, double kayaks, and kayaks that would take four people. We didn't actually get to sit in a kayak and paddle in the Danube until well into the spring.

One day at home, I caught a glimpse of myself in the mirror

without a shirt on. Much to my delight, I noticed that I had muscles. I had finally lost my remaining chubbiness.

In the spring, we started practicing in the Danube River. The Danube was a big river with a strong current. The weather was cold and gray, and so was the water. Using the skills we learned in the incessant practice sessions, Gabi and I put our double kayak in the water, then slid into the seats and pushed off from the dock. Immediately, the current grabbed us and tried to sweep us backward. But once we started paddling, we overcame the force of the current and started moving upstream. There was great satisfaction in feeling our own strength.

A normal practice consisted of paddling around Margaret Island. We always started off by going upstream; then, when we reached the tip of the island, we turned and let the river sweep us downstream on the other side of the island. Paddling into the current past the tip of the island was hard. We were paddling against the full force of the open river, and making the turn was a delicate maneuver. We let the kayak come to a stop, held the stern steady while the force of the water swung the bow around, then felt a sudden acceleration as the current picked us up and swept us downstream. It never ceased to be a thrilling moment.

Adding to the thrill was the presence of a skeet shooting range at the tip of the island. The shooters were hidden from view, but we could see the clay pigeons being tossed in the air and we could hear the shots and watch the disks shatter above us, the fragments flying this way and that. In addition to keeping an eye on the current, we had to keep an eye on flying bits of clay.

One time I was in a single kayak rounding the tip of the island, and as I was about to turn into the current, one of these clay pieces burst right over my head. I instinctively ducked, and the next moment I found myself submerged in the water, being swept rapidly down the river. My training came in handy. Even as I fell out of the kayak, I hung on to my paddle with one hand

and grabbed the side of the boat with the other. When I surfaced, I furiously kicked toward shore. Every time I tried to stand up, the current swept me off my feet. I finally struggled upright in water that barely reached my knees. Then I bailed out my kayak, got back in, and paddled like a madman to catch up with the rest of my group.

At the southern tip of the island there was a big bridge connecting the island to Buda on one side and Pest on the other. (It was the bridge where the bus accident had occurred.) This was where we turned to complete the circuit around the island. We learned to sneak into an eddy behind a pillar of the bridge where the water was calm and the current practically stationary, take a rest, get set, then punch out of the eddy and attack the current again. It was very exciting.

Our club competed in a number of kayak races with other clubs. Gabi and I entered in the beginner doubles race. I wasn't any better at competitive kayaking than I had been at fencing. All our best efforts got us to the finish line not quite at the end of the bunch, but at least we weren't last.

In late spring, the kayaking club took a weekend tour up the Danube. We crossed the river from Margaret Island to paddle in the quieter water next to the shore. Barges and passenger ships blasted their horns at us, and we bounced in their wakes. The coach and his helper followed along in a little motorboat. After a while, we were paddling by farmland. I didn't pay much attention to the scenery. I had to concentrate on not tipping over.

After hours and hours of paddling upstream, we finally arrived at our campsite. We slept on tarps on the ground in the open. We were dead tired, but between the hard ground and the clouds of mosquitoes nibbling at us all night, no one got much sleep. The next morning, we got up early and got going again. I was irritated that I couldn't scratch my mosquito bites while I was paddling.

The trip was generally uneventful, with one exception. There was one girl kayaker in the club. When the coach and his helper set up their campsite a short distance away from us, they invited the girl to join them. Later, they invited her to join them in a ride on their motorboat. We had no idea what might be going on, but we were all jealous.

I had had no girlfriend since Eva from the literary club, but my interest in girls continued, albeit at a distance. One day, my friend Peter told me that he had made it with a prostitute. He reported on it in great detail. He wasn't exactly exuberant about the experience, but he encouraged me to try it nonetheless.

It didn't sound appealing and I was nervous, but my curiosity overwhelmed my hesitation. Peter gave me an address and assured me that the woman would be expecting me. With considerable trepidation, I set off one Sunday morning to walk to the appointed place. In my pocket was the sum Peter had indicated. I had taken it from my parents' communal kitty.

Several times I wanted to turn and go home, but I forced myself to march on. As I practiced what I would say when I got there, my trepidation turned into apprehension and the apprehension into overwhelming nervousness. By the time I mounted the stairway to the third-floor apartment, I was swallowing harder and harder. Finally, I arrived at the apartment and rang the bell. After some minutes, the door was opened by a scrawny, middle-aged woman. Her hair was unkempt and she was wearing a wrinkled bathrobe and, it seemed, not much else. The bathrobe wasn't tied around her waist, and she clutched the edges together with her hands. She stared at me. I stared at her. Before I had a chance to explain who I was and who sent me, she told me that she was busy and I should come back later. Then she shut the door in my face.

I felt a great rush of relief. I returned home in a much better mood than I had left and replaced the money in my parents' bureau. I never went back.

The end of the school year came, and with it the dreaded graduation exams. I accelerated my preparations. I stayed home every chance I had and studied incessantly. Our apartment was being painted during the last few weeks before the exams, so I had to scurry from room to room to stay out of the painter's way. My parents were both at work, so it was only the painter and me at home.

I envied the painter. From my vantage point, he had a finite job; when he was done painting a room, his task was finished. My task, on the other hand, was infinite; whenever I thought I had finished studying a subject, I would start all over again and discover parts I had missed.

The painter must have been observing me, too. At first, he had ignored me, as if we were two strangers doing our jobs in a common space. The only time we talked was when he asked me to move so he could put a dropcloth over some furniture. But as the days progressed and he watched me study and worry, he actually grew sympathetic. He was still painting our apartment the day of the actual test. When I left, he called down from his ladder and wished me *kalap szart* ("a hatful of shit"). I looked startled. He explained that this was the strongest way to wish someone good luck. His comment echoed in my mind all the way to school.

When I arrived at school, I found our classroom completely rearranged. A line of desks stretched across the middle of the classroom. All of our fourth-year teachers sat behind the barricade. Behind them were representatives of the Ministry of Education, who were there to audit and supervise the proceedings. The students stood outside in the corridor, waiting to be called in one by one to stand in front of the inquisition and answer questions.

Each day a few of us were called to appear, some scheduled for the morning and some scheduled for the afternoon. The exam took about an hour for each student. While we waited our turn, some people affected nonchalance, chatting about anything but the exam. I didn't feel like participating in their banter, so I stood away by myself and was quiet.

Finally, my name was called. I was nervous. But once I faced my teachers I saw goodwill in their eyes. I realized that they wanted me to do well, and that helped me immensely. I was asked questions covering just about every subject we had studied in gymnasium. I knew the answers to all of them, and I felt I did well. I got the results a few weeks later. I had passed with flying colors.

With the long-awaited torture of the final exam over at last, there was only one more task to fulfill at gymnasium: the graduation ceremony.

It was held in the courtyard, the scene of uncounted physical education classes, an even larger number of daily recess breaks, and an occasional talking-to by the principal. Now the battered arena was set up with a podium and neat rows of chairs, which were filling up with friends and relatives. My mother came and so did my aunt Manci.

True to itself to the last minute, the A class had planned a prank worthy of its reputation. Dressed in our best Sunday suits, we all arrived by taxi. Taxis were rare in Budapest. I don't think I'd ridden in one since the war. It was quite a job to find a sufficient number of them and coordinate things so that our class, three or four kids squeezed into each taxi, could arrive at the beat-up old building at the same time. As we got out of the taxis, we each donned white sheets. We then walked around the courtyard like a bunch of ghosts, sneaking up to people, startling them, and shattering the solemn decorum of the occasion, much to the consternation of the teachers and our principal.

I stole away for a minute to carve my name on a brick at the side of the schoolyard. Then it was time for the graduation ceremony.

Somebody hollered at us to get rid of the sheets—and, for once, we obeyed. We were handed the traditional little six-inch wooden sticks with tiny cloth bags hung on one end, like a miniature hobo's kit. We held them over our shoulders as a symbol of setting out into the world. We were herded into a formal line, and all the graduating classes processed around the courtyard and down to the front rows of seats. Then we sat down to listen to a bunch of speeches.

Afterward, we gathered around with our teachers for photographs. We solemnly shook hands with each other. Then we went on our separate ways. Gymnasium was officially over.

I left the courtyard with mixed feelings. I had had many fun times during the last four years and I'd had a few wonderful teachers, but for the most part I hadn't liked my class or the school. I was glad to leave it.

The story of the A class wasn't quite over yet, though. A few of the rowdier boys organized a night on the town to celebrate graduation. I decided not to join them. That turned out to be a good idea. The next day I heard that the group drank too much. On their way home, they were carousing and singing at the top of their lungs and got picked up by the police. The police manhandled and slapped them around before releasing them to their parents. It was an experience I was glad to have missed.

I was completely preoccupied with whether I would be admitted to university. Shortly after the final exam at gymnasium, I had taken the entrance exams for the university. These, too, were oral tests conducted by a panel of faculty members. In addition to asking questions about chemistry, physics, and math, they questioned me about Soviet history and literature. It was advisable to know something of Soviet literature, even though it wasn't required at gymnasium. Luckily, I had read the books they mentioned—*And Quiet Flows the Don* and other popular novels by famous Soviet authors. I thought I did well on the test, but I feared that my background was going to keep me out.

I had applied to the natural sciences branch of the University of Budapest. You were allowed to apply to only one school. I wanted to study chemistry, and the University of Budapest was the most prestigious academic institution for pure sciences. However, rumor had it that the chemistry class would be small—only twenty or so students. That made the odds of my getting in even smaller.

My parents and I set out to do whatever we could to increase my chances of acceptance. I hoped that some hands-on experience with chemistry might help, so that spring, I had applied for a job at Chinoin, a chemical factory on the outskirts of Budapest. Getting hired was an arduous process. I took the tram out to the factory—a long ride—asked the guard at the gate how to apply for a summer job, and was sent from one office to another before finally getting an application blank. I filled it out and handed it in. I went back several times to find out about its status but never got a definite answer.

I realized that I needed help. Everything, from getting a job to getting a telephone, required "connections." My father found somebody who knew somebody who knew somebody inside Chinoin. This person moved my application along, and I got hired as a laborer. My friend Bubi, who wanted to go into electrical engineering, had applied with me. My "connection" got him hired, too.

We started working the week after graduating from gymnasium.

I had a vague hope that I would learn something about

chemistry by working at Chinoin. During my repeated visits to the factory in the spring, I was enthralled by the chemical smells that permeated the area, and I identified them as a symbol of my chosen profession. Once I started working, I grew so accustomed to the smells that I no longer noticed them.

We worked twelve-hour shifts, four days a week. It was hard work, and the four days were like a blur. All I did was work, commute, and sleep. I got up early in the morning, took the tram to the outskirts of Budapest, worked all day, took the tram home, fell into bed, then got up and repeated it all. It was good to have a three-day weekend to catch up on sleep. I still went swimming at the Palatinus pool on my days off. But the three days were over quickly, and then it was back to work.

Our job involved tending a big machine that filtered out sludge from a chemical process. Bubi and I were supposed to take the machine apart, remove the canvas filter, scrape off the sludge, clean the canvas with a powerful hose, put it back in its place, bolt the machine shut, then repeat this process with the next machine and the next one and the next one. There were many machines. When we finished replacing the filter in the last machine, the sludge had built up again in the first machine, so we repeated the job over and over.

It was hard and boring work, but Bubi and I worked well as a team and we made it into a sport. We happily slopped around in the sludge, throwing our weight into turning the handles that tightened the bolts on the filters as if it were some kind of competition. We were covered from head to toe in rubber coverall suits, so mucking around in the slippery stuff was actually fun. Sometimes we slipped off the handles and fell backward into the sludge. We called this "the rubber ass exercise."

The man who was assigned to supervise us and make sure we didn't cut corners watched our enthusiasm with cold condescension. Like most of the other regular workers, he moved slowly and deliberately and took frequent cigarette breaks. At first, I thought he was cold to us because we were students. But then I learned otherwise.

Bubi had gone on an errand and I continued cleaning the sludge all by myself. Our boss came over and watched me work for a while. Then he said to me, "Your friend isn't Hungarian, either, is he?"

I was confused. What would Bubi be if not Hungarian? Then, as I looked at the man's unwavering, steady gaze, I got it. What he was asking was if Bubi was a Jew like me. I turned red and, in a mixture of embarrassment and anger, furiously attacked my sludge without answering. The silence was broken only when Bubi returned. After that, I didn't mind that our supervisor stayed away from us.

I was hoping that my experience at Chinoin would help with my admission to the university, but my parents and I knew that this was far from enough. Their search for "connections" continued.

Then we got lucky.

My father discovered that the brother of one of his mates from the worker battalion was a professor at the university. He checked on my application and confirmed my worst fears: I had been classified as a "class alien" and was being rejected.

Our "connection" did something. I never actually knew what it was that he did, but I suspect he removed the papers that caused me to be classified as a "class alien." Without those, I was reclassified as "other."

In late summer, a postcard arrived at our house. It briefly stated that I had been admitted to the natural sciences branch of the University of Budapest.

The postcard arrived in the middle of the day on one of my days off. I grabbed it and stared at it with my heart pounding. I stroked the words with my fingers to make sure they were real. I was going to university! I was going to be a real chemist! My life had a direction. A weight that I didn't even know I was carrying lifted off my shoulders.

I ran out of the house, jumped on the tram, and victoriously marched first into my mother's office, then into my father's office, to tell them the news. Both were ecstatic.

Soon after I got the admission postcard, I cleaned my last filter of sludge. I celebrated my university admission by joining my parents for a week's vacation at Lake Balaton, the largest lake in Hungary.

This was the first time my parents and I had ever gone on vacation together. I was hesitant at the prospect. Other than afternoon outings, I had never spent much time with them. Being cooped up at a resort with them for a week seemed like a long time. To my relief, I actually enjoyed spending the time with them.

We got rooms at the guesthouse owned by my father's company. Lake Balaton was farther away than Lake Velence, but it was much bigger and much more developed. It had been Hungary's traditional resort area and was surrounded by hotels, guesthouses, and fancy lodges that had once been owned by wealthy people but now belonged to state-owned companies. Their former grandeur was dulled by the transformation, but they were definitely a step up from the rickety fishing cabin on Lake Velence.

Our guesthouse was a good walk from the lake, but once we got there, there was a sandy beach with a long shallow bank. You had to walk a ways out before the water was deep enough for swimming, but you could float around in the sun-warmed shallows to your heart's delight.

My mother was a good swimmer. One day, we held on to a rubber air mattress and swam far out into the lake. We drifted, talking about everything and nothing. I felt very close to my mother.

When we got back to the shallows, I saw my father floating on another mattress with his eyes closed. I snuck up behind him and, as a joke, flipped over the mattress.

This didn't turn out to be a good idea. My father didn't swim at all. Furthermore, he had been deeply asleep. He thrashed around furiously before finding his footing. Then he steadied himself and slapped me across the face. He had never slapped me before. I was stunned. But when I looked at him, I noticed that he was as stunned by his action as I was. Neither of us said anything, not then and not later.

All of the guests at the hotel hung around together. Among the guests were two older teenage girls who worked for the company. They weren't particularly pretty, but given my lack of exposure to girls for most of my school years, it was fun to be in the company of girls of my age. We all went out for dinner and dancing every night. My father and mother would dance together; they were good dancers, and I was quite proud of them. Sometimes I danced with the girls. One night, I asked my mother to dance with me. She was very pleased.

When the week was over, I took the train to Lake Velence, where I met Gabi for a few days at the fishing cabin. After graduating from the wood industry technical high school, he had gotten a scholarship to a university in Romania that offered a special curriculum in wood technology. (I never really knew what that was about.) This was our last summer before we started on new and separate chapters in our lives.

I had brought a marble-size ball of potassium from my chemistry stash in a bottle. On our last night, we took the rowboat far out on the lake. I tossed the ball of potassium out on the water to create our own fireworks. It skipped along, then settled on the surface and reacted violently, forming big metallic blue flames that shot high above the dark water, making loud sizzling noises. Then the flames sputtered out and we rowed back to shore.

Summer military training: We were handed ill-fitting, well-worn, faded uniforms with no insignia and a plain, foldable cap. I am the one standing on the left.

Chapter Eleven

UNIVERSITY—FIRST YEAR

THE ORIENTATION CLASSES for the first-year chemistry students at the University of Budapest were held in a nondescript room in an ornate nineteenth-century building with high ceilings and tall, narrow windows. As I walked up the columned steps leading to the heavy entry door, I felt I had arrived at my promised land.

As rumored, the entering class was small—twenty or so students, about two-thirds boys and one-third girls. Many were bantering and chatting with each other while we all waited for the administrator to come in and tell us our curriculum and schedule.

I silently took in the scene, nowhere near as disinterested as I pretended to be. As I sat and listened to the excited conversations around me, I figured that about half of the class was made up of kids from outside Budapest. They stayed at a dormitory for out-of-town students and seemed to know each other. A number of the Budapest contingent were graduates of the Chemistry Technikum and knew each other from there. That left just a few who were not members of any group. I was one of them. It was scary not to know or be known by anyone.

It was even scarier to think that the kids in this room were the best students in the country. True, many of them would have been given preference for being descendants of workers or peasants. Still, my shaky confidence sagged even further.

I noticed that the boy sitting next to me didn't seem to belong to any group, either. While the rest of the boys looked like clean-cut, good-student types, with short-cropped hair and conventional clothes, my neighbor had long, shaggy hair combed to the side in what I assumed was an attempt to mimic Western style. He wore green-tinted glasses, which he had let slip down his nose, and he gazed out over them with an air of condescending boredom.

The administrator came in, and the orientation process started. As we filled out form after form, I peered over at my neighbor's papers. His surname, I discovered, was Zoltan. He was from Budapest and, like me, had attended one of the gymnasiums rather than the Chemistry Technikum. In the breaks between filling out forms, I started talking with him. He had a sardonic sense of humor and was quite ready to show it in pointed comments about the various administrators who paraded in front of us over the course of the day. He intrigued me. I also suspected he wasn't Jewish.

Classes started for real the next day. The way the university worked was that we would all have the same schedule of classes, so the twenty of us would spend our time traipsing from one lecture to another as a group.

The focus of the first year of study was inorganic chemistry. The lectures took place every day and were given by the senior professor, a tall, elegant figure whose name was Professor Lengyel. His entrance into the lecture hall was always preceded by a parade of assistant professors. After they had taken their places,

Professor Lengyel swept in, his spotless white lab coat swirling behind him. We all stood to greet him. He stacked his papers on the table in front of the blackboard with dignified precision. Only after he was settled did we sit down.

The textbook for the first year was two huge volumes written by Professor Lengyel himself. I had never known anyone who was the author of a book. The combination of his name on our textbook, which we had to buy, the deference his assistants gave him, and his royal bearing filled me with awe. He lectured in a deep, booming voice, which was wonderful because I had no trouble hearing him.

The lecture hall was a semicircular auditorium with rows of worn, wooden benches rising steeply toward the back. It could have easily held one hundred people. Our small class was scattered among the first few rows in the center, while the assistant professors took their positions off to one side. Otherwise, the room was empty. During the break, Zoltan and I speculated on why our class was so small relative to the size of the hall. Zoltan let his green-tinted glasses slip down his nose, shot me a look over the rims, and in a deadpan voice remarked, "The Central Planning Department figured that four years from now the country will need exactly twenty chemists." I quickly looked around, swallowed hard, and did not answer. But I began to like him.

We also had classes in math, physics, and political education. Math was fairly straightforward, and it helped that again the professor spoke in a loud, firm voice. Physics was another story. This professor was Professor Lengyel's complete opposite. He dressed casually, leaned against the blackboard throughout most of his lecture, and spoke in an extremely soft voice. The room was another large lecture hall, and even though I sat in the front row, my seat was a fair distance from the blackboard. I couldn't understand a word he said. I was panic-stricken. To make my terror more complete, there was no official textbook.

After class, I caught up with the professor and explained my predicament. He smiled and assured me that he would try to remember to raise his voice in the future. His assurance didn't reassure me at all. I had long ago discovered that people speak at their own particular sound level, and even when they sincerely try to accommodate you by raising their voice, within minutes their voice settles back into its natural level.

This was not good. Here I was on the first day of class with a nightmare situation: a tough subject, no textbook, and a lecture where I literally could not understand a word. I had to find other solutions.

I described my problem to Zoltan and asked if he could help out. He readily agreed to share his notes with me. So did several other students. I arranged to borrow two or three sets of notes after each lecture and started to compile my own notes from the different points of view. I didn't know if it would work, but at least it gave me a plan of action.

I had no such problem in political education. Our textbook was the *History of the Soviet Communist Party,* which was used as the Bible in political education courses. While I had never read it, my parents had had to study it as part of mandatory seminars held at their workplaces, so I'd seen it around the house and was familiar with it. The book described who did what to whom between the Russian Revolution of 1917 and the years leading up to World War II. With phrases like "The Mensheviks trembled when they found out that Lenin had come to town," the book read more like a child's story than a serious history book.

The instructor led us through it, chapter by chapter, page by page, sticking so closely to the text that he might as well have read it aloud. People said that this book got reissued from time to time and that depending on the latest Party dogma, new characters appeared or, more important, some characters present in earlier editions disappeared. I supposed that not sticking precisely to the current edition would have been a bad idea and adding extraneous material would have been dangerous. In any case, my hearing was not an issue here.

It was also not an issue in labwork. Analytical chemistry lab was the centerpiece of our schedule. It was held every day and took up most of each afternoon. The experiments underscored what we studied in Professor Lengyel's class. The idea was that by doing the experiments, we would get an in-depth and firsthand understanding of the lecture material. It was also our first exposure to practical chemistry.

The lab was supervised by one of the assistant professors, a youngish woman whose bouncy, jovial demeanor was altogether different from Professor Lengyel's formality. We called her by her first name, Hilda. She assigned each of us a bench space but encouraged us to move around freely and ask each other for chemicals, help, or equipment. Fairly soon, we were all comfortable with each other.

Before the autumn was over, I felt more at home with this class than I ever had at Madach gymnasium even after four years. Part of the difference was that I no longer had to be embarrassed about being a good student. At university, we were all there to learn and we all wanted to do well.

In addition to Zoltan, I became particularly friendly with two other students. One was a boy called Jancsi Lanyi. Like me, he was very interested in chemistry, liked opera, and was Jewish. We got on quite well; nevertheless, unlike with Zoltan, I was always extremely careful when making political comments or jokes.

As in gymnasium, boys called each other by their last names. Sometimes we never even knew each other's first names. Girls, however, we called by their first names.

One was a pretty, lively girl from Budapest named Marianne. She was not a particularly strong student because she was forever distracted by the ups and downs of her relationship with her boyfriend. None of us had ever met this boyfriend, but Marianne was quite clearly more in love with him, according to her stories, then he was with her. We often walked part of the way home together after class, and to my surprise, I found myself becoming her confidant. Being friends with a girl with no romantic involvement was something I'd never experienced before. I enjoyed it.

Zoltan continued to intrigue me. I had never had a close friend who was not Jewish before, and Zoltan had never had a close Jewish friend. Although about one-third of our class was Jewish and the group as a whole mixed very well, as far as I could see, no other close friendships developed across the Jewish/non-Jewish boundary. Zoltan's caustic wit and his sharp insights impressed me, as did his interest in Western literature and music—he was an accomplished jazz pianist. His attempt to look Western, I soon realized, wasn't an act at all but was completely consistent with his interests. I found all of this fascinating, and as he openly made cynical political comments to me, I found myself opening up to him more and more, too. From time to time, we got together outside of school. Sometimes he came to visit at my apartment, but more often we went for long walks through the streets of Budapest.

There was still this business of Jew versus non-Jew that hung between us. On one of our long walks, I took a deep breath and asked him if it bothered him to be friends with a Jew. He sent me one of his characteristic glances over his green glasses and said with a straight face, "Why would it bother me that you are a stinking Jew?" This was the epithet that rabid anti-Semites hurled at Jews, and his use of it stunned me. Then I collected myself and shot back, "Yes, and why should it bother me that I hang out with a dumb goy?" That was an epithet I had never used, but I perceived it to be equally nasty. Without flinching, Zoltan replied, "That's it, then. You are a stinking Jew and I am a dumb goy. So what's the problem?"

With that, the uneasiness disappeared. It even got to be a sort of joke. In keeping with our increasing familiarity with the periodic table of elements, we realized that the initials of the words *stinking Jew* in Hungarian almost matched the chemical symbol of the element bismuth, while the initials for *dumb goy* precisely matched the initials for the element mercury. So whenever we were traveling together on the tram and one of us felt like poking fun at the other in public, we would mutter the words *bismuth* and *mercury* at each other until we started laughing.

School kept me so busy that I had to give up kayaking. But I didn't spend all of my time studying. The Franz Liszt international piano competition was held that winter, and my mother and I got tickets. It took place at the Academy of Music, which was located a few blocks from our house on Kiraly Street, so we could just walk over to the concerts.

I had never been to a music competition before. Each contestant first had to play the same piece of music—a sonata by Franz Liszt. I thought listening to the same piece over and over would be boring; instead, I became fascinated by the nuances of the piece, and I started to notice differences in the performers' playing styles and technique. By the end of this part of the competition, I was humming Liszt piano sonatas as I walked down the street.

My mother and I attended together. We had good seats on the first-level balcony. We could look down over the shoulders of the performers and watch their hands in action. In the intermissions, we compared notes and ranked our favorites. When the judges announced their decisions, we reacted with approval or horror, like soccer fans reacting to the referee's call. A Russian pianist won. Rumor had it that he used his prize money to buy a winter coat—right there in Budapest. It seemed that the selection in our stores was better than what he had at home. I found this strange.

My fascination with opera also continued to grow, so much so that I decided to take singing lessons. This wasn't the first time I had tried to get involved in singing. Some years before, I had tried out for a folk-singing group. I liked the sound of my own voice, and I fantasized that I would be discovered as a latter-day Chaliapin. I showed up at the audition, but when I belted out one of the few Hungarian folk songs I knew, the chorus director cut my performance short and sent me home. After this rejection, I didn't try to sing for a long time.

It took courage to try out again, but some years had passed and my voice had changed, and to me, at least, it sounded much better than before. The audition was longer this time. I sang, then the accompanist played some chords and I had to break out each of the notes of the chords to demonstrate that I had a measure of musical aptitude. This time, to my relief, I was accepted.

The lessons were half an hour long, two evenings a week. They were outright boring. The teacher made me practice singing scales. She was pretty matter-of-fact about my voice and paid a lot more attention to the advanced singers. I didn't care. I was learning real singing, so I persevered with vigor, using the times when I was alone in the apartment to practice. I would have been mortified if anyone at home heard me. My singing was not meant for friends and family, only for me and my teacher.

After several months of scales, during which my singing voice got smoother and more flexible, I was promoted to simple Schubert songs. The particular songs my teacher chose must have had great pedagogical value because they were just as dull as the scales. I persistently asked to sing something more interesting, and eventually my teacher took pity on me and allowed me to choose the next song. I asked to learn my favorite aria from Mozart's opera *The Marriage of Figaro.* In it, Figaro explains the realities of army life to a young boy who is anxious to join up. The music varies between lyrical and military melodies, between cajoling and aggressive tones, representing the variety of drama that I craved.

This was a lot more intricate than the Schubert songs, and it took months to get it right. Not only did I have to control my voice through the range of the aria, but I had to learn to pace the music just right. I had never really learned to read music, and I always had trouble with timing. But I loved every minute I spent on it, even when I had to sing particular parts over and over.

One winter evening after school, I got involved in a deep discussion with one of my schoolmates when I realized it was time to go to singing class. He came with me and we continued our argument all the way there and even while sitting in the anteroom until it was time for my class. I went in and practiced the Figaro aria. My classmate had told me he didn't know anything about music and wasn't interested in opera, so I was surprised that he was still there when I came out. We resumed our walk, but before we could resume our argument about chemistry he asked, "What was that stuff you sang? I could hear you through the door and it sounded really neat."

When my singing went well, it made me feel better about everything, even if things at school were tough. I thought I had made an important discovery. I realized that it's good to have at least two interests in your life. If you have only one interest and that goes sour, there's nothing to act as a counterbalance to lift your mood. But if you have more than one interest, chances are something will always go okay.

During that winter, a friend introduced me to one of his friends, who was a pianist. The pianist loved opera and liked to accompany singers. This was a rarity. Most pianists I knew wouldn't condescend to accompany singers. I jumped at this opportunity and started to show up at this fellow's house along with a small group of other students. We were ambitious and decided to learn the first scene from the first act of Mozart's *Don Giovanni.* My voice best fit the role of Don Giovanni, and I threw myself into his persona with relish. Don Giovanni's figure, his ease with women, his devil-may-care attitude, captured my imagination.

The scene was only a few minutes long, but it involved several singers in intricate interaction, and it took several months for us to get it right. When we did, the music was so beautiful that it gave me shivers.

Another song that I liked and learned was a Schumann ballad called "The Two Grenadiers." It's the story of two of Napoleon's soldiers rising from the dead to come to the defense of their embattled emperor. The range of the music was just right for me, allowing me to sing it quite well, and I especially liked the drama. I tried to act it out using only my voice, but my face and arms often got into the act, too.

One time that spring, my parents and I were visiting a friend who had a piano. Somehow it came up in the conversation that I was learning "The Two Grenadiers" and that I had the music with me. My parents' friends persuaded my mother to sit down at the piano. I had seen how the boy who accompanied us on *Don Giovanni* had to struggle with the music even though he worked on it for many weeks. So I was stunned when my mother, although initially reluctant, took the music, put it on the stand, and started playing without a moment's hesitation. I sang "The Two Grenadiers" and my mother accompanied me perfectly, following my cadence and adjusting her playing when I lost my timing. Singing while she played made me feel very close to my mother. Even so, I was never able to talk her into accompanying me again.

That spring, I had another chance to sing. It was for Class Night at the university. Class Nights were a tradition where each class put on some entertainment for their professors. Snacks and dancing would follow. It was a very small affair, held in a room in the university building. There was a piano in the corner. My classmates and I put together a number of short skits, and other people told jokes. In addition, I rounded up my singing buddies and the accompanist, and we sang the first scene from *Don Giovanni*. Even though most of the class had never heard the real thing—or maybe because of that—our performance was well received.

To top off the evening, Hilda came over to us with a proposition. She had caucused with some of the senior staff and they had an idea: How about if our class, which was obviously talented in matters of this sort, put on an opening act for the graduating class's traditional performance at the end of the year?

This proposition blew us away. The performance was held at a big theater off campus and was the social high point of each university year. It was attended by many hundreds of people, and tickets were always oversubscribed. Lower-class students were not even invited to attend, so the notion that a first-year class should be asked to perform was extraordinary. We accepted on the spot.

I suggested that we work up a pantomime around our experience in the analytical chemistry lab. That would be familiar to all chemistry students, as it was everyone's first exposure to practical chemistry. I already had an idea, so I volunteered to write the script.

In fact, analytical chemistry had already become my main focus, and not just from the point of view of writing the script. In the fall semester, chemistry lab had started out as a place where we would merely do experiments that brought home the lessons of what we had learned in class. In the spring semester, however, the lab changed and focused on experiments whose purpose was to identify unknown compounds. That's what analytical chemistry is about.

The early assignments were simple and we could complete them in a single class, but as the semester progressed, the compounds that we had to look for became more complex. To make matters worse, they were combined with other compounds, making the task a lot more complicated. Sometimes we worked in teams, other times we worked individually. More often than not, we needed several lab sessions to come up with the answers. Just to ratchet up our anxiety several more levels, we were told that our performance on these assignments—whether we identified the right substances and how long it took to do it—counted significantly toward our grade.

While some considered this analytical lab drudgery, I loved it, and I was good at it. Maybe my home tinkering helped a little. I particularly liked the deductive process involved in figuring out how, if one experiment gave one set of results and another experiment gave another set of results, it followed that the compound in question had to be *X*.

Hilda urged us on in her cheerful, energetic way. Her way of consoling us when we got stuck was to assure us that this was a trivial task, particularly compared to the final assignment. That one, she warned us, was so very complicated that nobody had yet gotten it completely right.

The warmth of late spring arrived and with it came the dreaded final assignment. We were each given a mystery solution containing half a dozen or so compounds. Each solution was different. Our task was to identify the compounds. The grade depended on how many you could identify. Mine was a clear solution with absolutely no clue to its ingredients. We had four weeks to decode it.

There were two different ways of going about the analytical process. One was by following preordained steps, rigorously identifying some compounds and eliminating others step by step by step. If you did everything correctly and interpreted your results correctly, this was bound to lead to the correct result—eventually. However, this rigorous process was extremely cumbersome and time-consuming, and there was a danger of running out of time.

Alternatively, you could make your own path. You could start with the rigorously mandated, conventional process, but as the results unfolded, you could take an intuitive leap and make up your own sequence of experiments, adjusting them as more results became available. This method had the advantage of being much more direct and faster, but it was more risky because if your experimental flow went in the wrong direction, you could blow the whole assignment.

I was confident enough in my grasp of inorganic chemistry to choose the high-risk option. After a few steps, I departed from the predetermined flow and, keeping careful notes, struck out in a direction that seemed logical to me. At first, I made rapid progress. I identified several components in my compound and eliminated many others. Then the going got tougher. Experiment after experiment yielded no new information. I became increasingly obsessed with the task at hand. It loomed monumentally large.

I was completely alone in this task. Each of us had a different compound and each of us chose his or her own path and everyone was completely preoccupied with his or her own problem, so I couldn't brainstorm with any of my classmates. Nor could I ask Hilda for advice. I had taken such unorthodox steps to get to where I was that she couldn't have helped me even if she'd been allowed to. Increasingly, I lived in my own little mental cocoon, inorganic compounds and elements dancing in front of my eyes day and night. We had one more week left, and I was seriously worried.

I was heading home after a late afternoon at the lab. I took the tram. I liked to let other people crowd on first so I could hang on the outside steps with the spring air blowing in my face. It was a slightly dangerous position, but a very refreshing one. This evening, I was hanging on the outside as usual, looking ahead in the gathering May dusk, but I didn't see the traffic or the familiar streets going by. My mind was filled with atoms and molecules and experimental schemes.

Then, all of a sudden, I got it. I don't know what set it off. The experimental results that were floating around in my head suddenly jelled and the confusion of the previous weeks coalesced into a solid vision of where I was and where I needed to go. I jumped off the tram and ran home. I took out my notes and checked to see whether my recollections of the past experimental results were correct. They were. I couldn't wait to get back into the lab the next day. With complete confidence, I planned the next sequence of experiments to confirm my hypothesis. They worked.

I cleaned up my notes and wrote them up into finished form, listing all the inorganic chemicals that made up my sample. Early on the day of the final lab session, I walked up to Hilda and handed her my lab papers. She looked at them with an inscrutable smile, then glanced up at me and said, "Are you sure, Grof?"

I said, "Yes." But all of a sudden, I wasn't as sure as I thought I sounded.

The next day, we all gathered around Hilda as she read out the correct answers to each of the compounds. Mine was the only analysis that was completely correct. In fact, according to Hilda, it was the first time that anybody got all aspects of this assignment right. My classmates looked impressed. Hilda looked proud. I was ecstatic.

The news of my accomplishment ran ahead of me. In several of my other classes, the instructors congratulated me with a smile. It was a wonderful way to end the academic year.

There was still one more task to accomplish before the university year was over: to perform our pantomime at the graduation ceremonies. I wrote and directed it and had a part in it, so I was almost as preoccupied with our skit as I had been with the final experiment.

The graduating seniors were performing a spoof of the Russian opera *Prince Igor.* Their version was called *Prince Szigor,* which is the Hungarian word for "discipline." They would sing their way through their university experience, making fun of their courses and teachers. The event usually consisted of only their performance, so inviting us to open for them was a break with tradition. The eyes of the entire university would be on us, and we wanted to do well.

Our script was about the behavior of chemical elements during the torture of laboratory analysis. Each member of the class represented a particular chemical element. To the accompaniment of classical ballet music, played on the piano by my friend Zoltan, they mimicked how the elements reacted to each other, to heat, to filtering, and to other scientific manipulation. The whole thing was a big in-joke and the fact that our class had just been through analytical chemistry gave it extra spice.

It was also a big in-joke about our class. For instance, two of the students—a guy and a girl—represented two elements that are almost identical; these elements always act the same way and are very difficult to distinguish from each other. These students were short and looked alike, rather like those elements, but the real joke was that they were actually dating each other and were inseparable. So when I tickled their feet with a Bunsen burner—actually, a larger-than-life paper cut-out of a flame—they jumped up on a chair and sat down in unison, holding hands with each other all the while. The first time we rehearsed this, everyone roared.

We held numerous rehearsals, squeezed in between our time

in the lab. Even though we were all preoccupied with our labwork, the rehearsals were great fun. Everyone had something to add to the script, so the end product was a class effort.

Despite our enthusiasm about our performance, outside of class I felt very awkward about my prominent role in it. Consequently, even though my parents badly wanted to attend the event, I was adamant that I didn't want them there. I told them their presence would make me even more self-conscious. My parents reluctantly accepted this but were very, very unhappy about it.

The big day came and we all gathered backstage. To my surprise, I was asked to make a few introductory remarks. I was not prepared and felt frightened by the thought of speaking in front of a big crowd. But when I came out in front of the curtain and saw the sea of expectant faces, I felt a curious calm. I suddenly had the impression that I was talking to a group of people who were there because they were interested in what I had to say. I managed to describe what the audience was about to see, and they responded with lively applause.

Then the curtain went up and we began our show. Zoltan hit the opening chords of *Swan Lake,* and our class paraded out. Everyone was wearing similar clothes, distinguished only by the signs hung around our necks telling which elements we represented. The audience, many of them chemists, appreciated the humor, and there was lots of laughter as the elements showed their true colors.

And so the first year ended with a big bang. The pantomime was a giant success. My academic work was promising. Even more important, for the first time I could remember, I felt at home in a group. I was no longer an outsider. I started the summer break on a real high.

I had been so happy and preoccupied during the year that I had almost ignored what was going on outside of my classes.

That year had also been marked by a series of traumatic political rumors and developments. Ever since Stalin died, there had been a succession of new names and faces in the top positions in the Soviet Politburo. None of them had acquired the same image or reputation that Stalin had while he was alive, and none stayed in power very long.

But early in 1956, a rumor started circulating about one of the new Russian political leaders, a man named Nikita Khrushchev. According to the rumor, Khrushchev in a speech at a big meeting of the officials of the Soviet Communist Party denounced the terror and cruelty perpetrated by Stalin over the years. I never saw a detailed description of Khrushchev's comments. Every rumor was different from the others, but their persistent nature made you believe that there was some truth to them.

The changing of the guard in Russia was mirrored in Hungary, too. Rakosi, who represented the Hungarian Communist regime at its most repressive, was replaced by Imre Nagy, a popular political figure who was also considered more independent of the Russians. Nagy lasted only a short time before he, too, was deposed and replaced by a member of the Rakosi regime. But this time, even the Rakosi followers seemed less repressive.

Altogether, there was an unmistakable easing of the political climate in Hungary. Many people who had been imprisoned for political reasons were released. But what made the most visible impression on me was the change in the tone of the newspaper and radio commentaries. Discussions of politics and the economy were more open. Voices of criticism and analysis appeared, seemingly with impunity.

The trend seemed to have been driven by journalists and writers. A number of these belonged to a discussion group called the Petofi Circle, named after Sandor Petofi, the poet of the 1848 revolution. I was only vaguely aware of the existence of this group. Then in June 1956 there was a buzz about their organizing a public discussion about the journalistic practices of the day. Some friends of mine suggested that we attend.

There was so much talk about this session that we decided to go several hours before it officially started. This was a good thing. Already the cavernous hall was almost completely full. By the time the session started, people filled every nook and cranny of the auditorium, crammed the stairways, and overflowed into the courtyard of the building. Loudspeakers had to be hung so that the sessions could be broadcast to the crowds waiting outside. Hundreds of people were packed in, sweating in the early summer heat and occasionally cheering at a shouted remark. In addition to other university classmates, I ran into several high school classmates and some of my parents' friends. Later I found out that both my parents were there, too, but I never saw them in the crowds.

My friends and I managed to find a place inside the auditorium. A long table was set up on the stage. At it sat a panel of writers and journalists. One of them was my cousin Marika's husband.

One by one, they stood up and, facing the audience, described the many ways in which each had worked to mislead the Hungarian public through lies, distortions, and exaggerations. A lot of the discussion involved subjects that didn't mean much to me. But one confession that I understood was by the editor of the major Communist daily newspaper. He told how he had doctored the weather forecast to promise clear skies for each May Day in order to encourage people to turn out in large numbers for the annual parade.

While a lot of the comments may have been lost on me, they were not lost on much of the audience, who greeted each confession with increasingly exuberant cheers, approving comments, and energetic applause. I was stunned by the enthusiasm, but I also noticed something peculiar about the applause. Communist political speeches and pronouncements were always acknowledged by rhythmic clapping, slow, measured, and always in unison. I had grown to expect such clapping at political meetings. Now I found it ironic that the speakers were acknowledged by the same rhythmic clapping that I associated with the Communists.

The meeting started in late afternoon and went on for hours. There seemed to be no end to the revelations and confessions. It was fascinating to listen to, and I couldn't help but feel that I was witnessing something unusual and significant. I sensed that I was witnessing history being made.

Afterward, my friends and I walked home, talking excitedly about the events of the evening. None of us had seen anything like this before. We were optimistic about what it might mean for the future. Then a thought occurred to me. The whole thing reminded me of a pressure cooker whose lid had been weakened. The danger was that as more steam was generated, the weakened lid might very well explode.

A few days later, I had to report for military training, as did all the boys from my university class.

We took the train to a dusty, hot army camp near a town called Orgovany, a few miles from Kiskoros. Every summer, over the four years of university, we would train in antiaircraft artillery; at graduation, we would become reserve officers. This, our first summer, was devoted to basic training. It was very basic.

We slouched off the train and were handed ill-fitting, well-worn, faded, greenish brown uniforms with no insignia and a plain, foldable cap. Then we were greeted by a sergeant, a wiry guy with a coarse face, who looked us over with undisguised disdain and announced that he was going to make men of us. I don't know what I did, but the sergeant somehow singled me out of the first lineup. Later, I wondered what happened. All I could come up with was that I looked straight at him when he lectured us—it helped me understand him—while the other guys all looked at their feet. In any case, right from the beginning, I was assigned all the unpleasant tasks, like washing dishes, cleaning latrines, peeling potatoes, and the like. The sergeant picked on me for several weeks, then I guess he got tired of it and spread his attentions more broadly.

There also were students from other universities at this base, but our group from the Chemistry Department was assigned to a small platoon that trained together. The training consisted of marching in formation, learning to salute, and waiting, waiting, and waiting some more. It was very hot in Orgovany, and waiting around in the sun was miserable and boring. Occasionally, we were lectured on how to calculate airplane speeds so we could hit moving targets. An instructor held up terribly simplistic charts of trajectories and formulas. They were on par with counting "One and two and three . . ." from the time you see lightning to when you hear thunder to figure out how far away the strike is. He was bored, and so were we. And we were hot.

The highlight of our training involved loading dummy ammunition—a wooden bullet—into a World War II–vintage antiaircraft gun. We did this over and over and over, one person pulling back on the breech and the other loading the ammunition. Then the next pair repeated it and the next after that. We did this hour after hour after hour. The greatest danger was the possibility that when the contraption closed, it might take your thumb with it, so we were taught slowly and carefully to fold our thumb into our fist as we shoved the bullet into the gun.

Once or twice, we practiced aiming the gun, cranking away to track a model airplane that was suspended on a wire and was pulled back and forth across the firing range. Even though the model plane moved slowly across the horizon, we had a hard time keeping it in the gunsights. I remembered the two jets that had zoomed above Gabi and me at Lake Velence and wondered how we would keep track of those with this gun.

In the four or five weeks of our military training, we never did get to fire the antiaircraft gun. The only time we ever got to fire anything was in rifle training. We were each handed three live rounds and were instructed to fire at a target placed against a hillside some distance away. My experience with my air gun came in handy. To my sergeant's amazement, I did very well at target shooting. Momentarily, I had a bit of his respect.

The single overwhelming element of our weeks of military training was abject boredom. When we weren't marching or attending lectures or practicing with the antiartillery gun, we would drag a blanket under the shade of a tree and sit and chat and play endless games of Twenty Questions, while watching the regular soldiers lifting weights during their time off.

Sometimes, for a change, we sat near the boundary fence of the army base. Outside the fence was a dirt road, and every once in a while the camp commander's wife would walk past. We could look at her surreptitiously, but it had to be very surreptitiously, because rumor had it that someone in an earlier group had wolf-whistled at her and all hell had broken loose. I usually hung around with my friends Zoltan and Jancsi Lanyi, but even Zoltan couldn't muster more than a couple of halfheartedly sarcastic comments.

As the August days grew shorter, we counted the hours to our liberation. Unfortunately, the end wasn't that crisply defined, so the closer we got, the more anxious we became. Rumors started flying that because of some unspecific offense we had committed, they would keep us three days extra. No, it was five days. No, maybe it was only two. It was very painful. Finally, it was over. We were promoted to the rank of corporal and allowed to go home.

Right: Hungarian flag, with the Communist emblem cut out. Just about every building was decorated with one.
Below: Demonstration: The crowd thickened, occupying entire avenues. Everyone was hollering and shouting happily as more and more people shared in the increasing excitement.
(Hannes Betzler & Ernest Laue)

Left: I saw burned-out trucks, occasionally even a burned-out Russian tank. Wherever a tank still smoldered, it was surrounded by gawking passersby.
(Hannes Betzler)

Chapter Twelve

REVOLUTION

I FELT VERY DIFFERENT walking into the university that September of 1956. I had just turned twenty. I felt happy and at ease, and I was looking forward to seeing all my classmates again. Even though I had just spent over a month at military training camp with some of them, it would be nice to see them out of uniform.

I was looking forward to my classes, too. The second-year curriculum was similar to the previous year's, but where the first year focused on inorganic chemistry, the second year would revolve around organic chemistry. Once again, the core chemistry course was taught by a chief professor, like Professor Lengyel another godlike figure whose textbook would be our course bible. Labwork, too, followed a familiar path. The year before, we had done labwork in qualitative analysis, in which we learned to identify the compounds in our samples. This year, our labwork would involve quantitative analysis, in which we would figure out the amounts of those compounds. This promised to be even more challenging than qualitative analysis, but having conquered qualitative analysis, I was looking forward to it. I thought I would have fun in this lab.

Everybody knew of my achievement in the first-year qualitative analysis lab, including my teachers in quantitative analysis. They implied that they expected me to do equally well in their class. I worried that I might not be able to live up to my reputation, but it was nice to be famous.

Early in the semester, our class organized a mixer for the first-year students. I met a girl in the new class whom I liked. Her name was Viki. She came from a small town in the country and was a little lost in the big city. It gave me an opportunity to offer my services as a tour guide, and to my delight, she accepted without hesitation. I enjoyed showing her around Budapest and taking her to my favorite haunts. She was petite, quiet, unaffected, and easy to be with. I asked her out a number of times, and I always looked forward to seeing her.

While the school year was getting off to a good start, outside of the university, the world was running off course. Earlier that summer, there had been rumors of antigovernment riots in East Germany that were supposedly put down by the East German police, aided by the Russian army. Other rumors claimed that anti-Russian demonstrations had also taken place in Poland at that same time and that demonstrations were again erupting in Poland in October. In late October, a buzz spread through the university about a march that was being organized to express our support for the Poles.

The plans were solidifying as some classmates and I headed off to lunch in a decrepit old restaurant that served as the college cafeteria. The restaurant was about a fifteen-minute walk from the university, but that day it took longer than usual to get there. We kept running into groups of excited students. They were all yelling, "Are you coming to the march?" When we arrived at the restaurant, I wrote the date, October 23, 1956, with my finger on a dusty mirror near the entryway and put a circle around it to emphasize the significance of this date.

Lunch was a rushed affair. We had decided that instead of going back to class we would join the demonstration, so we hurried back to the university, where the march was gathering. In a sign of solidarity with the Poles, we were all going to walk from the statue of Sandor Petofi to the statue of the nineteenth-century Polish general Jozef Bem. General Bem was revered as a friend of Hungary's for the support he'd given the Hungarian revolutionaries during the war against the Austrians and the Russians in 1848, the war in which Sandor Petofi gave his life. As we headed off to the Bem statue, students poured out of buildings and side streets. With every step, the crowd swelled like a river being fed by tributaries. At first it was only students, but then more and more adults joined in.

The crowd thickened, occupying entire avenues. The trams were forced to stop running, because people overflowed onto the tracks in the street. Everyone was hollering and shouting happily as more and more people shared in the increasing excitement. Every window facing the street had someone hanging out of it, waving madly. After all the years of sullen, silent May Day marches, there was something magical about a large spontaneous demonstration. I kept looking around, soaking it all in, feeling that I was in a dream.

All of a sudden, a Hungarian flag was unfurled from a window along the way. The Hungarian flag has horizontal stripes of red, white, and green. The original flag had the emblem of St. Stephen, a gold crown with a cross on top, in the center. During the Communist years, this emblem was replaced by the crossed hammer and sickle of the Soviet Union surrounded by sheaves of wheat. The flag now waving from the window had a hole in the middle. The Communist emblem had been cut out. Pretty soon, we saw more flags like that, then more flags, until just about every building was decorated with one, all with a hole in the middle.

The sight took my breath away. Those flags were permanently altered. The act seemed unequivocal and destined to provoke a reaction of some sort. The demonstration had started as an act of support and celebration, but now I felt we had crossed a line of no return. I began to feel a little nervous.

In the ebb and flow of the crowd and amid all my gawking, I got separated from my friends. I found myself being swept toward the big square in front of the Parliament building. Every inch of the square was jammed with demonstrators—thousands of them. After a while, they started chanting, "We want Nagy! We want Nagy!" Imre Nagy had been deposed as prime minister the previous year, but after a period of disgrace, he had been included in the government again. We stood and shouted, then waited, then shouted and waited some more. By now, it was early evening; it was getting dark, but nobody was leaving. Finally, Nagy appeared on the balcony of a building near the Parliament. People cheered wildly. He gave a short speech. I couldn't understand a word of what he said. People cheered again, but not as wildly as before. Clearly, whatever he said didn't seem to be enough.

A wave of excitement swept through the crowd. It seemed that the students who originally organized the march had formulated a twelve-point program of political reform, along the lines of a similar program formulated during the 1848 revolution. The buzz was that we should head to the main radio station and demand that the twelve points be read over Radio Budapest. Meanwhile, I also heard people saying that a crowd was trying to topple the gigantic statue of Stalin at Heroes' Square. I was excited but also increasingly scared.

The building in which Radio Budapest was housed was more or less on my way home, so I joined the stream of thousands that was flowing slowly in that direction. But before I could get there, a rumor ran through the crowd that the security police were firing on demonstrators at the radio building.

I decided to head home. The events had gone way beyond the exuberant demonstration of the afternoon. Now I was really scared. It took me a while to break out of the crowd. I peeled off to a side street, but even the side streets were crammed with people, all milling around. It was quite late by the time I got home, but my parents were still waiting up. They were very relieved to see me in one piece. We sat around, comparing our experiences of that day. It had been a day unlike any other.

We were up and out early the next day. On the street, strangers were shouting the latest rumors to each other. There had been a battle at the radio station. Security police had fired on the crowds, then trucks loaded with rifles arrived from the industrial suburbs, manned by workers who distributed the rifles to the crowd. The firefight between the demonstrators and the security police had raged all night. We still heard sporadic shooting from a distance. I decided to stay home.

We had one of the two telephones in our apartment house, so all day long neighbors kept coming in to call friends elsewhere in the city, and I was busy answering calls from people wanting to know what I'd heard. People dropped in to exchange news, then left again to pass it on. We heard that another demonstration was planned for the next day.

When I looked out the window the next morning, the trams were not operating. By midday, open-air trucks jammed full of people were shuttling up Kiraly Street. Clusters of more people clotted the sidewalks. A few hours later, I saw the trucks coming back. This time, the truck beds were full of wounded people being taken to a hospital in our neighborhood. There had been another big gathering in front of the Parliament and, depending on whom you listened to, either the security police or Russian soldiers had opened fire on the crowds. Later, people said, the Russians withdrew from Budapest.

I woke up the next morning, wondering what extraordinary events would happen now, but over the next week, life on the streets returned to normal. The trams started running again and people returned to work. But not everything was the way it had been before. A new government was formed by Imre Nagy, who became prime minister again. Political parties that had long been disbanded came back to life, and dozens of newspapers sprang up to publicize their beliefs. It was as if the gradual thaw that had slowly been taking place over the past couple of years had suddenly turned into a flood.

We could hear Radio Free Europe and the Voice of America on our radio. Previously, these stations had been regularly jammed and we could make out only fragments of phrases behind the static of the jamming. Both these stations gave us a lot more information about what was going on in Budapest than Radio Budapest did, but more important, they gave the impression that what happened over the last few days was getting attention all over the world. The announcers were calling it "the Hungarian revolution."

These days were exciting, but they had their scary side, too. Not too far from our house, I ran into a crowd of people craning their necks to see something happening in a side street. I joined them. I saw civilians, all with determined looks on their faces, armed with rifles and walking toward an apartment house. A small group broke off and went inside; the rest remained outside the front door. People next to me explained that they had located a member of the security police who was trying to hide in that house. The thought crossed my mind: How did they really know that the person they were hunting was, in fact, a member of the security police? What if he wasn't? I didn't wait around to see what happened.

A few days later, Radio Budapest announced that it was going to air a speech by Cardinal Mindszenty. The Communist regime had imprisoned him some years earlier as a representative of the reactionary clergy. The radio said that a Hungarian army unit had freed him a few days earlier. Even though Mindszenty had been in prison for years, he was still the top-ranking religious figure in the country, and his release seemed very significant. That night, Cardinal Mindszenty gave a speech in which he expressed his support for the revolution. Although there was nothing explicitly threatening in his speech, I found the speech vaguely ominous. It reminded me of when I first saw the hammer and sickle cut out of the Hungarian flag. Like that act, this speech signaled another escalation in the revolution.

I had mixed feelings about the whole thing. On the one hand, I was happy to see the Communist regime toppled. On the other hand, I worried about where all this liberation might lead. The war years were not that far in the past. I went to bed filled with uneasiness and anxiety.

Early the next morning, I woke up to the sound of wooden planks being dropped. It sounded familiar, but it took me a few minutes to think why. Then I remembered the sound from eleven years ago. It was the sound of heavy artillery fire.

My heart started pounding. I jumped out of bed and ran into the Big Room. It was still dark outside, but my parents were already up and wrapped in their bathrobes. My father was intently fiddling with the radio. No one said anything. We all knew what was going on. We were just waiting to hear official confirmation.

An announcement came over Radio Budapest. Soon, the announcer said, Imre Nagy was going to address the nation. We dressed quickly so that we could stay glued to the radio. Imre Nagy came on and gave a very brief address. He said that Soviet troops had attacked before dawn, but he assured us that the government was still functioning. That struck me as a bit dubious. I continued to hear the planks thudding louder and louder. The artillery fire was getting closer and closer. Nagy's statement struck me more like a call for help to the outside world.

As it got light outside, a strange rumble approached on Kiraly Street. I ran back to my room and flung open the window so I could see what was happening. Before I had a chance to lean out, I froze. A vehicle that looked like a tank without a cover was coming to a stop right in front of our house. Russian soldiers inside the shell were manning machine guns pointed in all directions. I heard shouting in Russian, and one of the machine guns slowly turned toward my window. I was too frightened to move. I stared down, petrified, as the muzzle swung toward me. There was a moment when it seemed to stop, then the machine gun continued to turn, moving past my window and scanning the other apartments. There was some more shouting in Russian, and then the vehicle rumbled on.

When my heart started beating again, I went back to my parents' room and in a shaky voice told them what had happened. We decided it was time to go to the cellar. I had a sour taste in my mouth. I wanted to say, "Not again."

We packed a bag of belongings and some food and headed down. Other tenants were doing the same thing. Without firing a shot, the troop carrier had jolted the entire house.

The air raid shelter had long since been dismantled, so we settled down on some wooden stools in the coal bin allotted to our apartment, wrapping blankets around ourselves and hanging more blankets around to try to make a warm corner. Occasionally, someone went up to check what was going on. Whenever he or she returned, we all circled around to get the latest news of the world above us. We didn't learn much.

We continued to hear shooting nearby. We half expected

Russian soldiers to show up at any minute. Stories of how the Russians treated people—especially women—during the war were on everyone's minds. The women had bundled themselves in their oldest clothes and wrapped their heads in kerchiefs, trying to look as old and unattractive as possible. My mother did, too. No one said anything.

That night, we slept in the coal cellar, huddled in coats and blankets. It turned out to be a wise thing. The next morning, I heard two mortar rounds *whoosh* and crash overhead. They had landed in the attic of our building. All the men ran upstairs, grabbing buckets of water from their apartments on the way in the hope of extinguishing any fires that the shells might have started. I went with them. When we got up to the attic, we saw that the roof was shattered in two places. Broken tiles and splinters of wood were scattered on the attic floor. Bits of the shell were still smoldering on the floor. Luckily, the floor was covered with sand, so instead of throwing water on the embers, we shoveled more sand over them and the fire was quickly extinguished. The sand had been spread in the attic in anticipation of an attack by the American imperialists during the Korean War. The irony of the situation didn't hit me until later.

A third mortar round crashed into the courtyard later that day. One of the fragments hit a tenant in the leg as he was on his way back to the cellar. A group of neighbors took him to a hospital a couple of blocks away. We stayed in the cellar another night.

Some people went upstairs to listen to the radio. We learned that Imre Nagy was no longer prime minister. The Soviets had replaced him with Janos Kadar. Radio Budapest began broadcasting messages from the new regime. In its old cheerily positive voice, it reported the defeat of the counterrevolutionaries and the restoration of order in the city.

The next day, Russian soldiers showed up at the house. They

came down to the cellar with their machine guns in hand and looked around. We looked back at them, waiting wordlessly.

They said something, gesticulating toward the upstairs apartments. I remembered enough of my school Russian to help translate. They wanted to get into the apartments facing the street. One of the apartments they had chosen was ours. They shoved some furniture out of the way to set up their machine guns in the windows. Then they waved us back into the cellar.

I wished there were no mortars falling on our house and no Russian soldiers in our apartment. I wanted the trams to run again. I wanted to go back to school. I wanted life to go back to normal.

A few days later, the shooting around us subsided. The Russian soldiers left our house and we moved back into our apartment. There were dirty footsteps on the rugs and the floor in the Big Room and handprints on the walls. The furniture was jumbled together where they had shoved it. Luckily, there was no other damage.

We could still hear sounds of fighting in the distance, so we didn't dare leave the house. The phone worked, however, so we scrambled to call other people who had a phone to find out what was happening elsewhere. I called my friend Peter from the Madach gymnasium, whom I had kept in touch with through my first year at university. He lived on Ring Street, and he had a girlfriend who lived in another part of Budapest and also had a phone. By looking out of the windows of our respective homes, we could give each other updates on where we heard fighting and where we saw troops coming and going.

I frequently talked with Jancsi Lanyi on the phone. He lived outside of Budapest, in the suburbs. Even there, he had experiences similar to mine.

My parents tried to call my aunt Iren and uncle Sanyi to get news of them and their family. There was never any answer. My aunt Manci didn't have a phone, so we had to wait until it was safe to go out on the streets to see how she was doing.

To try to get real news, we listened to Voice of America and Radio Free Europe. Mostly they were jammed again with so much static that we couldn't make out the words. Sometimes, though, we could hear them clearly. From the safety of Western Europe, their Hungarian announcers aggressively urged Hungarians in Hungary to continue their resistance to the Russians. They painted a hopeful picture of our situation, implying that the world was ready to support us. I found this irritating. I was sure they hadn't woken up to a Russian troop carrier aiming a machine gun at their bedroom window.

For a while, I could see Russian troops standing guard at the street corners whenever I peered out the window. After some days, the sentries disappeared. That's when we started foraging for food—bread, potatoes, and whatever we could find in the few stores that had started to reopen. But we stayed in the neighborhood, not daring to go very far.

As I walked around the streets, I realized that we had been lucky. Many houses in the neighborhood were marked by artillery fire. Some houses were completely demolished, their front walls ripped open so you could see everything inside. I noticed something strange about the windows in other houses. Often, the rectangle where the window ordinarily was placed was gone. In its place was a large circle. Cannon fire had shot into the house and all you could see was the ragged edges of bricks in a round frame around the window. I thought of a week or so earlier, when the gun on the troop carrier below slowly swung past my window.

A huge department store that occupied an entire city block not far from us had collapsed into a heap of rubble. I had never seen such devastation, not even from the bombing during the war. It was a heap of concrete, bricks, and mangled steel. Nothing was recognizable. Bystanders told me that Hungarian resistance fighters had stored ammunition in the department store and Russian tanks had shot at it until it blew up and brought the whole structure down.

I managed to find a few loaves of bread and brought them back to our apartment. Then I wrapped up one loaf and set off to bring it to Viki at her dormitory. The trams weren't running, so I walked. I was reminded of the time when my mother and I walked home from Kobanya, except that this time there was no snow. Abandoned trams sat in their tracks, their antenna whips disconnected from the overhead wires and dangling to the side. The electricity must have gone out at some point and left them stranded. Elsewhere, I saw burned-out trucks, occasionally even a burned-out Russian tank. Wherever a tank still smoldered, it was surrounded by gawking passersby, huddled around and staring. Nobody said anything. They just stared.

Makeshift posters had been pasted on the walls. Many of them called for United Nations troops to come into Hungary and oppose the Russians. Among the small clusters of people reading the posters, one man was passionately arguing against anyone coming in. He shouted, "Do they want to turn us into another Korea?" I agreed with him but didn't say anything. I didn't feel comfortable joining in.

Viki's dorm was in the same general area as the university. This neighborhood, too, had been damaged by Russian shelling. The university, of course, was closed.

I was relieved to see Viki. She was well but told me she was thinking of going home to her family. She had talked to a truck driver she knew who was planning to set off in the next day or two. As I said good-bye to her, I wondered if I would ever see her again.

My aunt Iren and her family had disappeared. We didn't

know where they were. My parents telephoned and telephoned, then went to visit. No one was home. The neighbors didn't know anything. It was very disquieting.

Manci, however, reappeared and was a frequent visitor. She would tie a kerchief around her head, bundle herself up in her winter clothes, grab a string shopping bag, and go from shop to shop, searching for food and the latest information. She was the most effective source of news we had.

After a week or so, the trams started running again. My parents went back to work. The university was still closed, so I stayed home except when I ran errands for my parents and bought bread and milk. I tried to keep in touch with whomever I could to get a sense of what was happening elsewhere in the city.

We started to hear of people who took advantage of the chaos to escape across the border to Austria. Escaping became a recurring topic of conversation between my parents and me. I was very tempted, but I didn't know how to go about it. My parents thought I should go but were terrified about what might happen to me if I got caught. So I agonized: Should I go? Did I dare go? Should I go alone? If not, with whom? How would I start? What if I got caught?

As my unanswered questions multiplied, I rationalized that things weren't so bad here after all. I really liked university, I liked my class, I liked Viki. Maybe I should stay. But then the lure of the opportunity of getting out to the West started the circle all over again.

My father contacted various friends to see if they knew of an adult who was planning to escape whom I could go with. He spent days chasing down leads. None of them materialized.

Right: Hungarian refugees were distinguished by mud-covered clothes—we got splattered as we crossed the border by walking across plowed fields.

Left: Refugees in a schoolhouse. Straw was strewn on the floor, providing a bit of cushion. (United Press Photo/Corbis)

Left: The most crucial visit was to the United States consulate. Everybody wanted to go to America. The line for registering stretched out to the chilly street. (Dickey Chapelle)

Chapter Thirteen

CROSSING THE BORDER

ONE AFTERNOON in early December I was reading near the window of the Big Room when my aunt Manci stopped by. She had been out shopping and had her usual nylon string bag hanging from her shoulder with a loaf of bread and something wrapped in brown paper in it. As always, she was dressed in a heavy coat with a kerchief tied around her head, but she was too agitated to take off her coat. She came right over to me and without any greeting said, "Andris, you must go."

I stared at her. "You must go," she repeated, "and you must go immediately."

On her way back from shopping, she had seen several Russian trucks, the kind that were covered with canvas and usually carried troops. The trucks had pulled up at an intersection. Russian soldiers had jumped out, rounded up young people who happened to be in the neighborhood, herded them on the trucks, closed the canvas flap, and left.

This was not altogether new news. Stories of such roundups had been going around Budapest since the Russians returned. But all the stories were thirdhand, hearsay. I had never talked to anyone who had actually witnessed such an event. Given the climate of rumors and exaggerations, one part of me believed the worst, but another part of me wasn't sure that these events actually took place.

Manci's visit changed all that. She was an Auschwitz survivor and had seen the worst that could be. She was not a hysterical woman and had absolutely no reason to exaggerate.

The news hit me at a time when I had been going back and forth in my mind about whether to leave the country. Ever since the Russians had returned some three weeks ago, the number of young people who had set off to cross the border had grown by the week. Some clearly made it across because they sent back word from Austria. Others disappeared. They either were captured and interned or made it across and didn't report back home. Nobody knew which. Still, as it became more and more commonplace to hear about acquaintances who had gone, the thought of leaving occupied me more and more.

Those thoughts led to endless discussions between my parents and me and between myself and my classmate Jancsi. Of all my friends, he was the one I had stayed in touch with the most during the turmoil of the revolution. Our discussions were all of the "what if" type: What if we could catch a ride on a truck on its way back to Austria? What if we got a travel permit to go to the vicinity of the border? And so on. None of them had a realistic chance of being translated into action. Still, my father obtained the name and address of the Viennese business associate of a friend of his—just in case. The friend wrote a little note, saying, "Do everything possible to help the bearer of this note." Then he signed it and gave it to my father to safeguard for me, if and when I should need it.

I knew where I would go if I did leave: Of course, it would be America. Or, as the Communist regime put it, "imperialist, money-grubbing America." The more scorn they heaped on it, the more desirable America sounded. America had a mystique of wealth and modern technology; it was a place with lots of cars and plenty of Hershey bars. In addition, there was a more pragmatic consideration. Manci's sister, Lenke, and her brother-in-law, Lajos, an aunt and uncle I'd never met, lived in New York City. Manci was positive they would take me in.

My parents didn't have a lot of confidence in Lenke and Lajos. Just after the war was over, we had received a package in the mail from America. It was a big tin filled with flints for cigarette lighters—thousands and thousands of them. In her accompanying letter, Lenke expressed her hopes that my father would come back alive and explained that she was sending the flints as a way to help him get started in business again. My father had laughed contemptuously: "Does Lenke want me to stand on a street corner and sell these?" The box of flints had disappeared someplace, but my parents' doubts about Lenke remained.

In any case, there were two more immediate problems holding me back from leaving: I didn't know how to do it, and I was scared.

Manci addressed the second problem in a roundabout way when she told me that I would be in danger if I stayed. If I could be picked up merely for being at the wrong street at the wrong time and taken away to heaven knew where and for who knew how long, I might as well take my chances and try to get out of Hungary.

Manci also proposed a solution to my first problem. Always a collector of acquaintances and connections, she told me about someone she knew who came from Szombathely, a small town about fifteen miles from the Austrian border. This woman had a daughter named Angela who was about my age and was also looking to get out. Angela had never actually been to Szombathely, but her family would equip her with the name and address of friends who still lived there so that we would have a jumping-off point. It wasn't exactly a smooth plan of getting across the border, but it was better than anything I could come up with on my own.

I called Jancsi and told him my aunt's scheme and asked him if he was ready to strike out with Angela and me. Without hesitation, he said yes.

We went over to the railroad station that afternoon and looked up the schedule of trains leaving for Szombathely the next day. Then we arranged to meet Angela at the station.

My parents had encouraged me to leave as long as the discussions were theoretical. Now that reality hit, they became extremely somber. My father said in a tone of earnest determination, "You should do it. You may never have a better chance." He gave me the note with the message to his friend's Viennese business associate, as well as the name and address of Viktor, a friend of his and Manci's from their Kiskoros days who now lived in Vienna. I folded them up as small as possible and put them in my wallet. My mother agreed with my father, but her tone was shaky. I felt that if I changed my mind, she would have been elated.

That night was very tense. I was busy figuring out what clothes I was going to wear, what I was going to take with me, and how I was going to dispose of what I left behind. I asked my mother to go to the university when it reopened and find out what grade I got in my latest lab project. Despite all the turmoil in my life, that organic chemistry lab was still very important to me, and I wanted to know whether my success in the first-year lab was a fluke or whether I could repeat it. My mother wrote down the information about whom she needed to see and what she was to ask.

We were trying to be thorough and efficient in our preparations, but we were just going through the motions. It was difficult to concentrate on these details when we were struggling with the unstated fact that we might never see each other again.

That night, before I went to bed, I walked quietly around the apartment. I looked over every room. I straightened up my chemistry set. I checked with my hand under the windowsill in the light shaft to make sure my prized bullets were still safely hidden. I silently said good-bye.

Early the next morning, I dressed in the warmest outfit I had: a baggy pair of brown corduroy pants that a neighborhood tailor had lined with my mother's old padded silk bathrobe and a jacket also lined with the remains of the bathrobe. Underneath, I wore my best winter suit. It would get wrinkled, but in the meantime it would give extra warmth and might come in handy if I needed another pair of pants and a jacket. I packed a change of underwear and some extra socks in my school book bag and put on a short winter coat. My father gave me all the Hungarian currency he could scrounge up on such short notice, and I hid the notes inside my clothes. Then Jancsi showed up and it was time to go downstairs, Jancsi and I to head off to the station and my parents to go to work.

We said good-bye at the corner as if it were any normal morning. We didn't dare make a big production of it; it would not have been a good idea to suggest that I was doing anything out of the ordinary. We parted, then I stopped in my tracks. I had automatically put the key to our apartment in my pocket. Now I fished it out, turned around, and ran after my parents. I handed it to my mother and said awkwardly, "I probably won't need this anymore." My mother nodded. She looked as if she wanted to say something, but she didn't speak. I saw that there were tears in her eyes. I turned and ran back to Jancsi.

We set out for the station. We met up with Angela, bought our tickets, and with great self-consciousness headed for our train. We had concocted all sorts of elaborate alibis as to why we were going to Szombathely, but when we got to the platform, these alibis suddenly appeared ridiculous. Everybody boarding the train looked like us, all dressed in their heaviest winter clothes and all seemingly on a similar mission. It was a train of would-be emigrants, all heading to the country but showing their origin as city folks.

The train ride was quite long—the train never went very fast, and it stopped many times, sometimes for no apparent reason. For a while, people kept to themselves and avoided even looking at each other, but as time went on and nobody interfered with us, everybody dropped their guard a bit. People started making oblique references about getting out, usually talking about friends or acquaintances who had made it and the adventures—or misadventures—that had befallen them. I struck up a conversation with a girl about my age, who said that she had been talking with the conductor, who turned out to be from Szombathely, and that for a small amount of money he had offered to guide her to wherever she wanted to go. The girl's problem was that she didn't have anywhere to go. We did. So we promptly formed an alliance. All four of us would have the conductor guide us to the address that Manci's friend had given Angela.

A little later, I introduced myself to the conductor and asked him how hard it would be to get out of the station. He was not very encouraging. I wondered if he made it sound worse than it was in order to justify his fee.

Eventually, we arrived at Szombathely station. The sun set early in December, and it was already dark. People got off the train and started heading to the exit, a gate at the end of the platform. The conductor came for us and motioned for us to follow him off the other side of the train onto the tracks. He led us to another platform, away from the Budapest passengers. He whispered that there were soldiers at the main entrance examining everyone's papers, but he would take us out a different way. We held our breath as we followed him through a series of back doors and deserted corridors behind the public part of the station; then suddenly we were out on a dark street. The conductor told us which direction to go in and said that he would follow us.

"Don't worry," he assured us, he would keep us in sight and tell us when to turn.

It sounded like a strange arrangement, but he was emphatic, so we followed his bidding. For a while, we kept glancing back and he was behind us. Then, he was gone. We stopped and huddled together and waited. There was no conductor. Other than an occasional passerby, nobody was on the street. It was now seven-thirty and there would be a curfew at eight o'clock; we couldn't wait any longer. We stopped someone to ask for directions to our address. He told us where to go—it turned out that it wasn't very far away—then he quickly headed off. We started walking rapidly, too.

Just about eight o'clock, we found the house. We knocked on the door. A middle-aged woman opened it. There was some discussion between her and Angela. The woman checked the street to the left and to the right, then quickly motioned us into the house. We could stay overnight, she said—in fact, we had to because the curfew had already started—then in the morning she would take us to someone who would give us directions to the border. Meanwhile, she fed us dinner, gave us some blankets, and left us to settle down for the night. We each took a corner of the room. No one slept much.

At daybreak, the woman walked us a few blocks to the house of a relative who was a railroad engineer for a spur line. He knew the area very well. He had just come back from a night shift and was already in bed, but the woman woke him up. Once he understood what our situation was, he agreed to help. The woman motioned us into the room. He stayed in bed, yawning, with tousled hair and in his underwear.

The engineer told us he would give us the names of a sequence of villages. There was, however, one condition: We had to commit it to memory. Under no circumstances would we be allowed to write it down. Quite clearly, he wanted to ensure that there would be no incriminating evidence against him if we were captured.

The four of us memorized half a dozen or so very strange-sounding names, muttering them to each other to keep the memory fresh. Then we set out toward the first town in the sequence. We took back roads, because the railroad engineer had told us that the main roads were patrolled by Russian troops. The back roads weren't paved. Within a short while, we were splattered with brown mud up to our knees.

In each town, we asked someone for directions to the next town, then we hurriedly walked on. And on. We may have walked ten or fifteen miles, but we were so tense that we were hardly conscious of being tired. By midafternoon, we reached the last village on the list. It was already getting dark and we quickly left in the general direction of what we thought was west. Pretty soon we were walking through an area of small woods alternating with plowed fields and pastures. It didn't look like we were about to cross a border. It looked like we were lost.

In one of the fields, a small man was plowing using a plow pulled by a single ox. We approached him, trudging through even more mud. When he heard us, he looked at us without the slightest surprise. He straightened up and we saw that he was a hunchback. We asked for directions to the border. He looked around in the dusk, peering at the surrounding woods for any possible eavesdroppers. Then he gestured in a particular direction and in a quiet voice, which seemed unnecessary as nobody was around us in the field, said his house was over there and we should go in and wait for him. We thanked him and set off in the direction he indicated. Soon we found the farmhouse.

We knocked. A voice told us to come in. A stunningly beautiful woman was cooking dinner. She was dressed in an elaborate traditional peasant costume that reminded me of folk dancers I'd seen in shows in Budapest. We told her, "The man outside sent us." She nodded and invited us to sit down for dinner. In short order, the man appeared, cleaned up some, and joined us at the table. They seemed to be husband and wife.

The whole scene—the four of us city people from Budapest, sitting around a table in a small house with mud floors and a tiled roof, eating dinner with a hunchback peasant and being served by a colorfully dressed, beautiful woman—seemed like a fantasy. But we were not very inclined to marvel at the strangeness of the scene. We had only a single abiding interest: to get to the border.

The man told us that he got some of his income by smuggling and knew this area like the back of his hand. He could take us over, he said, but it would cost us. He left us to ponder what we would do. We really didn't have a choice. Between the four of us, we came up with the amount he wanted and handed it over. My share took half of what my father gave me. The man told us to settle down and wait; we would set off at midnight.

Time moved slowly. The man and his wife went about their business without a word. The four of us sat deep in thought.

As it got closer to midnight, I had to use the toilet. The man took me to the door and pointed out a shack with a door hanging open. Inside was a hole in the ground with a tree trunk fixed horizontally in front of it. You crouched on the tree trunk and did your business into the hole; there were a few pieces of newspaper for toilet paper. I had never seen that kind of latrine before, and it was pitch dark inside. But I managed. I looked up at the bit of sky barely visible through the doorway and I thought, This is probably the last of me that I'll leave in Hungary.

Shortly afterward, the man said it was time to go. As the train conductor in Szombathely did, he started us off in a particular direction and told us he would stay behind us and seek us out from time to time to guide us to the next post. Given our experience in Szombathely, this was not very reassuring, but again we did not have any choice. He was firm about how he wanted to do this, and we needed him.

We would walk for five or ten minutes in a field or through the woods, then he would materialize from the dark, tell us to head in a slightly different direction, and then disappear again. After another five or ten minutes, he would catch up with us again and direct us to the next step. And so it went. Every time we thought he had abandoned us, he would materialize out of thin air and give us our next instruction. It was cold and dark, so dark that sometimes we had to feel our way among the trees.

I lost track of the time. After a while, we emerged from the woods. I could see some faint lights far across an open field. The man came close to us. "Those lights are Austria," he whispered. "Head toward them and don't take your eyes off them. This is as far as I go." And he was gone.

I didn't take my eyes off those lights. I trudged toward them as if they were a magnet. The muddy field seemed endless. The lights never seemed to get brighter.

We stumbled across some ditches, then crossed a dirt road. We heard dogs barking at a distance, and suddenly a flare lit up the sky. We threw ourselves to the ground, holding our breath. Then the flare burned out and it was dark again. We picked ourselves up and continued.

After what seemed like miles and miles, the lights finally came close. Had we made it? We snuck up to the first house that we could see. Dogs immediately started barking in the dark. We again threw ourselves to the ground. A man came out of the house, holding a kerosene lantern over his head, and called out—in Hungarian—"Who is there?"

My heart stopped. I'd heard stories of people who had attempted to cross the border, gotten lost, and meandered right back into Hungary. Had this happened to us, too?

"Who is there?" the man repeated. We hesitantly picked ourselves up from the ground and forced ourselves to approach. When he saw us, he smiled a big, warm smile and said, "Relax, you're in Austria."

For a moment, my mind went blank, then I started breathing again, almost panting with relief. My clothes were suddenly drenched with sweat.

He invited us into his house and served us each a shot of slivovitz, a plum brandy. Then he told us what would happen next. Austrian gendarmes patrolled the area regularly. They would soon be by and would take us to the village schoolhouse for the rest of the night. Sure enough, the gendarmes soon appeared. We had been walking all day and half of the night, but we wearily got to our feet and started walking once again. After half an hour or so, we got to the village with the schoolhouse. The benches in the rooms had been cleared to the sides and straw was strewn on the floor, providing a bit of a cushion. There were no blankets. Several people were sprawled in the straw, asleep. Between Jancsi, the girls, and me, we spoke enough German to understand that the gendarmes wanted us to stay there until morning.

There was no heat inside the schoolhouse. Jancsi and I huddled next to each other and tried to sleep. A couple of hours later, I woke up shivering. I was worried. I didn't like the whole idea of the gendarmes and whatever procedure they had in mind. Now that we had made it across the border, I just wanted to get to Vienna, to the address that my father had given me. I noticed that Jancsi was awake also. I gestured to him that we should get out of there. We tiptoed out of the schoolhouse, leaving the two girls and everyone else behind.

It was deep, deep dark and bitterly cold as we explored the village, looking for the railroad tracks. All we could see was dark houses. Finally, we came upon a house that had a light in the window. We knocked on the door. A peasant woman, dressed to go out in an overcoat with her head wrapped in a kerchief, opened the door. She, too, spoke Hungarian. We asked her where we could get the train for Vienna, and she told us that that was where she was going, too. She was taking some foodstuffs in a wicker basket to the market there. She had a little girl with her, and in a few minutes, they were ready to go. The four of us walked in the dark and freezing cold until we came to the railroad tracks. There was no station, not even a sign indicating where we were, but the woman said, "The train will stop here."

About fifteen minutes later, a train came along and it did indeed stop for us. The woman explained to the conductor in German that we were *fluechtling*—escapees, refugees. The conductor shrugged and patted us on the shoulder, then continued through the car without demanding our fare. We were on our way to Vienna.

It was midmorning when we arrived at the Vienna railroad station. The woman directed us to the streetcars, and after some trial and error, we found somebody who told us which streetcar to take to the address I had fished out of my wallet. We told the streetcar conductor in broken German that we were *fluechtling*—we learned quickly. He looked us over, smiled at our mud-splattered clothes, and said, *"Ich sehe"* (I see). Then he said something about a *graue karte*—a gray card. It seemed we needed to get gray cards. Meanwhile, he didn't make us pay the fare.

It didn't take long to find my father's friend's business associate. However, his reaction was not at all what we anticipated. While all the strangers we had encountered up to that point had been helpful and encouraging, this man was quite clearly not pleased to see us. When I showed him the note my father's friend had written, he waved it away with the comment, "I know, I know, he gives that to everybody." He could put us up for the night in a boardinghouse, he said, but beyond that, we had to find our own way. He told us how to get the gray card, which would enable us to ride the streetcars for free, and told us about various refugee organizations that might take care of us. Then he gave us a sandwich, took us to the boardinghouse a few blocks away, made the arrangements, and left.

Despite his sour attitude, he booked us each our own room. After our experiences of the last two nights, the rooms seemed incredibly luxurious. There was a bed with a thick comforter, frilly curtains on the windows that looked out onto a busy Viennese street, and a sink with a bar of soap. My first priority was to clean up. I undressed, took off my underwear and my socks, washed them out in the sink, and hung them up to dry. Then I washed myself as well as I could in the sink. When I finished, I was reasonably clean except for the mud that was caked on my corduroy pants. I sat on the edge of my bed, looked around at what would be my home for the night, and thought, I would be ecstatic to settle in a place like this and go to the university. If I could just do that, it would be more than I could possibly want.

But the daydreaming didn't last very long. We had to acquire the all-important gray card. The gray card was the identification card given out by the Austrian authorities to Hungarian refugees. We hardly needed identification, because Hungarian refugees were all distinguished by dirt-covered clothes from the border crossing. But the gray card entitled us to the most important privilege of all—free travel on the trams. And travel was a must.

I stood for five long hours in a long, slowly moving line of Hungarians—mainly young men, but also families with young children. They were all mud splattered and looked tired and confused. Everyone kept asking all the strangers around them for tips and advice.

I quickly found out that the key thing was to register at every relief organization that one could reasonably apply to for help. I registered with several, including the Joint, which was the nickname for a Jewish relief organization, and another one called the International Rescue Committee, which was referred to by its initials, IRC. The offices were scattered all over Vienna, but by speaking a combination of English and a few words of German, I was able to ask directions, and the gray card allowed me to get from one place to another without too much trouble. There were lines everywhere.

Some of these relief organizations gave us food vouchers, others gave us little packages of toiletries and some secondhand clothes. And most important, some gave us vouchers for places to stay.

I got a voucher for a *studentenheim*—a youth hostel. It was in the outskirts of Vienna in a two-story private building converted for the purpose. We would be bunked twelve to a room with barely adequate toilet facilities, but I was very glad to get in. Lodging was so scarce, I heard, that some Hungarians were put up by kindly policemen in the city jail because there wasn't any other place for them. This was better.

The most crucial visit of all was to the United States consulate. Everybody wanted to go to America. The line for registering at the consulate stretched out to the chilly street. We stood for hours, stomping our feet to keep warm. I finally made my way inside. The Hungarian translator asked if I had any relatives in the United States. I gave the name of Manci's sister, Lenke, and her husband, Lajos, and their address in New York City. The officials told me they would let me know when they had any news for me and asked for an address to reach me at. The only address I had was the one for Viktor, my father's friend from Kiskoros, so I gave them that.

Standing in line, I often encountered Hungarians offering to change Hungarian money into Austrian currency. After some bargaining, I exchanged my leftover forints for Austrian schillings. I was very happy to have real money in my pocket, although a few days later, I realized that I had been taken to the cleaners.

Fortunately, since I was now equipped with vouchers for most of the necessities of life, I didn't need much money. I traveled for free, I had a roof over my head, and with the food vouchers I could have a decent meal in a restaurant chain for just a few schillings. But I needed money to send two very important telegrams.

The first telegram went to my parents, telling them that I had arrived and was safe. Then I started wording the telegram to Lenke, telling her I had made it out of Hungary and that I would like to come to America. For a moment, I felt strange about approaching people I'd never met with a request for help. But as I glanced back at the long line behind me in the telegraph office, the feeling disappeared. I couldn't afford luxuries like embarrassment. I sent the telegram, and I again gave Viktor's home as a return address.

I had arrived on a Thursday morning, and all of this was done by Friday afternoon. That evening I went to visit Viktor. I didn't have his telephone number, so I just showed up out of the blue and introduced myself as Gyurka's son. He had half expected me, he told me, just as he half expected a lot of people those days.

In complete contrast to my father's friend's business associate, Viktor and his wife were very kind to me. They first asked me where I was staying and were relieved that I had found a place because they were already putting up a refugee at their house and had no more room. They peppered me with questions about my parents and Manci and about the situation in Budapest. Then they fed me a fantastic meal.

It was a genuine Hungarian meal, the first that I'd had in weeks. What with sheltering in the cellar and the food shops having been closed or empty, I hadn't had a really good home-cooked meal since the revolution started. For dessert, Viktor's wife put out a bowl of oranges and bananas. To me, these were incredible delicacies. I had had oranges no more than two or three times in my life. I loved them! Bananas, on the other hand, I had never encountered. Viktor's wife had to show me how to peel them. I eyed them with some suspicion, but when I bit into them, I loved them, too. I was off to a good start in the West!

Viktor had a ten-year-old son, who stared at me with great curiosity. He spoke Hungarian pretty well, and we got into a big discussion about what he planned to be when he grew up. I told him that I was studying chemistry and explained what chemistry was about. Viktor overheard our conversation. He offered to write to a friend of his, who was associated with a university in England, to see if he could get me a scholarship. I was grateful for the offer, but when I thought of England, it struck me that it wasn't far enough. Now that I had escaped, I wanted to get as far away from Hungary and even from Europe as I could.

Afterward, I went back to the *studentenheim* and wrote a letter to my parents. I did not address the letter to them, however. I suspected that their mail might be watched, because I figured that by now it would be known that their son had escaped illegally. Instead, I addressed the letter to Manci and in a bit of a code language asked her to share my story with her nephew, meaning my father. I made sure that my letter was resolutely nonpolitical. I confined my comments strictly to describing my arrival and what I had done so far, my reception by the surly man who put me up at the pension, and my warm welcome from Viktor. I said I had contacted Lenke and was waiting for an answer, and that I would write again soon. Then I went out, bought a stamp at a corner store, and mailed the letter.

Over the next few weeks, I continued to spend most of my time standing in lines to see if my case had moved forward at either the refugee organizations or at the U.S. consulate. The lines became my daily occupation. They represented the hub of the Hungarian refugee social life. In these lines, I met Imre, Peter, Bubi, and several other acquaintances. Jancsi had gone his own way. He had contacted some relatives in the United States who were well-off. They sent him money and were expediting his affairs.

Once Jancsi and I split up, for the first time in my life I was completely on my own. Even though I ran into Imre or Bubi and other friends from back home, no two of us were following the same path. Each of us was making his own way and looking out for his own luck. We were like so many Ping-Pong balls bouncing around independently of each other.

When I wasn't standing in one line or another or visiting relief organizations, I took the opportunity to explore Vienna. Vienna was fabulous. Unlike Budapest, there were no signs of the war anymore. The streets were clean, people were well dressed and friendly. To my utter amazement, even the police were friendly, a stunning contrast to any expectations I had of someone in uniform. They greeted us Hungarians on the street with a smile and were ready to struggle with language barriers to give us directions when we were lost, which was often. In fact, one off-duty policeman walked about twenty minutes out of his way to make sure I got to my destination, then waited until he was sure I had found the right address.

Vienna dealt me only one disappointment. As the days went on, I discovered I could buy cheap standing-room tickets to the Vienna Staatsoper. I saw three operas: *Fidelio, Don Carlo,* and *The Magic Flute.* The performances were good, but I thought they were not as good as their Hungarian counterparts.

The other standees were intrigued by my presence. I suppose I was easy to spot as a refugee, since despite my best efforts, my clothes were still mud stained, even the pants I had worn underneath my corduroys. They were friendly, though, and we managed to have a rudimentary conversation, in a mixture of German and English, interspersed with lots of pantomiming, comparing the opera here to the opera in Hungary. One of the people I chatted with was a cute girl. We walked out of the performance together, but then she said good-bye. I trudged back to the hostel a little sad.

I visited Viktor and his family often. Their house was like a home away from home to me. On one of my visits, he greeted me happily waving a telegram. It was from Lenke. Her answer couldn't have been warmer. She said that she and Lajos were looking forward to my becoming another son to them and added that their young son had put my framed picture on his desk in anticipation of his "brother's" arrival. I was greatly relieved. I had a place to go, if I could just get there.

One day, a notice was posted on the bulletin board at my hostel. Representatives from one of the refugee organizations where I had registered, the International Rescue Committee, were coming the next afternoon to interview refugees who wanted to go to the United States. I signed up and eagerly awaited their arrival.

The next day a group of young Americans arrived. I was surprised by how young they all were. They could easily have been fellow students of mine at the university.

They set up a long table in one of the rooms and began to interview the line of candidates who had signed up. Each candidate was interviewed by the whole group. When my turn came, they were surprised that I was able to conduct my interview in English, and to my happiness, I saw one of the interviewers jot on my file, "Good English." Then the questions moved to my activities during the revolution. They asked me if I had fought. I said no, I had participated in some demonstrations, but I had not fought. They looked at each other and at me with surprise. Everyone else whom they talked with had fought, they said. Why hadn't I?

I didn't know what to reply. I had my doubts about the others' claims. A sarcastic thought came to mind: If all of those people had fought, we would have won and I wouldn't be here. I didn't say this, however, and I was reluctant to fabricate a story for the occasion. The interview soon ended, with a promise that the next day they would announce who had been selected. I was tense. I knew from my visit to the consulate that there was a quota for admission to the United States and that requests for admission were already way oversubscribed.

By the time I got back to the hostel the next day, after the usual stint of standing in lines, the representatives from the IRC had come and gone. They had read off a list of names. According to people who heard the list, I wasn't on it.

I felt as if someone had socked me in the stomach, then my heart started beating so hard that I could barely breathe. "Where are the IRC people now?" I asked. Someone said they were conducting another series of interviews at a school some distance away. I took off like a madman. I ran all the way through the cold, dark streets. My heavy shoes hurt my feet as I ran, but I didn't care.

Sweat was pouring down my face by the time I reached the school. There was a familiar long line of people waiting to be interviewed. I didn't wait. As the next person emerged from the interview room, I brushed past the person whose turn it was supposed to be and pushed in to stand in front of the table.

The IRC representatives were a different group of students than the ones who had interviewed me the day before. They stared up at me blankly. I didn't give them time to say anything. I swiped the sweat off my face with my hands and, still panting, started talking in English as fast as I could.

I explained that I had been interviewed yesterday, that I was not selected, but that I really, really wanted to go to the United States. One of the interviewers asked me why. I told him I had relatives in New York City who would take me in, that I was a chemistry student, that I thought I would become a good chemist, and that I belonged in the United States. The words poured out, not eloquently or coherently, but I talked and talked as if I could overwhelm their objections by the sheer volume of my words. I almost didn't dare to stop talking, but finally I ran out of things to say. I stood there, panting slightly and still sweating profusely.

The students looked at each other and smiled, then one said, "Okay, you can go to the United States."

I was speechless. I couldn't believe my good fortune. I wanted to hug every one of the young men sitting on the other side of the long table.

They gave me a voucher for lodging at another student hostel in the outskirts of Vienna, where the IRC-sponsored students were put up while waiting for the paperwork to go through. I stuttered my thanks and, clutching my precious voucher, backed out of the room and left. The cold air hit me on the face. I was still sweating, but now it was from relief.

The next day I moved to the new hostel. There were some eighty of us who had been accepted for sponsorship by the International Rescue Committee. A lot of us were students. As it turned out, moving to the hostel was an important step, but only one step in the process. We had to go to the U.S. consulate to fill out more forms, have a medical exam, get photographed, and fill out still more forms. Then we waited day after day for the papers to clear. When they finally did, we had to wait some more to find out when we were going to be flown to the United States.

I spent the days washing my clothes, getting my few belongings packed and ready, then unpacking them, then packing them up again. I dropped by Viktor's house whenever I could. I was still tense with anticipation, but I was immensely happy to have gotten this far. It occurred to me that my father's insistence ten years earlier that I study English was a critical ingredient in my good luck. In my next letter home, I made sure to thank him.

The notification finally came. We were going to leave the next day. However, instead of going by airplane, we would take a train to Germany that would take us to a ship that would then take us to the United States. I was disappointed. Everyone I knew who left for the United States had gone by plane. The process was going to take a whole lot longer than I had anticipated. Still, I was glad to get moving in the right direction.

I took the opportunity to change all my remaining money into American dollars. It came out to $20.

The next morning, a bus pulled up in front of the hostel and took us to the train station. We were joined by other busloads of Hungarians of all ages. We settled into the compartments. There were six plastic-covered bunk beds in each compartment, three on each side. I chose a middle bunk that was about the level of the window and spent the time looking out at the winter countryside going by.

The train moved fast, but it still took hours, and the hours went by excruciatingly slowly. At some point we stopped. It was the German border. Uniformed border guards went from car to car, looking at all of our papers. It was the first time I had seen a German officer since the war. Their caps were peaked, in much the same style as I remembered the caps of German officers from wartime. My mouth was dry. They took my papers, looked at them, saluted, then gave them back and went on. But I continued to feel tense.

The tension didn't leave me until we got to the first stop in Germany, the city of Passau. German students lined the platform, cheering us exuberantly and offering us hot chocolate, coffee, sweets, and cakes. They were kids like us, just better dressed. That broke the ice.

After Passau, the train went at a good clip. It was dark outside, so all I could see were occasional lights. I couldn't sleep. I was overwhelmed by the momentousness of what was happening to me. I was truly in the West. Every hour, I was farther from my birthplace, my family, my world, heading toward America.

The thought hit me: After all the years of pretending to believe things that I didn't, of acting the part of someone I wasn't, maybe I would never have to pretend again. The train went on, and I finally fell asleep.

As we neared land, the ship stopped heaving and gradually all the Hungarians regained their equilibrium and came up on deck. We stood in silence and just stared. I thought, These houses have never heard bombs or artillery, not ever. I marveled at this. (Louis Lanouette)

Chapter Fourteen

ABOARD SHIP

I WOKE UP when the train stopped. It was dawn. We were at a port. Through the window, I could see a nondescript gray ship at the far end of the platform. The ship's name was *General W. G. Haan.* I looked at it with excitement. It was going to take me to America.

We were told to get off the train, and we slowly formed a long, snaking line to the gangplank leading to the ship. It was a cold, damp day, and everything—the ship, the port, and the sky—was shrouded in shades of gray.

There was a strange smell in the air. I realized it was salt water. It was the first time that I had ever seen the sea. It was not particularly beautiful. It, too, was a mass of gray. The smell, however, was mysterious, exciting, and wonderful.

Despite the early hour, a military band had assembled and was playing the Hungarian national anthem. But rather than playing it with the measured solemnity that we were used to, they played it like a military march. The brisk pace of the music contrasted with the slow movement of the line as we shuffled toward the gangplank.

Each of us had been given a little name tag with our name and a number on it. We were told to affix it with a string to a button on our overcoat. As we reached the bottom of the gangplank, one sailor looked at the tag and read the number out loud in English. Another sailor made a note of it in a ledger. Oddly, instead of reading the entire number as a single unit, the sailor read it digit by digit—one, seven, oh, seven, and so forth. I wondered if perhaps Americans didn't know their numbers and had to break them up into individual digits, and I wondered if "oh" was the same as zero.

The *General W. G. Haan* had been used as a troop carrier during World War II and was very Spartan. We were led down metal stairways deep into the bowels of the ship to large enclosures filled with hammocks suspended four deep from the ceiling. I took a hammock second from the bottom. The hammocks were very close to each other; when we were all lying in them, there were perhaps twelve inches between my nose and the bottom of the hammock above me. Sitting up was out of the question.

In fact, sitting anywhere was not something I was going to have much opportunity to do on this trip. The recreation room had tables securely fixed to the walls, but no chairs. A sign was stenciled above the tables: "Do not sit on the tables." Someone had penciled in an "h" after the "s." Of course, the humor of this was lost on most of the passengers, very few of whom knew English.

The only place you could sit was in the toilets, which were rows of stalls with no doors, or in the dining halls, where everything was bolted to the floor, including the very narrow benches around the tables. I soon found out the necessity of these arrangements.

It took most of the day to get us settled in. In the afternoon, the ship finally pulled in the gangplank and we left. Slowly, Germany receded. Most of us were on deck, looking back as the continent where we grew up disappeared. Nobody said much.

As we moved out into open water, the ship started to sway from side to side. Some people got seasick. Refugees clung to the railings on deck and threw up over the side, or they huddled miserably in their hammocks down below. Luckily, the swaying had no effect on me. In fact, I kind of enjoyed it. I took the opportunity to roam the ship, from front to back and top to bottom, exploring every nook and cranny and marveling at the enormous polished wheels and pistons in the engine room.

The next morning, I noticed a gathering of people on one side of the deck. They were staring at something white in the distance. Somebody said it was Dover. The thought struck me: I'm looking at England. The momentousness of everything suddenly hit me: leaving Hungary, traveling through Germany, seeing the sea for the first time, seeing England. Each event by itself would have been unthinkable just a couple of weeks ago. Now they were happening in quick succession. I was overwhelmed.

Even as I watched, England slipped out of sight. Soon we were out in the open Atlantic. The ship started to act differently. In addition to swaying from side to side, it now acquired an up-and-down motion as we headed into big swells. Most of those who weren't already seasick got seasick now. In just a couple of hours, the ship looked like a hospital ward.

I still felt fine. I tramped all over the ship. It was like being in a funhouse at an amusement park. I had to watch out for doors suddenly swinging open and slamming on me, and I had to hang on for dear life on the staircases. Drinking out of a water fountain became a real challenge. The water flow would disappear one minute and shoot six feet in the air in the next.

The stench down below was unbearable, so I spent most of

the time up on deck. I was bundled up to my nose against the cold, but I enjoyed the air and the motion.

Food was plentiful, but it was different from what I was used to. The coffee we got was made from real coffee beans. In Hungary, "coffee" was made from ground, roasted hickory nuts. Since coffee wasn't produced in any of the Communist-bloc countries, we didn't have it. Real coffee tasted very good.

Before leaving Hungary, I had eaten oranges only two or three times. On board the ship, orange juice came with breakfast, along with half a grapefruit. Much as I loved oranges, I quickly discovered that I couldn't stand grapefruit. The rest of breakfast was inevitably scrambled eggs with fried bacon. The smell of the bacon permeated the air, even on the deck, as it came up through the air vents. I grew to associate the smell of bacon with the smell of vomit, and I hurried through breakfast just to get it out of my nose.

As the ship swayed and heaved up and down, eating also became an increasingly difficult physical task. There were little railings on the table to keep the food trays from sliding into our laps, but they didn't keep them from sliding sideways. You had your choice of trying to steady your tray or hanging on for dear life to the table or to the narrow benches that fortunately were firmly fixed to the floor. The tray usually lost. It was a good thing there weren't too many people in the dining hall.

After a while, I found I could socialize with members of the crew. I started to hang around them just to practice my English. This led to a real job. Somebody approached me with a white helmet that had the letters *MP* painted on it and asked if I would be willing to stand guard at the crew's quarters to keep people away so the night crew could sleep during the day. I eagerly accepted. Besides feeling terribly important with the MP helmet on my head, I had a legitimate reason to camp out at the crew's quarters.

In Hungary, I had seen black or Asian people only in the movies. But the crew here consisted of white people and black people and in-between people who were neither black nor white but had unusual facial features. I later found out they were Filipino. The crew members were all glad to chat with me, but I had a hard time understanding them. It seemed as if they were talking with their mouths closed. Many of them chewed gum incessantly, which didn't help either.

I made friends with two crew members in particular. One was a wiry, dark-faced fellow. I found out he was Puerto Rican. The other was a husky white man of Italian extraction. The Puerto Rican was a typist for the ship's office. The Italian was a mechanic. His real job was working in a shipyard, but he had decided to come to sea so he could see more of the world. Both of them lived in Brooklyn, which, I found out, was near New York.

They took me under their wing and started to tutor me in the American way of speaking English. They could understand everything I said; I couldn't understand anything they said. It took me several days to figure out that what sounded like a single syllable stood for "That's right" and represented agreement. It seemed as though they said it in every sentence. They also said "yeah" instead of "yes," which confused me because I thought they borrowed that from the German *ja.*

The crew's quarters were at the stern of the ship, which was my favorite spot to ride the waves. When my friends weren't around, I liked to sit on a coil of rope near the railing. As the ship swooped over the unending swells, the stern went up and down and my seat in the rope coil was like an amusement park ride. I was practically weightless on the way down, so much so that I had to hang on to the railing so I wouldn't fly out, then I would feel the cold rope slam into my rear end as the stern kicked upward. I loved this ride and I loved watching the wake that the ship left behind. The cold notwithstanding, it was almost hypnotic.

My new friends explained to me that this ship was one of many that had been built after the war for the sole purpose of bringing the troops home from England. It seemed incredible to me that ships would be built for just one purpose, but they assured me that this was the case.

They also assured me that the ship was safe, which was getting increasingly difficult to believe as the waves grew bigger and bigger and the ship hardly seemed to make any forward progress. It was just climbing the waves and sliding down them, again and again. It turned out we were in a major storm.

After some days of stalled progress, my friends told me we were altering our course and taking a southern route to try to get out of the storm's path. For a while, it worked and the weather got better. Then we encountered more storms. The crossing was originally supposed to take about a week, but the arrival date was delayed and delayed again. Altogether, it was delayed three times as a result of the storms and the longer path. In the end, the trip took two weeks.

There wasn't much to occupy us during the trip. One day, some official-looking people set up some tables in one of the recreation halls and interviewed each of us, one at a time. When my turn came, they asked me who I was, what had I done in Hungary, and what I intended to do in America. Then they asked lots of questions about the revolution and its aftermath. They, too, asked whether I had fought in the revolution. Once again, I told them I had not. These people were as surprised as the IRC people. Like the IRC people they told me that I was the first person in all of their interviews on the ship to say that I had not fought. Once again, I didn't comment.

Another day, we were all told to line up to get shots. I didn't know what the shots were for, but I lined up along with the rest of the passengers. There were two stations, one manned by a young white doctor, the other by a black doctor. I had learned that there was a lot of prejudice against blacks in America. I quickly calculated that the black man must be really good to have become a doctor, so I chose to get my shot from him. Whether I computed rightly or not, the shot didn't hurt.

The storms, the delays, and the boredom got on the nerves of many of the Hungarians. Anti-Semitic comments started to be heard. There were a number of Orthodox Jews among the refugees who dressed in their idiosyncratic way and kept to themselves. They were targets of derisive comments, but soon so were the rest of the Jews on the ship. One of the men who bunked near me said, "You Jews all have it made. You speak English, you've got rich relatives in America. The rest of us will be in deep trouble." Then he pulled out a hunting knife and started sharpening it in front of my nose.

An American minister of Hungarian descent had traveled to Austria to accompany the refugees back to the United States. Enough such incidents took place that he called a gathering of all the Christian refugees. He gave a sermon and told them that as we entered a new world, old hatreds and prejudices needed to be left behind. The guy with the knife grumbled about this, too. "How can he say such a thing?" he said about the minister. "I hate whoever I want to hate, and I will not change."

There was an American rabbi on board as well. I noticed that the minister and the rabbi often talked together and seemed to be close friends. I took that as a good omen. Meanwhile, I stayed away from the other Hungarians as much as I could. My MP duties were a real blessing.

One day, to break the monotony, the authorities arranged for the Hungarian women to take over the kitchen. They cooked a meal with lots of paprika and seasonings. This briefly cheered everyone up and temporarily changed the smell in the air for the better. But it didn't last very long. The next day, we were back to ordinary food, which, as the days went on and on, became more and more dreary.

It got to the point where I welcomed any change in the menu. One day at lunch, they served a dessert of vanilla pudding. I had loved vanilla pudding at home and eagerly went back for seconds. Big mistake. Half an hour later, my stomach started to act up, and shortly after that, I was draped over the railings, throwing up into the Atlantic Ocean. I stayed away from vanilla pudding or anything else unusual for the rest of the trip, and my stomach behaved.

On New Year's Eve, the crew put on entertainment for us. They played jazz records and started dancing with each other. I was particularly impressed by the black crew members, who clearly danced more energetically and gracefully than the others. Some Hungarians joined them, but they were very awkward by comparison.

Finally, after four storms and three rescheduled arrival dates, we arrived in what we were told was Brooklyn. As we neared land, the ship stopped heaving and gradually all the Hungarians regained their equilibrium and came up on deck. It was evening and the lights of the city were shining. We could see the headlights of moving cars and street lamps and lights in the windows of houses. We were looking for the Statue of Liberty, but we couldn't see it. I wondered why. We stood in silence and just stared. I thought, These houses have not heard bombs or artillery, not ever. I marveled at this.

We had been told to prepare to disembark in the morning. I gathered my things, returned my MP hat, and said good-bye to my two friends. We exchanged addresses, and the Italian fellow promised that he would look me up at my uncle's place and invite me home for dinner. On shore a military band was waiting for us, playing jazz. After a while, they switched to a few bars of the Hungarian national anthem, followed by another serious-sounding piece, which I figured might be the national anthem of America. None of us paid much attention to it. We were silent and tense.

We began to disembark, luggage in hand, filing off the ship to a big warehouse. Our luggage was taken from us and sent toward officials on a conveyor belt. I had never seen such a contraption before. I wondered if America was so advanced that it was using machinery to make even trivial physical work obsolete.

The customs agents were looking for only one thing—Hungarian salami. A lot of Hungarians brought some with them from Hungary or Vienna, having been told that it was a precious item in the United States. Unfortunately, Hungarian salami has a characteristic smell. The agents unerringly pulled out logs of salami from bag after bag and, with a friendly smile, confiscated them.

We gathered our luggage and piled onto buses. We were told we were going to Camp Kilmer, an old prisoner-of-war camp in New Jersey. None of us were pleased about being taken to a camp, let alone a prisoner-of-war camp. We were told this would be for just a few days, but it still seemed like a step in the wrong direction.

My first impression of the United States was not very good. Even though it was midmorning, there wasn't a single person in sight. All I could see were cars parked in an unending line on both sides of the street. I'd never seen that many cars in my life. I wondered where all the people who drove those cars were, because nobody was in evidence. The streets and the buildings were ugly. The buildings were peculiar, too; they had metal stairways attached to the front leading down to the first-story level and then stopping in midair. None of us could figure out what they were for.

I did notice that every building had a television antenna on the roof. Cars, ugly streets, TV antennas, and no people—America was a strange place.

The bus suddenly swooped into a tunnel. The tunnel was brightly lit and lined with gleaming white tiles. It went on for a long, long way, which impressed us. There were tunnels in Hungary, too, but they were very short by comparison.

On the other side of the tunnel, we drove along a road that was elevated above a gray marshland extending as far as I could see in both directions. It was depressing. We stared at it in silence until a voice from the back said, "This can't be true. It's got to be Communist propaganda."

Eventually we arrived at Camp Kilmer. The camp consisted of rows of plain wooden barracks. Inside, though, they were surprisingly clean, neat, and comfortable, with only four beds to a room, a luxury after the ship and the crowded refugee hostels in Vienna.

As we were assigned our rooms, we were handed a package of razor blades and toothbrushes and toiletries. I guess we all looked as though we could use them. I had given up shaving on the ship. The constant heaving motion had made it almost suicidal to try. So notwithstanding the profusion of razor blades that had been showered on us by various refugee agencies in Vienna, I and most of the other men had heavy-duty stubble. I thought that I could open a drugstore with all the toiletries I had been given as a refugee.

We were told we would be processed in a few days and then would be free to leave. Meanwhile, there were still more interviews and paperwork. As I was waiting my turn for one of these interviews, I noticed a black soldier sitting at a desk with a phone in front of him. I went over and asked if he would help me make a phone call to New York City. He looked at me with amusement and asked whom I wanted to call. I said I wanted to tell my uncle that I'd arrived. He said, "Sure, why not?" with a big smile. I whipped out the phone number. It started with the word *Kingsbridge,* and I watched him dial KI and then the number. He handed me the phone and a minute later I was talking with my uncle Lajos.

He was very excited to hear from me, and I was no less excited to be in touch with the man who would be my guardian, if I ever got out of Camp Kilmer. He said that he and his son, Paul, would come visit me the next day. I was jumping with joy at the prospect of making contact with somebody who would be permanent in my life.

The next day, they showed up. Lajos was a short, husky guy with thinning hair and a friendly face. He was my father's age and looked a bit like him. He gave me a firm hug, then introduced me to Paul, who was standing shyly to one side. Paul was twelve years old and slight, and he looked a lot like pictures of his mother. He, too, gave me a hug like he meant it.

I had a rolled-up newspaper in my hand when I embraced Lajos and Paul. In my joy, I kept hitting Paul in the rear end with the newspaper.

We all started talking at once. Paul spoke only a few words of Hungarian and his accent sounded really funny, but he understood everything. Lajos spoke English with a heavy Hungarian accent, so I had no problem understanding him. The conversation among the three of us was a chaotic combination of my bad English, Paul's bad Hungarian, and Lajos's switching between the two languages. We kept looking at each other and breaking into happy grins.

Finally, Lajos turned serious. He told me that he worked at Brooklyn College and that he had my admission all arranged with the college authorities. All I had to do was get out of Camp Kilmer.

I was allowed to leave the next day.

Above: I had to study a lot for my technical courses. After my morning classes were over, I would go back to the empty apartment and work until it was time to return to City College for my evening classes.

Below: Lajos took me to get outfitted with new clothes. They were good clothes, they fit well, but they looked and felt somehow different. They made me feel American.

Above: There was a short underground tram in Budapest but it was nothing like the Manhattan subway.

Above: My friend Jerry (*right*), who took me under his wing. In particular, he decided to punch me in the shoulder every time I mispronounced a well-known word.

Left: My New York family (*from left*): Lenke, Paul, me, and Lajos. From the first moment, I felt at home with them.

Chapter Fifteen

NEW YORK CITY

LENKE AND LAJOS'S apartment was in the Bronx, on the fourth floor of an apartment house. It consisted of two rooms, a kitchen, and a bathroom. The living room had a fold-out sofa, which at night was turned into a bed for Lajos and Lenke. The arrangement reminded me of the Big Room in my parents' apartment, except this room was smaller and the central piece of furniture was a television set. I had read about television, but this was the first one I had ever seen.

The other room belonged to Paul. It, too, was a small room, smaller than my room at home. It had a bed, a small desk and some bookshelves, a birdcage with a canary, and Paul's bike. This was going to be my room, too. Paul had already set up a sleeping bag for himself on the floor. He insisted on giving me his bed. No amount of protestation would change this arrangement.

As soon as I arrived, Lajos took charge of me and guided me to the bathroom, where he filled the tub with steaming hot water. It looked inviting. I hadn't taken a bath since leaving home. After I climbed in, Lajos picked up the corduroy pants and jacket I had worn for the past month and marched off somewhere, holding them at arm's length. That was the last I saw of them. Later on, he told me that he'd tossed them into the incinerator. That was another mysterious contraption I had never seen before, but, unlike the television, I had never even heard of it. When I first put some garbage down its chute, the strange, strong draft that hit me when I opened the door actually scared me.

While I was luxuriating in the bath, the phone rang. I heard Lajos speaking in excited Hungarian, then heard him say, "Your son is here." I was in shock. Moments later, he opened the door and said, "Come quickly, it's your parents." I jumped out of the bathtub, wrapped myself in a towel, and ran for the phone. My parents had managed to beg their way to an international connection, which was very difficult to get. We heard each other's voices for the first time since I'd left. My mother was breathing quickly, and I was so excited that I could barely speak. Our incoherence was furthered by the fact that my parents had to huddle around the one telephone receiver we had, so neither one could hear me very well. I had to repeat myself quite a bit.

We finally calmed down enough to talk clearly. After assuring my parents that I really was all right and hearing their reassurances in turn, the conversation turned to day-to-day details. I asked my mother to pack up some of my chemistry textbooks and mail them to me. She agreed, then sheepishly confessed that she had disposed of my treasured stockpile of chemicals. I asked her how. After a moment's pause, she said she had flushed them down the toilet. Horrors flashed in front of my eyes. Depending on the order in which she had dumped them down the toilet, the process could lead to disaster. Sure enough, my mother added, "I probably shouldn't have done that." The combination of chemicals had overheated the water and the toilet bowl had cracked.

The minutes clicked away and we had to finish the conversation. We promised that we would write to each other in detail. I had been writing a diarylike letter on board the ship, which I figured I would send to Manci. My parents assured me that no harm would come from sending letters directly to them.

My excitement lasted long after the conversation ended. Lenke had returned home from work by now, and she and Lajos made me repeat the conversation several times, discussing every detail while I celebrated my arrival by snacking myself to the point of indigestion. In anticipation of my arrival, they had loaded up the refrigerator with a variety of foods. I particularly liked chocolate wafer sticks washed down with orange juice. The novelty of oranges was still strong.

Although she was Manci's sister, Lenke did not look like Manci at all. She looked like their mother, who had died before the war and whose picture I had seen at Manci's house. Lenke was an exceptionally warm person. She was determined to become a substitute mother to me and assumed this role with so much enthusiasm that it worked. From the moment I met her, I felt at home.

There was yet another treat in store. My parents had been writing to me in care of Lajos and Lenke before my arrival, and there was a pile of letters waiting for me. I eagerly settled down to read them.

The tone of their letters was worry, worry, worry about everything. Had I arrived safely in the United States? Was I eating? Was I sleeping? Was I able to understand people? Did they understand me? Would I get into a university? And on and on and on. I figured that the only way I could make them stop worrying was to let them know everything that was happening to me. I wrote a very detailed addition to my ongoing letter that brought them up-to-date with our phone conversation. Lajos agreed to mail the thick wad of scribble-covered paper for me.

Lajos took the next day off from work and devoted it to me. The first thing he did early in the morning was to march me down to the neighborhood doctor, who gave me a polio shot.

Polio was a scary disease. There were polio epidemics every summer in Hungary; the common belief was that the disease was transmitted primarily in swimming pools, so it always cast a shadow over my trips to the pool. I hadn't even known that there was a vaccine. I was very glad to receive it.

Then we took the subway to visit Lenke at her workplace. There was a short underground tram in Budapest, but it was nothing like the Manhattan subway. This was a huge network, deep in the ground. I was impressed by the complexity of the construction, the escalators, the stairs, the tunnels, and the distances the subway covered, but I didn't like the noise, the dirt, and the cramped and confining atmosphere. My expectations of a big-city subway system were shaped by pictures of the Moscow subway, which was spacious, bright, spanking clean, and filled with statues of heroic figures. The loud, decrepit tunnels of the New York subway gave me an uncomfortable feeling, reminding me of my first impressions of the city from the windows of the bus.

Lenke worked as a saleslady in a department store in the middle of Manhattan. When we surfaced from the subway, I stopped cold. I was surrounded by skyscrapers. I stared up at them, speechless.

The skyscrapers looked just like pictures of America. All of a sudden, I was gripped by the stunning realization that I truly was in America. Nothing had symbolized America more to me than skyscrapers; now I was standing on a street, craning my neck to look up at them.

Which also meant that I was an incredible distance from home—or what used to be my home. The cacophony of the traffic filled my ears. Mobs of people brushed past me. The perspective made me feel like an ant in the bottom of a canyon. I suddenly felt very, very insignificant in my new surroundings.

Lenke excused herself from her work area, and she and

Lajos took me to get outfitted with new clothes. Most of them were on sale, but all were new. They were good clothes, they fit well, but they looked and felt somehow different. They felt American. I left the department store, my old clothes bundled up in a package under my arm. It occurred to me that the package represented my past, neatly wrapped and tied with string, as easy to discard as my corduroys. I kept a firm grip on it.

When Lajos and I got back to the Bronx, we took my old clothes to a place filled with washing machines. For a few coins, a person could wash his clothes while he waited and could dry them, too. Then we headed home.

Lajos automatically turned on the TV as soon as we got back to the apartment. I was to discover that the TV was on a lot. Much of the time, Lenke, Lajos, and Paul just watched it out of the corner of their eyes. At first I found it distracting, but I soon just treated it as background noise.

Lajos rummaged for a copy of the Sunday *New York Times,* and the two of us spread the "Classified" section on the kitchen table. Lajos said that the many little items there advertised job openings. We didn't have this in Hungary.

We looked up jobs for chemists. I was delighted to find pages and pages of little boxes describing different positions for chemists. Most of them seemed to be in companies making cosmetics. Even so, Lajos and I were satisfied that my chosen profession was a good one.

I was still full of nervous and physical energy from the day's events. I was excited about everything that had happened. And scared—of everything and nothing in particular. I figured I would calm down by writing to my parents about my latest experiences.

Once I started, it occurred to me that I would never know if all of my letters arrived at my parents' home—they might be unintentionally lost by the post office or purposefully waylaid by some censor because of their American postmark. For the same reasons, I didn't know if I would get all of their letters. I devised a scheme where I would number my letters and suggested that my parents do the same. Then each of us would start our response by acknowledging the number on the last letters we had received.

Lajos decided to use that weekend to introduce me to the wonders of New York. We took the subway to Manhattan again. Lajos, Lenke, and Paul were all dressed up, as was I, wearing my new American clothes. On Saturday, we watched a Cinerama movie, which played on a huge, wide screen the like of which I'd never seen before. On Sunday, we went to see another movie and the Rockettes at Radio City Music Hall. In between, we walked around Manhattan, with me continuing to gawk at the skyscrapers and the crowded sidewalks.

I was astonished by the display of wealth. The store windows all looked fancy beyond belief, the mannequins in the windows beautiful and elegant. The people on the street, although not as elegant as the mannequins, still seemed well dressed. But what really impressed me was the number of big cars driven by uniformed chauffeurs. I watched some of these cars pulling up in front of a store, the chauffeur running around to open the door for the occupants in the rear seat. It looked like a Communist caricature of capitalism come to life.

We went to a Horn & Hardart restaurant. The arrangement was highly unusual. Instead of a waiter bringing you a menu and food, there was a wall of little glass-fronted drawers, each drawer containing a different dish. You put coins in a slot, then opened the little glass door to get your plate of stew or pie or whatever. I thought the food was bad and the surroundings unappetizing, but I didn't say anything because Lajos was so obviously proud of it.

The next day, using my newfound knowledge of how to use

tokens and navigate on the subway, I took off on an expedition of my own in Manhattan. While looking at the newspaper, I noticed that a new film version of *Don Giovanni* was playing in a Manhattan movie theater. It featured Cesare Siepi, a legendary singer whom I'd heard of but had never listened to. I had to go. Lajos gave me money for the tokens and the movie, and I was off on my adventure.

I easily found my way to the subway station, but then all of a sudden I wasn't sure if I had the right directions. I walked up to the man in the token booth and, in halting English, asked him if this was the right place to take the D train. When he answered me, I wasn't sure I'd understood him correctly. I could understand the "D," but what followed sounded more like "shrain." I asked him to repeat himself. I still couldn't understand him. Behind me, people were getting impatient and beginning to comment loudly. I decided to take a chance that this was the right train, but I thought that people here were not so friendly as in Vienna.

I did find the movie theater, however, and *Don Giovanni* was spectacularly good. What surprised me, though, was that I was almost alone in the movie house. A movie like this playing in Budapest would have been mobbed. Here, there were barely fifteen people in the audience.

I also took the opportunity to find the Metropolitan Opera House, a place of mythical status in my eyes. Several people directed me to a big, blocky building with a shabby, blackened-brick facade. I couldn't make peace with the fact that the home of the legendary Metropolitan Opera was this decrepit building that reminded me of the farmers market in Budapest. America was confusing.

But I didn't have much time to brood. I had to get on with my life.

I was getting increasingly comfortable navigating by myself in the city, so I went to visit the New York office of the International Rescue Committee, my sponsors. I was received very warmly. A middle-aged woman introduced herself as Mrs. Kadmon and invited me into her office. She had a file on me, which impressed me. She updated my address and phone number and asked me about my plans. She spoke English slowly and distinctly, and I had no trouble understanding her. I said that my uncle worked at Brooklyn College and, with his help, I was hoping to enroll as a chemistry student there. She noted that in the file. Then she asked me if my eyes and ears were good and when the last time was that I had visited a dentist.

I told her that I was slightly nearsighted and didn't hear very well, but that although I hadn't seen a dentist in many, many years, I had no problems with my teeth. She said I should see a dentist anyway, as well as visit a place for eyeglasses and another one for hearing aids. She wrote out papers for each of these. Then she told me that it wouldn't cost me anything; the IRC would pay for the dentist as well as any glasses and hearing aid that I got.

The visit to the dentist was another surprise. The office was gleaming, filled with all kinds of equipment that I'd never seen before. I'd never had a toothache or cavities, and the only problem I'd ever had with my mouth was that my gums bled a little when I brushed my teeth, so I thought I would be in and out in minutes. I wasn't so lucky. The dentist told me that my teeth were covered with "calculus." I was confused. Calculus was what I studied in math class. He explained that it was also a word that described deposits on my teeth that irritated my gums and eventually could cause real problems. Then he proceeded to scrape my teeth. My gums bled profusely. I thought my teeth would fall out. He took pity on me after an hour of torture, but only because I promised that I would come back the next day to let him finish the job. I dreaded it, but I did return, obedient and much chastened.

I also went to the eye doctor. He prescribed a pair of wire-rimmed glasses for me. I promptly stuck them in my pocket, feeling quite confident that I didn't need them.

Getting the hearing aid was a revelation. I had tried hearing aids in Hungary. They were bulky contraptions made in Russia. In addition to having to wear a conspicuous headset, I had to carry the batteries in my pants pocket and the hearing aid in my coat pocket. Both of them were heavy and dragged on my clothes. But worst of all, they really didn't help. I quickly gave up on them.

The hearing aids at the store here were astonishing. There was an enormous variety and the biggest one was barely the size of a matchbox, even including a place for tiny batteries. I was helped by a kind gentleman with a deep, booming voice that I could understand perfectly. He explained the different types of hearing aids, measured my ear, and picked out a number of models that he thought would work. I tried one after another in the store and got completely confused.

He suggested that I take home the two I liked best, then come back in a day or two to make my selection. I thought I must have misunderstood. Hearing aids were very expensive; the ones I chose were the most powerful and cost about $300. Yet this man would let me, a stranger, out of the store with two of them. But it turned out that I'd understood him correctly. I went home with two hearing aids, which I tested with Lajos, Paul, Lenke, and the TV. I chose the one that happened to be the most expensive hearing aid in the store. But when I reported this to Mrs. Kadmon with much embarrassment, she said, "Just choose the one that works the best and don't worry about the cost." America kept surprising me.

Lajos had arranged for an appointment for me with the head

of the Chemistry Department at Brooklyn College. When the day came, I got up very early so that I could take the subway with him to Brooklyn. I didn't realize what a long commute he had. We started from the top end of the Bronx, practically the end of the subway line, and because we were near the end of the line, at least we were able to sit down. Then we rode and rode and eventually changed subway lines. By this time the trains were full, so on the new train we stood sandwiched between other people. Lajos had developed a skill of folding his newspaper into eighths, so that he was able to read it even when fully surrounded. I whiled away the time by looking around the train, reading the advertisements over and over, and gazing at my fellow passengers. None of them returned my glance.

We got to Brooklyn College a few minutes after eight o'clock, after more than an hour of travel. Lajos first showed me around his workplace. He was a technician in the Botany Department, which was a logical job for him because he had been a gardener back in Hungary. Here he tended all kinds of exotic plants that were going to be used in the botany classes. His empire was like a jungle.

His colleagues greeted me with great exuberance. It was obvious that Lajos had told them about me and they were looking forward to meeting me. One of them showed me around the chemistry lab. There were no students around at the time because it was between semesters, but otherwise the room looked just like the chemistry lab at the University of Budapest. That was reassuring.

Somebody else showed me around what he described as a language lab. He explained that this was where students learned foreign languages. The lab consisted of little cubicles, each equipped with a tape recorder and a microphone; students could listen to phrases in foreign languages, repeat them into a microphone, and instantly hear their own pronunciation of the phrase so that they could compare their pronunciation with the correct one. I had never seen anything like this and was very impressed with the lavish setup. I sat in a cubicle and repeated an English phrase into the microphone. When I listened to my own version, I was appalled. I sounded like Donald Duck with an accent.

Then it was time for me to meet the head of the Chemistry Department. He spent a couple of hours with me, trying to establish what I knew about various subjects so that he could figure out which courses to enroll me in. It was an informal test, like a casual version of the oral exams I'd had to take at the university in Hungary. At the end of it, the professor told me that my knowledge of chemistry was "outstanding" and that I would do very well at Brooklyn College.

I also met with a professor from the Math Department and, because the college required the study of a foreign language, with a professor from the Russian Department. I was told to come back the next day, when they would tell me where I stood. I hung around until Lajos was ready to go, and we repeated the long journey home.

The next day, I again rode in with Lajos and went directly to the Chemistry Department for my results. I was pleasantly surprised. I got credit for a good number of chemistry courses and for five semesters of math, even though I had taken only two at the University of Budapest. I was told that I didn't need to take any more math at all. I also got credit for five semesters of Russian and again was told that I had fulfilled the foreign language requirement. The bottom line was that I could graduate as a chemist in one and a half years.

I was stunned. I considered myself a beginning student in chemistry, having barely started my second year of university. I couldn't picture myself as a professional chemist in just a year and a half more of courses. But the Chemistry Department chairman smilingly reassured me that I had not misunderstood. University education in Hungary was more advanced than here, he supposed.

Then he explained that although I had received credit for a lot of science and math classes, I would need to take courses in English literature, American history, and political science. My eyes widened. I quickly calculated that if I subtracted the required courses that had nothing to do with chemistry from the total number of courses I could take in the year and a half left before getting my degree, I would have the opportunity to take only two or three more chemistry courses. I stuttered, "How can I be a chemist with only two or three more courses of chemistry?" The professor patiently explained that I would be a chemist, but to be a real chemist, I would have to go on to further study for a master's degree or, even better, a Ph.D. A master's degree would take one extra year; a Ph.D. would take two or three years beyond that.

My aim was to acquire a profession that would enable me to become self-sufficient as soon as possible, so I could support myself and set aside enough money to help my parents get out of Hungary and join me in America. The picture that was unfolding was not what I expected.

I started negotiating. Could I do away with the English literature, the political science, and those other courses that wouldn't help me become a better chemist and take more chemistry instead? The professor shook his head with a slight smile. "No," he said. "Those courses are required for graduation."

I looked so crestfallen that he took pity on me. "If you want to take more scientific and technical courses, maybe you should switch your degree to chemical engineering," he suggested. He reached behind his desk and pulled out a little booklet listing the courses required by some engineering school for graduation. He flipped through it, muttering the names of the courses. They all seemed strange and mysterious. I took that as a good sign. If I signed up for a big list of such strange courses, I felt I would learn something that would make me capable of useful work. I said that I would be interested in switching to chemical engineering.

The professor sighed. Unfortunately, he explained, Brooklyn College did not have an Engineering Department. I asked who did. "Well," he said, "there's a school not far from here, Brooklyn Poly. That's a very good engineering school. Would you like to talk to them?" I quickly said I would.

He scribbled some directions on a piece of paper. Minutes later, having said good-bye to Lajos, I was on my way to Brooklyn Polytechnic. When I got there, I looked for the admissions office and in short order was sitting down with two admissions officers. I told them my story: I was a Hungarian refugee, a chemistry student, and I had a problem. They nodded their heads. They completely understood my predicament.

Brooklyn Poly, they said, was a private school where you had to pay tuition if you did not have a scholarship. The school had created two scholarships for Hungarian refugees. Unfortunately, both had already been given out. I asked how much tuition cost. They said, "Two thousand dollars." They might as well have told me it was two million. I stared at them, speechless.

One of them said maybe I'd want to consider City College. It had a good engineering school and, like Brooklyn College, was free. I perked up. "Where is City College?" A few minutes later, I had another set of scribbled directions in my hand and was on my way again.

I surfaced after a couple of long subway rides. It took me a few moments to get my bearings, then I started walking toward City College. I had been told that the subway station was ten city blocks from the college campus. After a couple of blocks, I realized that something was strange about my surroundings. I didn't see a single white face on the street. Everybody—storekeepers, passersby, children—was black. Since coming to New York, I'd seen plenty of black people, but I'd never been in a situation where everybody on the street, block after block, was black. I was very self-conscious about being different, but nobody paid any attention to me.

After fifteen minutes of walking down the windy, wintry streets, I arrived at a group of ornate, old-fashioned buildings. I asked somebody for directions to City College. I was there, I was told. I asked to see someone in admissions and was directed to the office of the registrar. I told my well-worn story to the receptionist and was sent in to see a friendly older gentleman. He invited me to sit down and started asking the usual litany of questions: What courses had I taken, what grades had I received, and so on. I listed my courses one after the other and, with slight embarrassment, told him that I had received the highest grade, equivalent to A in America, in each of them. I was telling the truth, but I had no transcript, no proof of any kind. Would the gentleman think I was making this up? If he did, he didn't let on.

That same afternoon, I was officially accepted as a student of the City College of New York in the Department of Chemical Engineering. I was placed in the category of upper sophomore, which meant that if I took a full load, I would graduate in three and a half more years. While here, too, I would have to take courses in English literature, political science, and such, I could see that I would have plenty of technical training before graduating. This was more like it.

There was still the problem of money for books and to cover the cost of living while getting my degree. The registrar gentleman explained that the school had no cash scholarships, but that he understood that an organization called the World University Service gave cash stipends to Hungarian refugees. The moment I left his office, I was on my way again with yet another set of directions, this time to Manhattan.

Before the afternoon ended, the World University Service had granted me a scholarship for the semester. It was not a whole lot, but it was still money. I no longer had to rely on an allowance from Lajos. In fact, by the time Lajos and Lenke arrived home from work and sat around the kitchen table as I recited the story of my day, I had figured that I should give them a third of my scholarship to defray the cost of my presence in their household. The rest would go for books and things.

I would also be able to start saving to help my parents come to America. I had no idea how they would get out of Hungary in the first place or, if they did manage to get out of Hungary, how they could get to America. I figured that money would be needed in either case, so I resolved to save every dollar I could.

Altogether it had been quite a day. Lajos and Lenke thought so, too. They were very proud of me. Late that night I sat down to report all of this in a letter to my parents. I felt quite proud of myself, too.

My timing was fortuitous. Registration for classes at City College was to start in a few days. It took place in a gymnasium. Crowds of young people milled around, jostling in front of tables set up for different classes where administrative paperwork was being handed out and collected. The sound of everyone talking, occasionally shouting questions, and rattling papers echoed in the cavernous space, adding to the confusion. Even though I was wearing my American best, I was immediately identified as a Hungarian. Students and staff helped me line up at the right places and fill out the right paperwork.

At one point, a friendly staff person tripped over my name for the umpteenth time. "Look," he said, "do you mind if I just call you Andy?" I assured him that I didn't mind at all. It had a good ring to it, coming from American mouths. By the end of the day, being called Andy sounded as natural as if this had been my name all my life.

The registrar had told me which courses to take. I was surprised to find that there was no such thing as a single class of chemical engineers who attended all the courses together, as we did in Hungary. Each student had a different list of courses, and we moved from one class to another, sometimes with students from other classes, other times not. It was a very different system from the one I was used to. I was reminded of how I felt when I first saw skyscrapers; everything at first seemed overwhelming. But within a few days, I was running from class to class just like everyone else.

Everything was different. Classes, students, and professors all were far more casual than in Hungary. In my very first class, I stood up when the professor entered the classroom. That was the custom in Hungary, but here I was the only one on my feet. All the other students turned and stared at me. I slumped back into my seat, my face turning red.

Once the class got going, I peeked around. The other students were sprawled in their seats as if they were lounging at a party. Every now and then, they stuck their hands in the air and questioned something the professor said. That was another difference. In Hungary, you reserved your questions for the junior faculty, and you certainly never interrupted a lecture.

The teachers were equally casual. To my amazement, the math teacher chewed gum all the time. I had a hard enough time understanding him in the first place; the gum certainly didn't help.

The most important class, one that alone made up one-third of my course load, was a physics class. Unlike his counterpart in Hungary, the teacher spoke in a firm, loud voice. Having situated myself in the front row, I had no problem hearing him. That was the good news.

The bad news was that at the end of the first class we were assigned thirty problems to solve before the next class, which was the next day. Thirty! The problems weren't terribly hard if you understood the language, but the language of mechanics included words that I had never encountered in Oscar Wilde. Without a dictionary, I didn't know what words like "vertical," "horizontal," and "perpendicular" meant, let alone "isosceles triangle."

As an engineering student, I also had to acquire an impressively complex slide rule. I had never seen a slide rule before and had to learn how to use it from scratch. I discovered that it contained an incredible wealth of information and, once I was skilled at it, allowed me to calculate much more rapidly than I could with plain pencil and paper. This turned out to be extremely useful with the many problems I had to solve for physics class.

In addition to my technical classes, I also had to take courses in English composition and American history to make up for what I hadn't studied in what I still thought of as gymnasium, although I quickly learned it was called high school here. These courses were given at night for adult students who worked during the day. I took the technical courses that were part of the regular engineering curriculum in the morning and English and history at night.

I had to study a lot for my technical courses. I tried to study in the library, but I couldn't concentrate with people milling around me. So after my morning classes were over, I would go back to the empty apartment, settle down at Paul's desk, and work until it was time to return to City College for my seven o'clock evening classes. After class ended, I would come back, turn on the lamp at Paul's desk, and, while he slept, study some more.

The commute from my home to City College was a good forty-five minutes—a fifteen-minute walk to the subway, fifteen to twenty minutes on the subway, then another fifteen-minute walk to the campus. The three-hour commute, added to my study time, made for a long day.

I used every minute to study, including the time I spent coming and going on the subway. Every once in a while, I rewarded myself by buying a paper cup filled with Coca-Cola from a machine in the subway station for five cents. But I tried not to do that too often because that would be five cents I wouldn't have for my parents.

The walk from my home to the subway and from the subway to City College was miserable. It was winter and it was damp, windy, and cold, particularly during my evening trips. Sometimes rain or sleet drove into my face. Winter here felt much nastier than winter in Budapest.

In addition to English composition and American history, I had to take physical education. There was no such thing at the University of Budapest. We started our first class by lining up in single file in order of descending height. To my chagrin, I found myself near the end of the line. In similar lineups in Hungary, I was always in the middle or close to the front. American boys were taller.

I was an unenthusiastic participant. Throwing big, heavy balls to each other seemed utterly pointless to me. In one of my PE classes, I heard somebody talk about a fencing team. I was intrigued, and my intrigue got elevated to outright enthusiasm when I learned that if I joined the fencing team, I wouldn't have to come to PE. A couple of weeks into the semester, I went for a tryout. To my amazement, the coach put me on the varsity team and asked me to come to the next meet on the coming weekend. We went to New Jersey to fence against Rutgers University, and the coach had me lead off. I won my first bout, but it was downhill after that. I didn't win any more bouts at that meet and never got to lead off again. Being Hungarian took you only so far in the fencing world.

The kids on my fencing team and, for that matter, most of the kids in my classes were all very friendly to me. My classmates and the other students called me Andy. Being called Andy made me feel that I was fitting in—at least, until I opened my mouth. My accent always made me stand out.

I stood out another way, too. I had a hearing aid. It was a bone conduction device, which was very rare. The hearing aid had to press against the bone behind the ear, so there was a headset with a spring that pushed it against my skull. I wore it in class, then took it off as soon as class was over, partly because the pressure of the headset hurt my head and partly out of vanity. It was an odd-looking contraption and drew furtive glances.

One way I did not stand out was by being a Jew. While I was visiting Brooklyn College, I had picked up a copy of the college newspaper. As I flipped through its pages, it struck me how many of the students' and professors' names were Jewish. I had a similar impression at City College. Many students and professors either had Jewish names or looked Jewish to my still-trained eyes. A couple of the students even asked me very matter-of-factly if I was Jewish. Once when I said yes, a couple of boys who were dressed in the manner of Orthodox Jews started to talk to me very enthusiastically, inviting me to join them in a group they belonged to. I didn't want to join. I said I was overwhelmed by my courses, which was absolutely true.

One boy who was in a couple of my engineering classes took a particular interest in me. His name was Jerry Rosenthal. He was fresh from the army. While in the military, he had been stationed in Germany; his unit was mobilized during the Hungarian revolution when the United States was deciding whether it would participate on behalf of the Hungarians. Jerry was very aware of the Hungarian revolution and its aftermath, and we started to spend more and more time together, studying and talking. To my delight, I discovered that he liked classical music. Not only that, his favorite opera was *Don Giovanni.*

Jerry took me under his wing. He started working on my pronunciation with a vengeance. He decided to punch me in the shoulder every time I mispronounced a well-known word. I had to tolerate multiple punches in my shoulder before I learned to pronounce "book" correctly—I was pronouncing it "boook." This was relatively easy. Learning to pronounce the "th" sound as in the words *the* and *they* was a lot harder. Lajos was no help. Although his English was fluent, he pronounced "the" and "they" as "duh" and "day." Jerry's fists had to work double time on the "th" sound. Some days I had a very sore arm, but my pronunciation improved rapidly.

Jerry also helped me warm to the American political system. In spite of my deep suspicions about what Communist propaganda said about the United States, some of the Communist teachings must have taken root. I horrified Jerry when I casually mentioned that "of course" the American government was in the pockets of big business.

Jerry argued with me vociferously but couldn't convince me. Then one day, he pulled out a copy of *The New York Times* and triumphantly waved an article in front of me. It reported on a Supreme Court decision forcing the DuPont Corporation to sell an interest they had in General Motors. If the Supreme Court were controlled by big business, he argued, how could they possibly rule against DuPont's interest? I grumbled skeptically, but I didn't have a good comeback.

Another young man I also got to be friendly with was a veteran of the Korean War. He, too, was studying to become an engineer, and we were in some of the same classes. After a while, I worked up enough courage to ask him if it was true that American troops used bacterial warfare in Korea. He got extremely angry with me and shouted, "You know me well enough to know that I couldn't possibly do such a thing! How can you even ask such a preposterous question?" I hastily retreated, wondering if anything I had learned in Hungary about America and Americans was true.

School was hard, but I thought I was coping well until my first big exam in my physics course. I had done reasonably well on all the homework, so I wasn't concerned. But when the exam came, I had two surprises. First, we had to finish the entire exam in fifty minutes. And second, we weren't allowed to open our books. There were no such tests in Hungary, and I was not used to having to memorize equations. I knew I did poorly, but I still wasn't prepared for the F that was written on the folded-over workbook that the instructor handed back at the next class. I was shocked and embarrassed. This had never happened to me before; I was used to being a straight A student. After class, the professor called out, "Gruff, come to my office this afternoon. I'd like to talk to you."

(My professors called me Grof, but half the time I didn't recognize my last name when they called the roll. In Hungarian, Grof is pronounced with a long "o"; here, everyone read my name as if it were written "Gruff.")

My professor was worried about me. This was a tough course even for people who had all the right preparation, he told me. It was the first serious engineering course that students encountered. Perhaps it was too soon for me. He offered that if I wanted to drop the class, he would let me do it without any penalty and I could take it again the following semester.

I was stunned.

It was bad enough that I got an F on my test. Even worse was being invited to drop the course. I thanked him for his consideration and told him, with clenched jaw, "I'm going to do better." From there on, the first subject I studied every day while I was fresh was physics. I studied for as long as it took for me to get on top of the material.

I kept writing to my parents. I had lots to report, but I would have written even if I hadn't, just to keep them informed so they wouldn't worry about me. My father was very happy about my shift to engineering. He was a practical man, and he thought he understood what an engineer did better than what a chemist did.

I started hinting that they should follow me to America. At first, my parents' reaction wasn't encouraging. By that time, the borders were sealed again. Getting across as I had was no longer possible. Furthermore, my father was deathly afraid of finding himself in a place where he didn't speak the language, which was anywhere but Hungary. I started lobbying for them to study English. After a while, they did, and I encouraged them by including English comments in my letters. I used my messy cursive writing when I wrote to them in Hungarian, but whenever I switched to English, I would print the phrases to make it easier for them to read.

In one of their early letters, my parents mentioned that Gabi had returned to Hungary from Romania and visited with them often. I asked if it would be all right for me to write to Gabi directly. I was afraid of any repercussions resulting from his keeping in touch with a dissident friend. My parents didn't think there would be a problem.

After a few exchanges, though, Gabi's letters dried up. I kept writing to him, but I had no answer. My parents reported that he had stopped coming by. Then one day, my parents were walking down the street and saw Gabi walking toward them. But when Gabi saw them, he crossed the street to avoid having to say hello. I stopped writing to him after that.

Jancsi, Bubi, Imre, and Peter all got to America. We went our separate ways, but we kept occasional contact with each other. Jancsi ended up across the country at Stanford, where he had relatives. Bubi got a job as a TV technician in New York and was studying English. Imre got a scholarship to the University of Michigan and was on his way there. Peter was enrolled at Princeton, where an uncle of his was a professor.

I also heard from the friendly crew member on the ship. He called to invite me to dinner, and one Saturday night, his wife drove up from Brooklyn to collect me. We had dinner in their sparsely furnished apartment, with their two little kids playing in the corner. They were very impressed with my progress on the college front.

Another day, a woman telephoned for me. Her name was Magda. She said she was my mother's niece and lived in New York. My mother had never told me about her. When I wrote to her about Magda, she answered that she had lost contact with her after the war. Magda, however, did not forget about us. She thought that some of us might have made our way to America in the wake of the revolution, so she checked with Camp Kilmer for the names of my father, my mother, and other relatives until she came across mine.

She came to visit. She was younger then Lajos and Lenke, a single woman, good-looking and sophisticated. She said she would have gladly taken me in. I liked her a lot. It was good to know that I had another relation in this huge place.

Some weeks later, the time came for the second big physics exam. My rigorous regimen paid off. This time, I got an A.

I was feeling better about my academic prospects, which was just as well because I got word that my faculty advisor, Professor Kolodney, wanted to see me. Professor Kolodney was a lean, middle-aged man whose low-key demeanor was at odds with the perpetually amused glint in his eye. He asked how I was doing in my classes. I was glad to be able to report my good news in physics. Then he asked me the question that just about everybody else asked: "How do you like America?"

Ordinarily, my answer would be a short and perfunctory, "Fine, I like it very much." This time, something made me go beyond that. Having just braved the elements on a particularly nasty day, I burst out, "America, I love. New York, I hate."

The whimsical eyebrows raised. "And why is that?" he asked calmly.

"Because it is cold and wet and ugly," I said.

Professor Kolodney thought about this for a little while. Then he asked me about Budapest. I described it as a beautiful city where water and mountains meet, where the sun always shone and the wind never drove rain into your face. Of course, this was not the case, but from the distance of space and time it seemed to have been so, at least for me on that grim, gray day. Professor Kolodney thought again, then offered, "Maybe you want to move to California. You're likely to find what you describe in San Francisco more than any place else in America." He then switched the subject to discuss which courses I would have to take the next semester, but the idea of California buzzed in my brain. I might want to live there after I finish, I thought. It sounded exciting.

But first I had to get back to my courses. In order to expedite my graduation, I needed to start taking the course sequence offered by the Chemical Engineering Department. The first course in the sequence was called "Chem E 128." This was a legendary course with an intimidating reputation; rumor had it that half the students flunked it. Only those who passed Chem E 128 could continue with the chemical engineering courses and become chemical engineers. Those who flunked, the condescending rumor went on, became physics or psychology majors. I wanted to get going with my sequence of courses, so I needed to get into Chem E 128.

Professor Kolodney wondered if it might be too soon for me to take it. He said that the only way I would be allowed into the course was if I got permission from the chairman of the department, Professor Schmidt, who taught this course. So I went off to see Professor Schmidt.

His office was guarded by a secretary who wouldn't give me the time of day, let alone an appointment. I waylaid Professor Schmidt after his class. He was a short man, middle-aged, with a fierce mustache and graying hair severely combed back. He wore a gray dress shirt and a tie. He was very intimidating. I got straight to the point.

I told him my predicament while all around us students were noisily milling about in the usual postclass hubbub. His piercing eye never left mine as he asked which courses I was taking that semester. When I mentioned my physics course, he asked who my teacher was. Then he asked about my grades. I swallowed and told him that I had flunked the first test but got an A on the second. He looked at me quizzically, then said that if I continued to do well in the physics course, he would let me take his class.

I took a deep breath and blurted out, "Professor Schmidt, I wonder if you could help me with my other problem."

My scholarship from the World University Service was only for the current semester, I explained. I needed to get another scholarship for the following year. He frowned, then said that I should come see him in his office later.

I showed up as instructed and smugly pranced by the disapproving secretary as Professor Schmidt gestured for me to come in. His office was minuscule, with barely enough room for him and his desk. I edged my way onto a chair. Professor Schmidt asked me how much money I got from the WUS. After I told him, he pulled out the longest slide rule I'd ever seen. It must have been more than two feet long. Without saying a word to me, he started computing something and muttering to himself. Then he put down the slide rule and asked, "How would you like a job instead of a scholarship?"

I didn't know what to say.

He explained that the Chemical Engineering Department had the budget for one student assistant who would help him and his secretary. The job paid $1.79 an hour, which was very good wages because the other jobs around the college paid only $1.00 an hour. Glancing at his slide rule, he figured that if I worked twenty hours a week, I would make as much as I got out of the scholarship.

I quickly calculated that by next semester, I would no longer have any physical education requirements, so I could drop out of the fencing team and gain some time that way. And the idea of working for this man really appealed to me. I said yes.

The job wasn't going to start until the next semester, but Professor Schmidt said it was mine.

Meanwhile, another important development took place. I applied for my green card. My official status in this country was as a parolee by order of President Eisenhower. That was signified by an identification card, a white piece of plastic with my name and personal data on it. The white card gave me the right to be in this country, but it did not give me permanent resident status. As I understood it, I had been let in but was still in limbo.

The green card would signify that I was here to stay and would be on track to become a U.S. citizen in five years' time. This was extremely important from the standpoint of bringing my parents here. As relatives of an American citizen, they would have preferential status in being admitted to this country.

Things were falling into place, but there was one detail that still bothered me: my name. I liked being Andy. I hated being Gruff. When I complained to Lajos and Lenke about it, they said I could change my name easily enough if I wanted to. They told me that a friend of theirs had Americanized his name some years earlier so that the pronunciation of the Americanized version sounded the same as the correct pronunciation of his name in Hungarian.

I started doodling with different spellings. The most obvious thing to do was stick an "e" after my name. G-r-o-f-e. I showed this to a classmate and asked him how he would pronounce it. He said, "Oh, Gro-fay, like the composer of the 'Grand Canyon Suite.'" I went back to the drawing board.

I tried another version. I wrote G-r-o-v-e. I took it back to the same boy. He said, "Oh, that's how you say it. Grove." It was a serviceable rendition of how G-r-o-f was pronounced in Hungarian and was certainly a lot closer than Gruff.

I went to see each of my teachers and told them that I was changing my name to Andrew Grove. For good measure, I added a middle initial: S. It stood for Stephen, the English version of István, the middle name that I had never used in Hungary. Nobody had any problem with my new name, except for my physics teacher, who again asked to see me after class. He solemnly told me that it was really not necessary to change my name, that I should hang on to my identity and not give in to any pressure to Americanize. I explained to him that my name was what people called me by, and when he pronounced "Grove," it sounded more like me than when he pronounced Grof as "Gruff." He shrugged and said okay.

Now I had to find out how to make my name change official. To my surprise, I was told that all I needed to do was start using the new name. When I became a citizen, my name change would take place formally. In the meantime, however, no papers needed to be filed. I just had to be consistent about using my new name. America continued to amaze me.

That night when I wrote to my parents, I ended my letter by carefully printing in English, "FROM YOUR SON ANDY, WHOSE NAME WILL SOON BE 'GROVE.'"

Epilogue

I've never gone back to Hungary.

To be sure, as the years went on, political and economic life both improved, at least as far as I could tell. Hungary even ended up becoming a member of NATO. But although I've retained fond memories of Hungarian music and literature, and I still look with some warmth at picture postcards of Budapest sent to me by friends who visit there, I have never desired to revisit it myself.

I'm not entirely sure why. Maybe I don't want to remind myself of the events I wrote about. Maybe I want to let memories stay memories. Or maybe the reason is something simpler than that: My life started over in the United States. I have set roots here. Whatever roots I had in Hungary were cut off when I left and have since withered and died.

Meanwhile, my life here has flourished.

I graduated from City College three and a half years after I started, at the top of my class. *The New York Times* even wrote a little blurb about it, with the headline REFUGEE HEADING ENGINEERS' CLASS. I got married. (My wife and I met when we both worked summer jobs in a resort in New Hampshire; she was a waitress, I was a busboy.)

Soon after graduation, we piled into an old car and drove out to California so I could go to graduate school at the University of California at Berkeley. Somewhere on Highway 40, I saw a sign indicating that we were nearing the Sierra Nevada. The words jumped straight out of the Karl May books I had read when I was a kid. Now, here I was, about to drive through these hitherto mythical mountains.

I fell in love with the San Francisco Bay Area from the moment I drove through a tunnel north of San Francisco and saw the city glittering in the sunshine. It was everything Professor Kolodney had suggested it would be. It was beautiful. It was friendly. It became home. I've lived in the Bay Area ever since.

Five years after I landed in the Brooklyn Navy Yard, my parents were allowed to leave Hungary and joined me in California. They got simple jobs: My father became a clerk at a title company and my mother a cashier/wrapper in a department store. They held these jobs until they retired in the 1970s.

Both of my parents learned English, my mother easily, my father with difficulty. Partly spurred on by his necessity to get along in America, but equally motivated by his desire to talk with my wife and his grandchildren (we now had two daughters), he finally overcame his difficulty with foreign languages. He was proud of his accomplishment.

My father passed away at age eighty-two. My mother is still alive and, in fact, has offered her critical views of the manuscript of this book.

My parents' friend Jani also escaped from Hungary at the time of the revolution. He ended up in Australia. He and his wife once visited my parents in California.

Romacz stayed in Hungary, retired, and lived out his days in a rented room in a friend's apartment. My father wanted to help him, but Romacz rebuffed all offers of financial assistance;

when my father insisted and sent him some money anyway, he returned it. He died alone, as self-sufficient as he had lived.

My aunt Iren and my uncle Sanyi both passed away. My cousin Marika is my only relative in Hungary who is still alive. My mother keeps in close touch with her.

Lenke died a few years after I moved to California. Lajos remarried; he passed away many years later, but not before he saw me succeed in the business world. Paul grew up and had a family of his own.

Of my friends from Budapest who escaped in the wake of the revolution, Jancsi and Peter both became professors at American universities. We've run across each other a few times over the years. Bubi became an engineer; he died of a heart attack in his fifties. Imre is also in California, where he is now retired. His son looks more like the Imre I remember than his father does.

I lost track of my friend Gabi after trying to contact him, as I described. He has become part of the closed chapter that Hungary represents.

I have loved my life in the United States. The doors that the International Rescue Committee and Professor Schmidt opened for me were just the first of many. I went through graduate school on scholarships, got a fantastic job at Fairchild Semiconductor, the high-flying company of its day, then participated in the founding of Intel, which in time has become the largest maker of semiconductors in the world. I rose to be its chief executive officer, a position I held for eleven years, until I stepped down from it in 1998; I continue as chairman today. I've continued to be amazed by the fact that as I progressed through school and my career, no one has ever resented my success on account of my being an immigrant.

I became a U.S. citizen. I was named *Time* magazine's Man of the Year in 1997. My two daughters now have children of their own. In fact, it was the arrival of the grandchildren that stimulated me to tell my story.

As my teacher Volenski predicted, I managed to swim across the lake—not without effort, not without setbacks, and with a great deal of help and encouragement from others.

I am still swimming.

I am extremely grateful to the International Rescue Committee for bringing me to the U.S. I have donated all of my royalties from this book to them so they can help today's refugees.

THE BONDWOMAN'S NARRATIVE

by Hannah Crafts

edited by Henry Louis Gates, Jr.

A historical and literary event, this recently uncovered tale written in the 1850s is the only known novel written by a fugitive female slave and, by all accounts, the first one by an African American woman. The riveting story recounts the adventures of a young slave on a Southern plantation as she escapes and makes her way to freedom. From a manuscript discovered and edited by noted African American scholar Henry Louis Gates, Jr., this book also feature research notes by Dr. Gates on Hannah Crafts's remarkable life and the history of her fictional work.

"A remarkable historical discovery . . . compelling . . . an immensely entertaining and illuminating novel."

—*New York Times*